# KIA HIWA RĀ!

# KIA HIWA RĀ!

Māori Journalism in Aotearoa New Zealand

ATAKOHU MIDDLETON

HUIA

First published in 2023 by Huia Publishers
39 Pipitea Street, PO Box 12280
Wellington, Aotearoa New Zealand
www.huia.co.nz

ISBN 978-1-77550-698-0

Copyright © Atakohu Middleton 2023

Cover images
Front cover:
Top row (left to right): Leonie Hayden – supplied by Leonie Hayden; Piripi Taylor – Whakaata Māori; Annabelle Lee-Mather – supplied by Annabelle Lee-Mather

Middle row (left to right): Kereama Wright – Whakaata Māori; Oriini Kaipara – Stuff; Arana Taumata – Jae Frew

Bottom row (left to right): Kirsty Babington – Whakaata Māori; Julian Wilcox – Whakaata Māori; Peata Melbourne – Whakaata Māori

Back cover image courtesy Simon Smith, AUT

This book is copyright. Apart from fair dealing for the purpose of private study, research, criticism or review, as permitted under the Copyright Act, no part may be reproduced by any process without the prior permission of the publisher.

A catalogue record for this book is available from the National Library of New Zealand.

Published with the assistance of The Faculty of Design and Creative Technologies Te Ara Auaha, AUT and Creative New Zealand.

# CONTENTS

| | | |
|---|---|---|
| | **ACKNOWLEDGEMENTS** | 7 |
| **1** | **KO TE HOROPAKI**<br>Setting the Scene | 8 |
| **2** | **KO TE WHAKAPAPA O TE MAHI TĀ HAURAPA KŌRERO**<br>The History of Māori Print Journalism | 24 |
| **3** | **KO TE WHAKAPAPA O NGĀ PURONGO IRIRANGI REO MĀORI**<br>The History of Māori-language News on Radio | 62 |
| **4** | **KO TE POUAKA WHAKAATA ME TE IPURANGI**<br>Māori News and Current Affairs on State and Commercial Television | 82 |
| **5** | **HE WHAKANGUNGU KAIKAWEKŌRERO**<br>Māori Journalism Training – Many Paths to the Newsroom | 100 |
| **6** | **KO TE ĀHUATANGA O TE MAHI**<br>Analysing News Values and the Māori Perspective | 138 |

**7**    **KO TE REO KIA RERE**
Māori Journalists as Agents of Language Revitalisation    162

**8**    **TIHEI MAURI ORA!**
Elements of Whaikōrero in News    184

**9**    **KO TE WERO**
Tikanga, Relationships and the Māori Reporter    214

**10**    **KO TE TAPU ME TE KAIRĪPOATA MĀORI**
The Influence of Tapu on News Work    244

**11**    **KEI MUA**
What Lies Ahead?    272

**ENDNOTES**    276

**BIBLIOGRAPHY**    292

**INDEX**    304

## ACKNOWLEDGEMENTS

Ehara taku toa i te toa takitahi, he toa takitini kē. A major enterprise like a book is not just the work of the person named on the cover. A non-fiction book like this captures and reflects the whakaaro, tautoko and aroha of many. I wish to acknowledge the many people in journalism and academia who shared my vision of presenting a first and comprehensive account of Māori journalism in Aotearoa New Zealand. In particular, he pīki mihi to the journalists at Television New Zealand, Whakaata Māori (since May 2022 the official name of the Māori Television Service), Radio New Zealand and Radio Waatea who made themselves available for interview and allowed me to film them for days on end in order to gain a fine-grained understanding of their work. For your tautoko, e hoa mā, I am eternally grateful.

This book started life as a 100,000-word doctoral thesis completed at Auckland University of Technology (AUT). I owe a great deal to my academic supervisors, Associate Professor Helen Sissons of the School of Communication Studies and Professor Hinematau McNeill of Te Ara Poutama. They are the best possible companions on a long academic journey.

He pīki mihi to AUT for providing a Vice-Chancellor's Doctoral Scholarship, which allowed me to cut back my paid work from 2017 to 2019 inclusive to focus on the research. I am indebted to other organisations that financially supported the work: to Waikato-Tainui, the Kate Edgar Charitable Educational Trust, the Māori Education Trust and the School of Communication Studies at AUT.

Finally, a mihi to my husband, Dr Andrew Balemi, who has supported this wahine and her mahi for more than twenty-five years. E te tau, e kore e mimiti tōku aroha ki a koe.

*Atakohu Middleton, Tāmaki Makaurau, June 2022*

# 1

## KO TE HOROPAKI

## SETTING THE SCENE

## A JOURNALISM OF TWO LANGUAGES

Māori journalism comes in two languages: te reo Māori, bequeathed by our ancestors, and English, the language of colonisation that nearly smothered te reo Māori. Māori journalists use both te reo Māori and te reo Pākehā to tell Māori stories in Māori ways, primarily to the iwi but also to wider Aotearoa. Since the Māori language newspapers of the 1800s, a uniquely Indigenous journalism culture has developed, branching into radio, magazines, television and now digital platforms.

To set the scene, let's turn to Māori language journalism. News and current affairs in te reo is provided by three primary players. National state television broadcaster Television New Zealand (TVNZ) presents *Te Karere*, on air since 1983. Indigenous national broadcaster Whakaata Māori, since May 2022 the official name of the Māori Television Service, produces reo Māori news bulletins under the banner of *Te Ao Māramu*. Urban Māori radio station Radio Waatea, based in Tāmaki Makaurau, produces *Waatea News* bulletins and a current affairs interview show, *Manako*, sharing these with the twenty other stations in the national iwi network.

These exist as a result of the landmark 1980s Tiriti o Waitangi claim WAI11, known colloquially as the Reo Maori Claim (see Chapter 3), which obliged the government to invest in promoting and protecting te reo and tikanga through various means, broadcasting among them. The money for Māori language and Māori-focused broadcasting is disbursed through Māori broadcasting agency Te Māngai Pāho (TMP), which has a reo revitalisation mandate. Therefore, it pays for news content with various levels of Māori language to enrich the reo Māori 'languagescape', rather than for the dissemination of news in and of itself. TMP policy is silent on what constitutes quality news and current affairs. It is not charged with assessing the quality of the journalism it funds, just the quality of the language used; the (problematic) assumption made is that news staff will be

*Te Ao Mārama* is the Whakaata Māori reo Māori bulletin, here presented by Peata Melbourne.

WHAKAATA MĀORI

appropriately qualified. We look at this conundrum more closely in Chapter 7.

### THE HEALTH OF TE REO MĀORI

Due to the effects of colonisation, te reo Māori is somewhere between definitely endangered and severely endangered. Just 11 percent of Māori claim they speak te reo "well" or "very well", but 55 percent say they can speak more than a few words or phrases. Nationally, just 4 percent of the entire population can speak te reo to some degree. Although some intergenerational transmission is occurring, boosted by the Māori language education system, te reo is yet to reach the critical mass that will ensure that it thrives and endures.[1]

In English, there's a variety of Māori interest news and current affairs available. Radio Waatea and Whakaata Māori both produce Māori interest news in English and te reo. On the two major free-to-air broadcasters, there are two Māori interest current affairs shows that include some Māori language: *Marae* (TVNZ) and *The Hui* (Three). Māori interest content in English is also produced by online platforms such as E-Tangata, a high-quality online magazine that promotes new and experienced Māori and Pacific voices, and Ātea, which is part of online magazine *The Spinoff*. Some funding for these programmes comes from government public media agency New Zealand On Air (NZOA), whose mandate is finding content that "connects and reflects our nation".[2]

Among mainstream media, the country's most heavyweight news sites are stuff.co.nz and nzherald.co.nz, both part of integrated stables of newspapers and radio stations. Both sites have Māori issues sections, but both are relatively new and prompted by relatively recent reckonings with the past. The stuff.co.nz Māori issues section, Pou Tiaki, has dedicated journalists and some bilingual content. It was launched in 2020, following the company's historic apology for its racist coverage of Māori over its 163 years of publishing. The apology followed an investigation, led by senior staffer Carmen Parahi, that saw around twenty journalists scrutinise their own company's portrayal and representation of Māori from its nineteenth-century newspapers to now. They found numerous examples of bias and prejudice that acted to deny Māori an equitable voice in their own country.

It is interesting to note that the self-scrutiny and apology took place only after the company passed from Australian ownership to Stuff editor-in chief Sinead Boucher in 2020. The shift to local ownership, Sinead Boucher said, provided the company with the opportunity to reset and reposition itself and its value system.[3]

The *New Zealand Herald*, part of New Zealand Media and Entertainment (NZME), launched its Kāhu section in 2021, also with dedicated staff. This section started after something of a crisis of conscience among senior leaders, provoked after one of the paper's regular columnists, Teuila Fuatai, who is of Samoan heritage, was commissioned to write a column about racism in Aotearoa. At the time, the Black Lives Matter movement against racism, started in the US, was gaining momentum in Aotearoa; Teuila Fuatai approached a Black Lives Matter Auckland co-leader for interview, but was rebuffed when the organisation realised she was from the *Herald*. The co-leader said the paper's coverage was racist and upheld structures of white supremacy – and Teuila Fuatai agreed. Her subsequent column detailed her concerns about the *Herald*'s record on racism and her efforts to raise those with

KIA HIWA RĀ! MĀORI JOURNALISM IN AOTEAROA NEW ZEALAND

How Stuff apologised to the nation for past racist coverage. This is the *Dominion Post* front page of 30 November 2020.
STUFF LTD

her editors. This was a catalyst: a footnote from the editor accepted the criticism and pledged to do better.[4] According to Lois Turei, who leads the initiatives that have emerged, Kāhu "is part of a low-key, long-term plan to build trust among our communities, recruit Māori staff, increase content relevant to Māori audiences, and tackle issues important to Māori health, welfare, education, and development."[5]

This book is timely: it comes at a time of major societal shift, with growing public interest in te ao Māori. A new generation of media leaders in Aotearoa, both Māori and Pākehā, are taking active steps to ensure news organisations work towards realising the aspirations embedded in Te Tiriti o Waitangi: Partnership between Māori and tauiwi; protection of language and culture; and fair participation in all spheres of life.

## TE REO IN MAINSTREAM MEDIA

This greater interest in and understanding of te ao Māori in general has been reflected by increasing mainstream-media use of words and phrases in te reo. For some years, bilingual journalists working in mainstream media have occasionally produced stories entirely in te reo with subtitles, usually during the annual Māori Language Week. In the past couple of years, a major change has been increasing use of small snippets of te reo Māori in English stories by Māori and non-Māori alike, both those who speak te reo and those who don't.

This appears to have accelerated from 2016, when Māori news staff at Radio New Zealand (RNZ), which has a mandate to promote Māori language and culture, encouraged fellow reporters to use greetings and sign-offs in te reo during Māori Language Week in July that year. Once the week was over, editorial managers encouraged staff to continue, and many have. In RNZ news, it's not unusual to hear reporters saying "Ko [name] ahau" (I am ...) without translation at the end of reports. Presenters may open a show with "Kei te whakarongo mai koe ki Te Reo Irirangi o Aotearoa, you're listening to Radio New Zealand."

TVNZ, which is run as a commercial enterprise with no particular mandate to promote te ao Māori, has nonetheless followed RNZ's lead. On *1 News*, the country's most-watched television news bulletin, you'll often hear presenters say "E whai ake nei – Coming up". To reporters who have just completed a live cross, presenters might say "Ngā mihi – Thank you". After an ad break, phrases like "Hoki mai anō" (Welcome back) are often not translated at all; the assumption is made that in a country where increasing numbers of people from all ethnicities are taking Māori language classes, context and the formulaic nature of news shows makes the meaning clear. Initial pronunciation of Māori words by presenters and reporters who are not reo speakers may not be perfect – but improvement comes with practice. The use of te reo in public is an important part of normalising and legitimising the language in the public sphere.

Local media-standards bodies have made their support for te reo very clear. In March 2021, the New Zealand Media Council, the watchdog for print and online media, refused to hear a complaint about Stuff's use of "Kia ora, Aotearoa" as a greeting on its website, saying it did not breach any principles of sound news practice.[6] The following month, the Broadcasting Standards Authority, which oversees television and radio, announced that it would no longer accept complaints about the use of te reo Māori on air. As te reo was an official language, it said, there were no standards issues to consider, and broadcasters therefore didn't need to respond to complaints about te reo.[7] This move shut down an avenue for those whose complaints about te reo were a thin veneer for ethnic prejudice. Then, in September, the Human Rights Commission announced that it would no longer consider individual complaints over the use of te reo Māori or the term Pākehā.[8]

## Keep your complaints about te reo Māori to yourself, BSA rules

How Ātea headlined the Broadcasting Standards Authority decision over complaints about te reo on air.

THE SPINOFF

### MĀORI JOURNALISTS: A SMALL GROUP SET TO GROW

Nationally, the tally of Māori in the national journalist workforce has remained low for years, and in 2016 was found to be in just 7.9 percent.[9] However, the number of Indigenous reporters is set to increase quickly, and this is partly, and rather perversely, due to COVID-19.

## TRADING COMPETITION FOR COOPERATION

There was a time when newspapers, television and radio news services existed in separate silos, competing fiercely against each other. However, in an era of multi-platform news companies, collaboration and cooperation is increasing, and we are beginning to see Māori content producers partner with mainstream outlets, delivering Māori stories to wider audiences. An example of this is a 2020 RNZ partnership with commercial television producer Great Southern Television and the Māori-focused Aotearoa Media Collective, which produced a compelling documentary series on the land wars of the nineteenth century titled *NZ Wars*. Created and presented by high-profile journalist Mihingarangi Forbes and funded by NZOA, it was produced as a video documentary, a podcast, a stills gallery and a series of extended interviews.

Mihingarangi Forbes presents *NZ Wars: Stories of Tainui* from the Waikato River.

AOTEAROA MEDIA COLLECTIVE & GREAT SOUTHERN TELEVISION

Mainstream media enterprises have long struggled to find sustainable business models in a digitally disrupted world. Many journalism jobs have been lost and the quality and quantity of news from the regions and public authorities has suffered. In 2019, industry group the News Publishers' Association, RNZ and NZOA responded to the paucity of local-body reporting with a project called Local Democracy Reporting (LDR), similar to projects in the UK and Canada to boost reporting on elected officials and bodies by putting dedicated journalists into partner newsrooms. At the time of writing, there were thirteen LDR reporters across the country.

The quality and quantity of regional news was also an issue in the Māori news sector, which had been severely underfunded for decades compared to its English-language state counterparts. A shortage of trained journalists, bilingual reporters in particular, had become critical. In the 2020 government Budget, TMP was allocated $3.5 million to try and remedy this. Four bidders won funding to mount a multi-platform, content-sharing pilot programme to provide local news, and they hired both experienced journalists and young people to train on the job. The successful bidders were:

- Te Reo o Te Uru, comprising Te Korimako o Taranaki, which serves eight Taranaki iwi; Awa FM (Te Reo Irirangi o Whanganui) and Kia Ora FM (Rangitāne)

- Tahu News, broadcast by Tahu FM, the iwi station of Te Rūnanga o Ngāi Tahu.

- Aukaha – Te Tai Puukoorero, comprising iwi radio stations in the central North Island: Raukawa FM (Ngāti Raukawa), Tūwharetoa FM (Ngāti Tūwharetoa), Maniapoto FM (Ngāti Maniapoto), Tainui Live (iwi of Waikato), Moana Radio (iwi of Tauranga Moana), Ngā Iwi FM (iwi of Hauraki) and Te Reo Irirangi o Te Arawa (iwi of Te Arawa)

- Tūranga FM, which broadcasts to the iwi of Te Tairāwhiti.

The pilot will be assessed and a decision made on its future.

The arrival of coronavirus in early 2020 and a consequent national lockdown threatened to derail an already frail news media. In response, the government in February 2021 announced a $55 million Public Interest Journalism Fund (PIJF), a response aimed at providing transitional support to the media sector over three years – and this led to significant numbers of jobs for Māori reporters. The scheme is administered by NZOA under the management of the agency's first head of journalism, former television reporter Raewyn Rasch, who is Māori.

Among the PIJF projects with the greatest potential to permanently increase the number of Māori journalists is Te Rito, a training collaboration between Whakaata Māori, Newshub, NZME and Pacific Media Network and eleven other media organisations. It is training twenty-five new journalists from Māori, Pacific and other communities traditionally under-represented in media. Ten of that number are fluent speakers of te reo. PIJF funding for 110 new journalist roles of one or two years' duration saw more gains for Māori interest and reo Māori news, with Whakaata Māori and Radio Waatea each gaining seven roles, and online magazine E-Tangata four. Mainstream news outlets such as stuff.co.nz, TVNZ and Three also won funding for Māori journalists. Although the PIJF is a short-term stop-gap, the hope is that these new journalists will become long-term members of the media.

## ABOUT THE WRITER: ATAKOHU MIDDLETON

I see myself as a child of Te Tiriti o Waitangi: my dad is of Ngāti Māhanga whakapapa and colonial English heritage. My mum is an Australian of Irish descent who migrated to Aotearoa New Zealand as a young adult. I trained as a print journalist in the late 1980s in my birthplace of Tāmaki Makaurau, then spent twenty years working in newspapers and magazines in both Aotearoa New Zealand and England. A return to university to pursue postgraduate papers in te reo Māori led, a bit accidentally, to a doctorate in Māori language journalism.[10]

In this book, my aim is to tell a story that hasn't been fully told: the vibrant history of Māori journalism, the personalities who fought so hard to carve out space for Māori voices, and how we actually do the newswork, because there are differences between Māori and mainstream ways of reporting, as we'll see. I wrote this book while

Atakohu Middleton.
SIMON SMITH, AUT

I was a senior lecturer in the School of Communication Studies at Te Wānanga Aronui o Tāmaki Makaurau Auckland University of Technology. I am now working as a reo Māori journalist for Radio Waatea.

## WHAT'S IN THIS PUKAPUKA

The big question overarching of this book is this: What is Māori journalism? The insights here are drawn from my journalism experience and my doctoral research. Chapter 1 sets the scene with a brief exploration of the Māori worldview, mātauranga Māori and tikanga and how these are reflected in Māori news. Chapter 2 provides a history of Māori language and Māori interest print journalism from the newspapers of the 1800s to the digital print publications of today. Chapter 3 outlines how Māori engaged with radio after it started in 1921 and Chapter 4 traces the impact of television after its arrival in Aotearoa in 1960.

Chapter 5 unpacks the history of journalism training focused on Māori and telling stories through an Indigenous lens. In Chapter 6, we look at real news stories, unpacking how standard news values are interpreted in a Māori paradigm and applying these to stories that have appeared online, on radio and on television. Chapter 7 examines how the work of Māori language journalists supports the national reo revitalisation agenda and Chapter 8 offers a deep dive into the ways in which elements of whaikōrero have transferred into news language and framing.

The challenges involved in maintaining relationships and tikanga in a fast-paced news environment dominate Chapter 9; Chapter 10 takes this further by looking at how tapu and noa influence Māori newswork. Finally, Chapter 11 looks to the future for Māori interest and Māori language news media in the digital age.

## SOURCES OF THE ORIGINAL TEXTS QUOTED IN THIS PUKAPUKA

Many of the newspapers and magazines referred to on this book are now available for free online through two sites: Niupepa: Māori Newspapers, a project of the New Zealand Digital Library Project at the University of Waikato, and Papers Past, an initiative of the National Library Te Puna Mātauranga o Aotearoa. They are treasure troves of information on the preoccupations of Māori through past decades and centuries.

## THE MĀORI WORLDVIEW, COLONISATION AND TWENTY-FIRST-CENTURY ASPIRATION

In Māori thinking, the natural and the spiritual are one; cosmology and life are framed by an interconnectedness that dictates relationships, whether with humans, the environment, or the gods. This is whakapapa, which means descent in the linear genealogical sense, but also encompasses the many layers of stories that map the nature of the unseen and seen worlds, and explains the nature of the relationships within them and between them. Whakapapa provides, as Cherryl Waerea-i-te-rangi Smith explains, "explanation for existence and also articulates the human role within that existence. Within whakapapa there are origins and explanations for trees, birds, parts of the human body, words and speaking, the cosmos, the gods, karakia, the moon, the wind and stones. All life is connected and interrelated."[11]

The many pūrākau or stories embedded in whakapapa also define the parameters of human behaviour, either literally, metaphorically, or through value judgments, while acknowledging that desired standards are not always met. As author and activist Ranginui Walker wrote, stories about the ancestors and their activities provided "myth-messages ... to which the Māori people can and will respond today".[12] In daily life, we call on a shared appreciation. An adventurous, risk-taking child might be compared to Māui the trickster demigod or the sea may be personified as Tangaroa, deity of the sea. To illustrate how these understandings are reflected in the ways journalists tell stories, let's turn to the best-known creation pūrākau to show how the perspectives it encodes can be reflected in newswork.

## PŪRĀKAU AND JOURNALISM

Although creation stories are broadly similar across all iwi, there are differences and even contradictions; what follows is a condensed narrative of a widely known version. It recounts that the cosmos emerged from an energy that evolved through various stages from Te Kore, a primal void, to Te Pō, which means darkness or night, to Te Ao Mārama, the world of light. In Te Pō, Ranginui, the male essence, and Papatūānuku, the female essence, were locked together in a tight embrace.

Between them in the darkness were a number of male children. These would become atua – gods, guardians and guides of the natural world. They included Tāne Mahuta, the god of birds, the forests and man; Tāwhirimātea, the god of winds, storms and rain; Rongo, the god of cultivated food plants and peace; Haumia tiketike, the god of uncultivated food plants, such as fern root; Tangaroa, the god of fish and reptiles; Rūaumoko, the god of earthquakes, volcanoes and thermal activity; and Tūmatauenga, god of war.

The brothers were unhappy about being wedged in the darkness, and a fierce discussion resulted about how they could get to Te Ao Mārama. Tāwhirimātea objected to separation, fearing the consequences; Tūmatauenga suggested that the brothers kill their parents. Various of the brothers tried to push their parents apart without success, until Tāne lay on his back, on his mother, and used his legs to thrust his father upwards, allowing Te Ao Mārama to flood in. Above, Rangi showed his love and yearning for Papa by weeping rain upon her, and below, her distress rose in mist.

Tāwhirimātea was so angry that he flew to support his father and waged war on his brothers with his winds, storms and rain. He snapped the branches of Tāne's children, lashed Tangaroa's oceans, forcing some of his lizard-children onto land, and made the helpless Rongomatāne and Haumia-tiketike cower in their mother's belly. Only Tūmatauenga stood firm, and in disgust for his elder brothers' weakness, chased and caught them all except Tāwhirimātea. He debased them by eating them or turning them into implements such as spears and sinkers.

Tāne then created the ira tangata, the human element. He used red earth to fashion the first woman, Hineahuone, and they had Hinetītama. Tāne later slept with Hinetītama, who was unaware that Tāne was her father, and they had a child. When Hinetītama learned the truth, she fled, distraught, to her grandmother, Papatūānuku, and descended to the world of darkness where she transformed into Hinenuitepō, the goddess of death.

An important message in the creation story is the necessary complementarity of male and female for life to thrive, but the narrative also sets limits – the flight of Hinetītama to the underworld tells us that incest is prohibited. The creation story also introduces the dichotomy between tapu (sacred) and noa (profane or everyday) so central to Māori thinking. Tūmatauenga's actions in eating his brothers and turning some of them into everyday tools describes the ritual and cultural significance of cannibalism as the ultimate humiliation of the conquered.

Te reo Māori, the Māori worldview and reo Māori reporting are intimately connected. As we think and speak, so we write. In Māori language news, the earth is routinely identified as Papatūānuku; native forest as te wao nui a Tāne, or the great forest of Tāne; and plants and trees as the children of Tāne. A common phrase in reporting the death of a leader is "Kua hinga te tōtara o te wao nui a Tāne", or the tōtara in Tāne's great forest has fallen. The tōtara is a sturdy giant often referred to as a "rākau rangatira", or chiefly tree; as Tāne is the god of the forests and of man, the metaphor is a perfect fit. The sea is often personified as Tangaroa, and sea life as "ngā tini a Tangaroa", the many children of Tangaroa. Weather reports are often titled "ngā tohu a Tāwhirimātea", the signs of Tāwhirimātea, the god of wind, storms and rain. These are just a few examples of the ways in which the creation story and other pūrākau important to Māori are referenced in news stories. Many more examples are given in Chapters 6 and 7.

## WHAIKŌRERO – THE FIRST NEWS CHANNEL

The ancestors developed a rich oral culture in which whaikōrero, or oratory, was a primary channel for transmitting important information between and within iwi. As academic Poia Rewi noted in his book *Whaikōrero*, oratory "helped people make decisions with regard to all matters affecting their living arrangements, their work, and their daily, monthly and yearly activities that would keep them safe. If there were any major issues to put before the people, each speaker would stand and air their opinion until all concerned had expressed what they had to say."[13]

Speakers built on each other's commentary, like a news story laying out points of view. Then, as now, speakers followed a structure and called on cultural knowledge to frame the 'news', using chants, allusions and stock phrases, drawing on imagination and wit, and often making references to whakapapa, people and places important to listeners.

Veteran broadcaster Tainui Stephens talks about whaikōrero as the origin of Māori news; Māori journalists are, he says, "the newest branch of a very old family tree".[14] Whaikōrero is one of the art forms that constitutes mātauranga Māori, and we explore the meaning of mātauranga next.

## INDIGENOUS WAYS OF SEEING, BEING AND DOING

Mātauranga Māori is not neatly defined in English. Academic Robert Wiri described it as encompassing "the Māori way; the Māori world-view; the Māori style of thought; Māori ideology; Māori knowledge base; Māori perspective; to understand or to be acquainted with the Māori world; to be knowledgeable in things Māori; to be a graduate of the Māori schools of learning; Māori tradition and history; Māori experience of history; Māori enlightenment; Māori scholarship; Māori intellectual tradition."[15]

The wide range of skills and activities within these headings also form part of mātauranga Māori, among them carving, weaving, house-building, genealogy, oral narratives, proverbs and song. In short, mātauranga Māori tells how we got here and who we are, and gives us guidance. Rooted in mātauranga Māori is tikanga, or the protocols and processes, rituals, obligations and behaviour in public and in private, for the individual and the group that are reinforced, validated and modified as they are passed down the generations. As a noun, tikanga means rule, plan or method; custom or habit; anything normal or usual; reason; meaning or purport; authority or control. The root of the word is tika, which as an adjective means straight or direct; keeping a direct course; just or fair; right or correct. The word embeds notions of doing the right thing in a Māori paradigm. Academic Hirini Moko Mead summarised it like this:

> Tikanga are tools of thought and understanding. They are packages of ideas which help to organise behaviour and provide some predictability in how certain activities are carried out. They provide templates and frameworks to guide our actions and help steer us through some huge gatherings of people and some tense moments in our ceremonial life. They help us to differentiate between right and wrong in everything we do and in all of the activities we engage in. There is a proper way to conduct one's self.[16]

In earlier times, wrote academic Meihana Durie, following tikanga was critical: "In a world where survival was a major consideration, there was little room for actions, practices or behaviours that compromised safety or wasted precious time, hours of sunlight or energy."[17] After the missionaries arrived, Māori discovered there was a new practice – the written word – and were very keen to grasp it.

# KO TE WHAKAPAPA O TE MAHI TĀ HAURAPA KŌRERO

## THE HISTORY OF MĀORI PRINT JOURNALISM

## MĀORI LANGUAGE NEWSPAPERS

Early missionaries and settlers had to speak te reo to survive – they were minorities in a Māori land. From the early 1800s, missionaries spurred the development of a reo Māori orthography, translating the Bible into Māori and using it to teach their converts to read and write in te reo. The newly literate often returned to their homes to teach others.

There are no reliable indications of the numbers of Māori who were able to read and write te reo in the first half of the nineteenth century, but it is claimed that by the 1850s, about half the adult Māori population could read Māori and about one-third could both read and write in te reo.[18] Indeed, Māori may even have been more literate in their native language than British settlers were in theirs.[19] As a result, there was a ready market for newspapers, and from the 1840s to the early 1930s, more than forty reo Māori newspapers debated ideas, reported news, advertised goods and services and generally recorded Māori life, traditions, opinions and language use; they are a fascinating insight into the past.

These newspapers fall into two broad groups. One comprises newspapers produced by the new arrivals, and included the government, which dominated publishing from the 1840s to late 1870s; churches of various denominations, which aimed to Christianise Māori; and private businessmen, often driven by religious faith to do likewise. The other group contains papers produced by Māori primarily for Māori. These proliferated from the 1860s, as tensions between tangata whenua and the British rose, and the newspapers publicly recorded iwi opposition to government encroachment on Māori land. However, all the papers, regardless of whoever was in charge, were opinionated propaganda organs with various political, religious and cultural agendas; the news business didn't start professionalising until much later in the nineteenth century.

## GOVERNMENT NEWSPAPERS

The colonial government was quick to exploit the power of print. The first Māori language newspaper was the monthly *Ko te Karere o Nui Tireni* (1842–46),[20] produced at the command of the country's first governor, William Hobson. The first paragraph in the new paper stated that it had been started "so Maori understand the laws and customs of the Pakeha and Pakeha also understand Maori ways".

The following paragraphs made clear the government's assimilationist agenda: The paper's focus would be "first, the Governor's decrees and secondly the Queen's laws; the means of applying justice and the crimes for which people are tried, and a great deal concerning Pakeha customs". This first paper, which ran to forty-nine issues, adopted a condescending tone that looks very jarring now, and became more strident as its publisher's ideology against Māori hardened.

Other government papers included *Te Waka Maori o Ahuriri*, a fortnightly produced in Napier between 1863 and 1871. It was succeeded by *Te Waka Maori o Niu Tireni*, a monthly produced in Wellington 1871–7. These papers also promoted assimilation, but that didn't mean Māori voices were silenced: Māori were keen correspondents to all the newspapers, and their contributions to the press are explored later in this chapter.

## CHURCH NEWSPAPERS

Church-based newspapers urged readers to keep the faith and promoted temperance and the value of British ways. The first Māori language church newspaper was the Wesleyan *Te Haeata*, which ran to thirty-seven issues between 1859 and 1861. It was typical of its breed, wrote Jane McRae, an expert in these early papers:

> Highly didactic – often using Māori proverbs and metaphors in support of its lessons – much of the paper was given over to exhorting Māori to keep the faith, abandon their customary beliefs, and live and be educated as the Pākehā. The reporting on local and overseas news and political matters – the King Movement, war in Taranaki and trouble in Waikato – is conservative, and contributions from Māori are primarily in support of the church and faith.[21]

The Māori clergy of the Church of England living on the East Coast established a noteworthy press, putting out *He Kupu Whakamarama* (1898–1902), *Te Pipiwharauroa* (1899–1913), *Te Kopara* (1913–21) and *Te Toa Takitini* (1921–32).

## PRIVATE PAPERS

Several wealthy Pākehā published newspapers in the late 1840s and 1850s, driven by their desire to inculcate Christian values in Māori society. One was Charles Davis, an interpreter with a "genuine liking for Māori"[22] who had previously been involved with government papers. He published three short-lived papers, *Te Waka o te Iwi*, which ran to two or three issues from October 1857, *Te Whetu o te Tau* (June, July and September 1858) and the bilingual *Ko Aotearoa or the Maori Recorder* (January 1861 and January 1862). Later on, W.P. Snow, a "pious and benevolent American gentleman of means"[23] launched a monthly newspaper, *Te Korimako* (1882–8), and appointed Davis as editor.

The lines between private, state and church papers blurred at times – unsurprisingly, given their common cause of 'civilising' Māori. As an example, a young Native Department official, Walter Buller, who had a background in government publishing, went on to establish *Te Karere o Poneke* (1857–8). Despite the government coat-of-arms in the masthead, it was a private enterprise that included Buller's father, a Wesleyan missionary. The paper was particularly active in promoting the "ritenga pai" of Pākehā,[24] a euphemism for the concepts of civilisation and progress – the law, religion and habits of the settlers – the Pākehā-run newspapers promoted to Māori.

It is tempting, when looking back at the collective power of the nineteenth-century newspapers through a post-colonial lens, to see collusion between the Pākehā-run papers and the Crown to promote Māori deculturation. There was certainly some sharing of information, particularly from the government to the church and private papers, but no evidence of an agenda; the publishers shared the belief that Māori would do better if they behaved more like Pākehā, and their newspapers echoed that conviction.

## MĀORI-OWNED NEWSPAPERS

Papers run by Māori, in Māori and for Māori flourished from the 1860s. *Te Hokioi o Niu Tireni e Rere atu na* (1861–3) was the first Māori-owned and Māori-run paper wholly in te reo; it was also the first and most radical example of Indigenous media activism in New Zealand.[25] The paper was founded and controlled by the Kīngitanga, the Waikato-based confederation of North Island tribes that united under a figurehead to resist colonial encroachment. Its name and stance referred to the mythical and fearsome hōkioi, a bird whose cry, heard only at night, was an omen of war.[26] The bird is believed to have been the giant Haast's eagle, now extinct.

But first, we need to ask a question: How did Māori get access to their first printing press? In 1859, two Waikato rangatira, Wiremu Toetoe Tumohe and Te Hemara Te Rerehau Paraone, went to Austria on the frigate *Novara* at the invitation of Austrian geologist, Dr F.R. von Hochstetter, who had met them while surveying Aotearoa. From the account of Tumohe, re-published in *Te Ao Hou* in 1958, the pair went to Vienna to learn how to print. The Emperor of Austria presented them with a press and type, which they brought back to Māngere where Pōtatau Te Wherowhero, the first Māori King, lived. This press, now in the Te Awamutu Museum, was used to print the King's proclamations and *Te Hokioi*.

The paper's editor was Wiremu Pātara Te Tuhi, an advisor to the King whose "articles were full of native wit and ability".[27] A total of ten issues, typically around four pages long, would appear over an eleven-month period, with most content criticising the colonial government and reminding readers of the agreements in Te Tiriti o Waitangi. Here's a translated example from the issue of 15 February 1863:

> The Waikato River does not belong to the Queen but to the Māori only … The word of our mother, the Queen, to those chiefs is clear indeed, that is: if the people of New Zealand don't wish to cede the mana of their lands, their rivers and their fisheries to me, that is fine; let them keep the mana: so this is one of our rivers we are keeping to ourselves.[28]

The messages published by *Te Hokioi* so enraged Governor Grey that he instructed a rival newspaper to be set up in nearby Te Awamutu, called *Te Pihoihoi Mokemoke i Runga i te Tuanui* (*The Lone Sparrow on the Roof Top*). Edited by local magistrate John Gorst, the new paper began publishing the government viewpoint in February 1863, but it would last only five issues. The paper quickly offended the Kīngitanga, leading to Māori calls for Gorst to be expelled and his newspaper shut down. The exchanges between the two publications became increasingly vitriolic in "a brief newspaper war".[29] The two birds sparred vigorously until Ngāti Maniapoto chief Rewi Maniapoto sent warriors to *Te Pihoihoi* to shut it down. Tensions were running high; on 12 July 1863, on a flimsy pretext, government troops invaded Waikato.

Tensions were rising elsewhere, with Māori concerned about dubious land sales to settlers. Several notable newspapers were published by the Hawke's Bay-based Repudiation movement, which wanted such sales disavowed on the grounds of fraud. Among them was the anti-government newspaper *Te Wananga* (1874–8). It demanded an end to land sales and leases, that the Native Land Court be abolished, that Māori representation in parliament be increased and that railways, roads and telegraphs not be built on Māori land.

Various tribes, mistrustful of the Pākehā-run national parliament, established Te Kotahitanga, a Māori Parliament, to seek constitutional authority of their own. Hastings-printed *Huia Tangata Kotahi* (1893–5) was the first of several newspapers published under the Kotahitanga umbrella. It provided coverage of parliament's proceedings, letters and notices, local and foreign news, and advertisements. A successor was the monthly paper *Te Puke ki Hikurangi*, producing more than 180 issues in the periods 1897–1900, 1901–6 and 1911–3. It covered a wide range of issues and was notable for the involvement of a woman who emerged as a major force in the Māori language newspapers: Niniwa-i-te-rangi, also known as Niniwa Heremaia. She chose and translated items from English-language newspapers for the paper and wrote numerous reports herself.

However, not all Māori were unhappy with the changing landscape. A coalition of twenty-five koroua (elderly men) established

*The Jubilee Te Tiupiri* (1898–1900), a bilingual, loyalist paper that commemorated Queen Victoria's 1897 Jubilee and ran to more than seventy issues. To give you a flavour of its stance, the first story in its first edition lists, in turgid detail, the reigns of the entire British monarchy from 1066. The same story also describes the "great European nation" as having "constant mana and chieftainship", while the Māori are "still in darkness, living through the want of energy in our dealings; for this reason, we, the elderly gentlemen belonging to this place set about establishing a newspaper".[30] These elderly gentlemen were aware that it had long been common for one person to buy a newspaper and read it aloud to many. This was clearly bad for business, and the first issue asked purchasers not to read out the content.

## WHO WERE THE JOURNALISTS?

The phrase 'citizen journalism' to describe ordinary people gathering and spreading the news may appear to be a development of the digital era, but it was thriving in the mid-1800s, with Māori contributing substantial content to the reo Māori newspapers. Newspaper proprietors, publishing before the advent of professional journalism and widespread telegraph transmission, faced a small population from which to raise subscriptions, a shortage of advertising and minimal staffing; they actively encouraged readers to send stories. For example, an editorial in *Te Pipiwharauroa* on 1 April 1899 exhorted readers to play journalist:

> Organisers, send in reports of your own areas: reports of meetings, money, description of the situation of your lands and of the people, or about your ideas, or sayings of ours, the Maori, and many other reports which are appropriate for our paper. Don't wait until the news is known and then send it in, but send in snippets of news; don't delay with the news.[31]

Māori responded enthusiastically, as academic Lachy Paterson wrote: "Men, women, the young, the great and the small wrote letters in the spirit of the long-held tradition of kōrero, of talk and debate."[32] Māori

> E nga kai whakahaere tukua mai nga korero o koutou na takiwa; nga korero hui, kohi moni, whakaatu mai i te ahua o koutou na whenua, o nga tangata, i o koutou na whakaaro ranei, i nga whakatauki ranei a tana a te Maori, me te tini o era atu korero e tika ana mo ta tatou pepa. Kaua e tatari kia wharona rawa te korero ka tuku mai ai. Tukuna mai nga pito-pito korero. Kaua e roa rawa te korero.

*Te Pipiwharauroa*, 1 April 1899, p. 6.

PAPERS PAST, NATIONAL LIBRARY OF NEW ZEALAND TE PUNA MĀTAURANGA O AOTEAROA

wrote in all genres – editorials, letters, articles, obituaries, reports of meetings and events, advertisements and notices. Publication conferred prestige: "Just as chiefs spoke for their hapū, so they often wrote on their behalf also. Getting letters to the editor published, in effect as an extension of a good whaikōrero performance, meant that the writer acquired mana."[33]

In the early reo Māori newspapers, men's voices dominate. One study of newspapers published between 1855 and 1863 claimed that women's voices were absent: "Men rarely discussed Māori women, except for expressions of concern about their health or morality."[34] However, we must add a caveat: this study covered just eight years of the forty years during which reo Māori newspapers flourished. In addition, we can't tell how much these women might have influenced debates before pen was put to paper. We do know that in the 1880s, in areas where women were politically organised, women of mana like Niniwa-i-te-rangi in Wairarapa were visible and sophisticated correspondents.[35]

You may have noticed from the illustrations above that the colonial-era papers used no macrons – short lines above a vowel that mark vowel length, which clarifies a word's exact meaning. In the 1800s, te reo was healthy and fluent speakers instinctively knew where to elongate vowels. Now, in a climate of reo revitalisation where many people learn te reo as a second language, reminders in the form of macrons help preserve the language's integrity. Macrons have been promoted by peak body Te Taura Whiri i te Reo Māori, the Māori Language Commission, since its establishment in 1987, and macron use is now widespread; however, a notable exception is tribal entity Waikato-Tainui, whose own publications use a double vowel. In this book, text is quoted as it was originally written.

## THE ORAL ARTS IN REO MĀORI PAPERS

A striking feature of all the ninteenth-century newspapers is how seamlessly oral culture translates to the page. Māori often wrote for the newspapers as if they were speaking in public, complete with the poetic and formulaic language of whaikōrero. To connect with Māori, Pākehā writers for the government's papers often did the same. As McRae noted, "Māori brought … the precedent and observance of performance and their oral arts, and implicitly, sometimes explicitly, the philosophy that underpinned them. The poetic language therefore found a place in the papers and Pākehā were attracted to the use of it."[36]

Anything that could be said, sung or chanted in public could appear on a newspaper page, including genealogies, songs, sayings, speeches, incantations and narratives. Newspapers were another marae ātea, a community space for views to be shared, debates held and communal decisions made. As on the marae, the wit, repartee and wisdom of oratory were evident. Letters might begin with an elaborate mihi to the paper or the editors. Newspapers contained debates about whakapapa and tribal traditions; letters might end with the words of a waiata or karakia.

A newspaper that ran to seventy-five issues between 1882 and 1888 provides several good examples of Māori oratory on the page. As previously mentioned, philanthropist W.P. Snow founded *Te Korimako* to promote Christianity. The bird was an astute choice of metaphor: "Māori admired its song. Its chorus at dawn announced the light of day that, in their thinking and poetry, represented life and success. It was

Ko te ingoa mo to tatou taonga, ko "Te Korimako Rere Haere" Ko tenei, ekoro ma, akona mai to tatou Manu Maori, whangainga hoki ki "nga hua o te tau" kia kaha ai tana kotete. Kei runga kei te hoka to tatou Manu, ko ana korero anake e rere atu ana ki rau-whenua, ki rau-iwi; koia hoki e kiia atu nei, whakaahurutia tenei mokai, kia puta ai ta tatou mahara, kia ara ai te kauwae o tenei motu, kia tamia iho te kino, kia whakamoiritia ko te pai.

The name for our valuable paper is "THE KORIMAKO." And now, oh Sirs, teach this our Maori bird, and feed it with "the fruits of the year," so that it may possess sufficient energy to speak out. Our bird is on the perch; its sentiments only fly away to many lands, and many peoples, hence my request to you is, nourish this bird, by which means we shall enable ourselves to carry out our project—the advancement of this island; the dethronement of evil, and the ascendancy of good.

Newspaper *Te Korimako* likens itself to a bellbird spreading news.

NEW ZEALAND DIGITAL LIBRARY, COMPUTER SCIENCE DEPARTMENT, UNIVERSITY OF WAIKATO

therefore a fitting image for early reports and news, and put the papers in a good light."[37]

In its first edition, the editor's welcome was translated to ensure that all readers would understand the paper's mission and its need for income.

The paper is likened to a bird winging its way from kāinga to kāinga bringing news from all corners but needing "the fruits of the year",[38] or a subscription, from the people in turn; similar metaphors recur in many nineteenth-century papers. A reader who sent subscription money and a congratulatory letter extended the metaphor (the original text appears on the opposite page):

A Message Sent to Us

To Te Korimako

Sir, greetings! The first bird to fly across this land, around all its bends and headlands, O bird, I am anxious that you land at my residence. I simply thought when I went after some birds, they would be caught forever. Well, in the end, I left off shooting them because they were not plump. But then I remembered your flying out to me in days gone by. And this is why I am again sending you a letter of invitation, so that you will fly again to me and in case you are upset at my abandoning you in those days. A saying of my ancestors goes like this, 'Uetahi's[39] deed will be returned'. So, I send fragrant seeds to entice you to fly to my residence. That's all I have to say. From your sweetheart

T. ERUETI MĀNIHERA, TANGOIRO, TŪRANGANUI[40]

Birds were an endless source of imagery and ideas in the newspapers. "Maori thought about birds a great deal," wrote academic Margaret Orbell. "Often they identified themselves with them."[41] The metaphor of the sweetly singing bird bringing news to all people had positive connotations for both Māori and Pākehā. However, for Māori, there was deeper meaning. There is "unmarked signification" in all genres of Māori communication, borne out of a shared culture based on a Māori

## Ki a Te Korimako.

E hika,—Tena koe! Te manu tuatahi nana nei i rere haere te motu nei, rauna noa ona kokonga me ona kurae. E manu tenei ano au te manukanuka nei ki ou taunga mai ki tooku marae, huanoa i whai atu ai au ki etahi manu, e mau tonu, kati, mahue ana i au te pupuhi i te momona kore. Heoi, no konei ka mahara ano au ki tou rerenga mai ki ahau i era ra kua pahure ake nei. Koia ka tukua atu nei ano e au he reta powhiri maku kia rere mai ano koe ki a au, kei manukanuka koe mo taku whakarerenga i a koe i era ra. He penei hoki te whakatauki a oku tupuna, "he mahi na Uetahi e hokia." A tenei ka tukua atu e au nga puakakara hei taki mai mou kia rere mai ki tooku marae. Heoi nga kupu na to Whaiaipo.

Na T. Erueti Manihera.

Tangoiro, Turanganui,

A reader likens his subscription monies to food for the newspaper *Te Korimako* – the bellbird.

NEW ZEALAND DIGITAL LIBRARY, COMPUTER SCIENCE DEPARTMENT, UNIVERSITY OF WAIKATO

metaphysical worldview.[42] In Māori thought, humans are intrinsically linked to the environment. Birds, fish, insects and plants, as well as phenomena such as the moon, mist, wind and rocks, all possess their own life force, or mauri. The land, its moods, its inhabitants and the places where important events have taken place shape Māori thinking and provide endless metaphorical anchors. Birds could be omens of death or messengers between the living and dead. A bird's song might mark a sacred place where chiefs lay; birdsong at daybreak was often seen as a sign of the triumph of light over darkness.

To illustrate a typical transfer of environment-related figures of speech to the page, we return to W.P. Snow, who died of a fever in 1883, aged twenty-six. His obituary referenced the bird of the masthead and contained typically Māori allusions:

### Roto i a Mate.

Ua moe, i tana moenga roa, W. P. Te No, nana ra i whakahuru te manu nei, a TE KORIMAKO. Tenei te noho-mokemoke ei taua manu meroiti, i runga i manga o te rakau. Titirohakatau ai, kaore e kite-wheriko u i te matua, na te mea, kua uaraia e te pae-maunga ki a po. tangi ana nga tai-whakatimu nga mata-tahuna o Aotearoa. auwhare ana mai te pukohu ki a tara o Ruawahia, ko te hoa kimihia nei, kei tana haere i te a pikipiki a Tawhaki.

An obituary for the proprietor of *Te Korimako*, W.P. Snow.

NEW ZEALAND DIGITAL LIBRARY, COMPUTER SCIENCE DEPARTMENT, UNIVERSITY OF WAIKATO

> W.P. Snow has come to the long sleep of the dead, he who gave the feathers to this bird, *Te Korimako*. And now the little bird sits lonely on the branch of the tree. Even if looking out intently, he will not see a glimpse of the father, because he has been obscured by the mountain range to Night. The ebbing tides cry against the shores of Aotearoa. Mist hangs over the peaks of Ruawāhia; the friend we seek is on his journey along the path climbed by Tāwhaki.[43]

The 'long sleep of the dead' is a common sentiment in te reo. The paper is, once again, anthropomorphised as a lonely bird. The feathers reference the whakataukī or saying 'Mā te huruhuru te manu ka rere, mā te kākahu te tangata ka tika ai', which translates as 'By feathers a bird flies and by clothing is a person presentable'. This originally meant to dress appropriately for the circumstances; however, like so many Māori expressions, this one found new meaning as times changed. In this context, the feathers are the money with which Snow funded the paper.

Finally, mountain ranges, raised high and hard to climb, inspired fear and awe. They were often thought to be the homes of spirits and were therefore used as a metaphor for separation between the living and dead. It was thought that dying people expired when the tide was ebbing, and outgoing tides were generally associated with misfortune. Mist often signified regret or disappointment. Ruawāhia is one of the domes at Tarawera, near where Snow and his wife lived. Tāwhaki is a demigod who climbed to the sky, so the path climbed by Tāwhaki is co-opted as the route to heaven.

## FROM ORATORICAL TO JOURNALISTIC

English-language newspapers in the 1800s were very wordy; according to journalism academic Christopher Scanlan, "stories were almost always told in the traditional, slow-paced (some might say long-winded) way."[44] This meant that the oratorical style of Māori language writing was fitting. However, change was coming. Telegraphy, invented in the 1840s, had revolutionised the newspaper business around the world, and, by the last two decades of the century, in Aotearoa. News was getting to and around the country in hours, not weeks or months.[45]

However, telegrams were expensive – senders paid per word. This led reporters in the English-language press, which was gradually becoming more professional, to adopt a clipped writing style focused on the new and factual. In his history of Aotearoa's colonial newspapers, journalism historian David Hastings observed that "such brevity was as far away from the verbosity of the 1840s, 1950s and 1860s as it was possible to get."[46] It also led to what journalists today term the inverted pyramid news-writing style, in which the most important and new information is broadly summarised first, with information of diminishing importance following. Even if readers don't finish the story, they have the most important detail; time-pressed editors can cut quickly from the end.

Correspondents writing in te reo quickly adopted the journalist's style: "They incorporated less of the manners and matter of traditional speech and were less rhetorical."[47] More stringent editorial gatekeeping also had an influence: "Newspapers ... sought to appeal by focus on the new. Editors turned down writing which was unclear; cryptic referents to a tribal tradition limited the chance of making a point widely understood (and thereby gaining sympathy); writing had to be explicit for a paper's many readers."[48]

Oral traditions remained on the page, but were truncated. Songs, sayings, genealogical stories, incantations and stories were still referenced, but "journalism, with its European literate conventions, enjoined them to rework those and use others."[49] We have a good example in the letter opposite to *Te Korimako*, in which Māori landowners complain about settlers stealing sand. There is just one Māori allusion, to Hawaiki, the ancestral homeland, believed to be in East Polynesia. Otherwise, the communication is largely free of ornament.

The allusion to Hawaiki here appears to mean that the complainants are witness to the thefts; they are not back in their ancestral homelands and thus unable to see that their sand is being stolen.

## THE BEGINNING OF THE END OF REO MĀORI NEWSPAPERS

An influx of settlers from the mid-1800s would spell the beginning of the end for reo Māori publications. By 1858, the Māori and

### Ki a Te Korimako.

E hoa,—Tena koe! E hoa, mau e tuku atu a matou korero kia kite nga Pakeha me nga Maori e noho nei i tenei motu, ara, he whakaatu na matou kia mohio nga Pakeha me mutu rawa ta ratou utauta i nga onepu ki runga ki o ratou tima, kaipuke, aha ranei e tae mai ana ki te kao nei. Notemea kahore matou e mohio ana heiaha ranei i mauria ai nga onepu, akuanei pea tera he taonga mo matou kei aua onepu, na konei ka whai kupu matou ki nga Pakeha me mutu te hari i nga onepu ki runga i o ratou tima. Ko te take no matou te whenua, a no to matou whenua hoki aua onepu. Mehemea he hiahia to ratou to nga Pakeha ki te onepu kaua e hari pokanoa, engari me haere mai kia matou ma matou te tikanga. E hara hoki i te mea kei Hawaiki matou e noho ana kia hari pokanoa i nga taonga o to matou whenua. E mohio ana matou ko nga tima o te kamupene o te makereka nohoia Akarana, nga tima e auau ana te mahi penei ki nga onepu, heoi he whakamutunga tenei. Kahore o koutou hea ki tenei whenua e tika ai te mau pokanoa. Mehemea he hiahia, kei konei ano matou e noho ana, haere mai pataia.

   Na Eparaima Kapa,
    ,, Keepa Horo,
    ,, Hemi Riumakutu,
    ,, Wiki Te Whai.

Te Kao, Parengarenga,
 Oketopa, 8, 1884.

Letter of complaint to the editor, *Te Korimako*, August 1885.

Pākehā populations had reached parity, at around 59,000 each. After 1874, Māori were less than one-tenth of the total population, and this remained the case for a century.[50] Such rapid colonisation was catastrophic for te reo and tikanga Māori. Anglo-centric education policies instituted from the late 1860s tied education funding to English-language instruction and later removed Māori language from the classroom altogether. To gain an education through the Māori-only native schools, children had to board away from home, inhibiting transmission of their parents' tongue and tikanga. This, wrote tohunga Māori Marsden, was "cultural genocide".[51] In 1913, a survey found that 90 percent of Māori children starting at a native school spoke te reo as their first language, learning English at school. A decade later, that figure was 82 percent.[52] In 1950, a survey suggested that just 54 percent of Māori children spoke "some" Māori at home.[53] Worse, in 1975, fewer than 5 percent of Māori schoolchildren could speak their heritage language.[54] By then, said the Waitangi Tribunal, English-language newspapers, radio and television created an "incessant barrage that blasted the Māori tongue almost into oblivion."[55] As English became the language of public life, the general-interest Māori language publications dwindled, and by 1913, most of the Māori language publications were church newspapers and niche-interest pamphlets. Meanwhile, the English-language press was thriving: by 1911, Aotearoa had sixty-four daily papers for a population of just over a million.[56]

## TAIHOA AKE! BUT WAIT ...

There were, however, two reo Māori papers that tried to swim against the tide of English in the twentieth century. The first was *Wairere*, about which we know little. Two copies have been found, dated February and May 1917. The masthead stated that the paper was a weekly. Also on the masthead was the name N.P. Kawiti (also known as Nau Paraone) who was, presumably, the publisher. Kawiti was a Whangārei boarding-house keeper who stood unsuccessfully for the Northern Māori seat in the 1914 and 1919 general elections. By this time, editorial cartoons in newspapers were common, and *Wairere* featured them on its front page. The cartoon below, which is not available online, shows warriors in waka trying to head off a crocodile that has its jaws agape as it heads for the North Island, labelled Aotearoa, the word commonly used at that time for the island.

The crocodile appears to be labelled too, though the word is unclear. The animal appears to represent a threat to sovereignty, either national, Māori or both. We could speculate that the crocodile is a metaphor for a submarine or for Germany; at the time, World War I

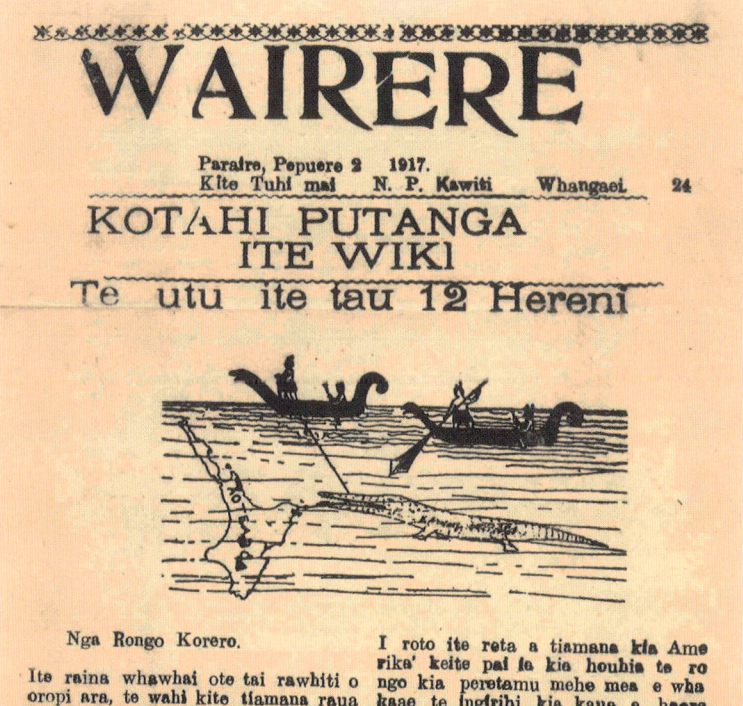

The front page of *Wairere*, February 1917.

TĀMAKI PAENGA HIRA
AUCKLAND WAR MEMORIAL
MUSEUM. NZ SERIAL
AP7.5 WAI

was raging between the Allies and Germany in Europe, and submarines had already come close to winning the war for Germany. In January 1917, Germany announced it was reneging on an international code that required merchant ships to be given warning of attack so sailors could escape; from then on, its submarines would shoot and sink. There was fear that the United Kingdom, reliant on food shipped from Aotearoa, would starve and that many merchant seamen would be lost.[57]

All the stories underneath the cartoon, whether local or international, concern the war and are written in clipped journalistic style. Curiously, the first story appears to be an early example of fake news. On the Eastern Front, it says, German and Russian troops called a truce so they could work together to eradicate packs of hungry wolves that had become a threat. This story appeared in various newspapers around the world – but the incident has never been verified by Russian sources nor thorough academic work on historical wolf attacks.[58]

The second twentieth-century newspaper of note was run by a woman, Rehutai Maihi of Ngāpuhi (1895–1967). Maihi trained as a compositor before working on papers such as the English-language *Northland Age*. In June 1932, with her elders' approval, she launched a general-interest Māori language newspaper, *Aotearoa*, an unusual

Rehutai Maihi.

ALEXANDER TURNBULL
LIBRARY, WELLINGTON:
JANET MARY CANDON
MCCALLUM COLLECTION
PA12-2207

The front page of *Aotearoa*, believed to be the last reo Māori newspaper.

NATIONAL LIBRARY OF NEW ZEALAND TE PUNA MĀTAURANGA O AOTEAROA

move given reo Māori papers had largely vanished. In her first issue, Maihi reprinted Te Tiriti o Waitangi and invited contributions from readers. Publication was initially weekly, but became less frequent and stopped in 1933. In following years, Maihi became the first Māori woman to stand for Parliament, as an independent, but was unsuccessful. In September 1940, the second year of World War II, she saw that Māori in New Zealand and soldiers overseas were hungry for information in te reo, so resurrected *Aotearoa* as a fortnightly, then a monthly.[59] Above is the issue of 1 February 1945.

The first cover of *Te Ao Hou*, 1952.

TE PUNI KŌKIRI

## PRINT MAKES A COMEBACK, BUT MAINLY IN ENGLISH

World War II was a catalyst for many Māori to move to cities in search of employment, and by 1951, a total of 19 percent of Māori were urban. The state policy of 'pepper-potting' Māori families in Pākehā communities further broke kinship and language links. For many of the new arrivals, city life brought dislocation and inter-racial tension and the government's assimilationist agenda intensified, with print media again one of its tools. The best known was *Te Ao Hou*, a quarterly, bilingual magazine launched in winter 1952 by the Department of Māori Affairs.

Under four Pākehā but largely pro-Māori editors, *Te Ao Hou* became a "veritable Māori institution"[60] and has been digitised. The magazine didn't appear to have dedicated journalists beyond the editor, instead relying on contributions, many from notable writers and leaders of the time. *Te Ao Hou* ran a wide range of articles about Māori life, history and tikanga, mostly in English. The first issue gives the flavour of that range: it carried, among others, an English article about Ngāti Mutunga doctor and politician Te Rangi Hīroa (Sir Peter Buck); a bilingual story announcing that changes to the law that meant "Māori marriages", or those without the licences required by Pākehā law, were no longer legal; a bilingual report on the second annual conference of the Māori Women's Welfare League; and an English feature on Māori sport. There was a story in English about the newly released film *Broken Barrier*, which told the story of a love affair between a Māori nurse and a Pākehā journalist, and a bilingual article outlining the aims and objectives of the Department of Māori Affairs.

However, the first editor, Erik Schwimmer, a migrant from the Netherlands, often butted heads with his bosses over content. They preferred instructional, condescending information as was commonly directed to Māori at the time; Erik Schwimmer believed in a bicultural Aotearoa. One of his regular contributors, pioneering poet and short-story writer J.C. Sturm, recalled that having to dispense paternalistic advice to Māori bothered Erik Schwimmer far more than it did his readers. "We … were very used to, indeed, expected to be told by all and sundry what we had to do to become respectable middle-class citizens, a lighter shade of brown, as it were," she wrote. "In fact, some of us had become pretty good at preaching ourselves."[61]

A few issues in, Erik Schwimmer was told that there was no room for opinions in the magazine beyond those of the government. From then on, he made *Te Ao Hou* a site of restrained resistance where writers shared ideas about self-determination in a careful and measured manner. They recognised, he said, that "this marae on paper was precarious and did not wish it to fall apart. Their attitude was protective."⁶² In "a period of apparent compliance," he said, "... many texts we received expressed hidden, indirect and symbolic resistance."⁶³

The magazine also became an influential publisher of English-language creative writing by Māori, among them Witi Ihimaera, Patricia Grace, Katerina Te Heikōkō Mataira and Arapera Blank. In these stories and poems, as in the journalism, ideas around identity, justice and politics were explored, subtly at first, and then more overtly as the writers started challenging the assumptions and policies that circumscribed their lives.⁶⁴ The last issue of *Te Ao Hou* was published in June 1975, without a word of explanation in its pages.

In later years, the Department of Māori Affairs and its successors would print a range of publications to inform and influence Māori thinking and, over time, as pro-Tiriti thinking gained ground in government, stopped trying to control the narrative. Among these publications was *Te Kaea*, an English-language magazine with some reo content that appeared five times between 1979 and 1981. Editor Graham Wiremu saw *Te Kaea* as a direct successor to *Te Ao Hou* with its emphasis on news, views and creative writing, and embraced contentious issues. His first issue contained stories about the poor state of te reo Māori, whether the four Māori parliamentary seats should be abolished and a story by land rights activist Eva Rickard about her campaigning. Lighter fare included stories on entertainer Sir Howard Morrison's new TV show and the kōauau, the Māori flute.

The next page contained two poroporoaki, and here we see tikanga Māori and Pākehā practice side by side. The first obituary, written by broadcaster Selwyn Muru in te reo, was for a high-profile welfare worker, Parāone Kawiti Pūriri. Muru addressed Pūriri directly, as is common during tangihanga, using all the flourishes of formal speech: pepeha (proverbs), kupu whakarite (similes and metaphors) and interjections to convey emotion, such as "Auē! Te pōuri, te tangi ē!" ("Oh, the sadness! The mourning!"). The final paragraph farewelled Pūriri to his ancestors in a fashion typical of such whaikōrero: "Haere, haere, haere atu rā ki te kāinga tūturu." ("Return to the true home", meaning where the wairua, or spirit, of the ancestors resides).⁶⁵

The first cover of *Te Kaea*, featuring Howard Morrison and Tina Cross.

TE PUNI KŌKIRI

Alongside was an English-language obituary by Māori Battalion captain Bill Herewini for Brigadier George Dittmer, a Pākehā and the Māori Battalion's first commanding officer. It follows the style of English-language newspaper obituaries: in the third person, it starts with when and where Dittmer died before turning to a chronological recounting of his life. But tikanga Pākehā then took a decidedly Māori turn – the final sentence, in te reo, farewelled Dittmer to his ancestors.[66]

The successor to the Department of Māori Affairs, Te Puni Kōkiri, was created in 1991 and since then has produced a range of publications to inform readers of its work and celebrate success stories, mostly written in English. However, and notably, three issues of its magazine *Kōkiri*, which ran from 2007 to 2016, were published in te reo only to mark Māori Language Week in three consecutive years (2007, 2008 and 2009). The Matariki edition in 2015 was a bilingual effort – each story appeared in te reo and English in a back-to-back magazine format. The magazine ceased in 2016. Te Puni Kōkiri's external communications are now all digital, provided through its website. Some content is bilingual.

## *TU TANGATA* MAGAZINE: "WITHOUT FEAR AND WITHOUT FAVOUR"

One of the high points of Māori print journalism was a co-production by the three organisations that dominated Māori development at the time – the Department of Māori Affairs, the New Zealand Māori Council and the Māori Women's Welfare League. *Tu Tangata* (1981–7) was a bi-monthly magazine that came into being as part of the Department of Māori Affairs policy Tu Tangata, which aimed to empower Māori communities to be self-reliant. The first issue stated that the magazine would "inform the Maori people of the things of today, without fear and without favour".[67]

Editor for all but the first two issues was Piripi Whaanga, who had a background in mainstream newspaper and radio. Whaanga was a self-described stirrer, and the magazine was reflective, high quality and outspoken, with professional journalists among its contributors, some of them Pākehā. In-depth reports on the doings of Māori entities and discussion of political, cultural, economic and social issues accompanied success stories, letters, creative writing, poetry, crosswords, tips for people learning te reo, and poroporoaki. Obituaries and tributes to the deceased were often in te reo only and displayed all the oratorical flourishes of Māori speechmaking.

Whaanga believed that mainstream media needed an influx of Māori journalists to influence and improve the way Māori were portrayed, and used the magazine as a platform to encourage change. He actively

Piripi Whaanga, editor of *Tu Tangata*, in 1981.
TE PUNI KŌKIRI

promoted one-week taster courses in journalism for young Māori, run at the time by the Department of Māori Affairs and the Journalists Training Board (see Chapter 5), and profiled young journalists. As broadcaster Derek Fox wrote in the magazine, "We can only break the monocultural view of our society by being able to offer a Maori view at the time of writing and production. And that can only be done by being inside the system in sufficient numbers to have an impact."[68]

In the thirty-third issue of *Tu Tangata*, Whaanga described the magazine as having "changed its outlook over the years, from writing about Māori people to writing for Māori people."[69] However, the magazine fell victim to cost-cutting three issues later. In his final editorial, Whaanga said that it was a "blow" to lose the magazine: "It was the only independent voice for the people." While the publication "had its knockers and critics" because it was published by a government department, that same department was

> only too aware at times that *Tu Tangata* was not a departmental propaganda tool ... and the Maori people, from rangatahi (young people) through to kaumatua (elders) have responded over the past six years with letters of support and criticism, articles, jottings, poems and appeals ... it is rather tragic that at a time when many Maori and Pakeha people are acknowledging a thirst for information about Maori take (issues), *Tu Tangata* magazine has to close.[70]

## INDEPENDENT, PAN-TRIBAL PUBLICATIONS

In the late 1980s and 1990s, private, Māori-run newspapers and magazines sprang up to serve both iwi and pan-tribal audiences. Their publishers were united in the belief that mainstream media focused on Māori in only negative terms, and that many stories of interest to Māori and the wider population were simply not being told. Some of the papers explicitly wanted to inform and include Pākehā as well. The majority were wholly in English, but some had sections in te reo. Many periodicals of this era were run by people who had passion and political nous, but minimal journalistic, editorial and management experience. As journalist and educator Ian Stuart explained, "these papers, often radically pro-Maori or ultra-Māori, frowned upon writers who had what was perceived as 'Pākehā' media training. Often this was seen as a colonising process and therefore not desirable."[71]

By the late 1990s, more than a dozen pan-tribal periodicals were running at once. However, as with their nineteenth-century counterparts, funding was a perennial problem and appeals for government support were fruitless. By 2000, just a handful of the periodicals were still in business. Below, we'll look at several notable publications, both past and current.

## *TE IWI O AOTEAROA:* BLACK POWER TURNS PUBLISHER

In October 1987, Abraham Wharewaka, the entrepreneurial leader of the Auckland branch of the Black Power gang, set up a newspaper, *Te Iwi o Aotearoa*, which ran to forty-four issues until August 1991. He explained its aim in the first issue:

> This newspaper came into being because there has always been a shortage of Māori magazines, newspapers, etc, that give us the freedom to express ourselves without fear of being misinterpreted. Only the more negative aspects of our people are highlighted by the media machine. Yet there is a lot of positive work being done in Māoridom. We have a lot to contribute to this country in all aspects – given the opportunity. TE IWI O AOTEAROA will be an excellent vehicle to help establish a bicultural understanding so that TAU IWI (other people) have a clearer view of the issues surrounding the Māori people.

Black Power had a trust called Tatau te Iwi that ran government-funded employment skills schemes, and one of those paid for eight trainees to work on *Te Iwi o Aotearoa*. The paper gave plenty of space to its own events, such as gang conventions, but also covered a range of Māori issues, such as land rights, politics and Māori broadcasting.

## THE TUMAHAI STABLE

Publisher Anaru Tumahai was responsible for a string of periodicals between December 1992 and August 2005, predominantly newspapers in English with some Māori content. The focus, he told me in an interview, "was to publish Māori social and economic development in a positive light, which was, at the time, non-existent within mainstream publications." At the time, Tumahai saw publishing as a commercial investment that would be sustainable. Many advertisements published in his papers came from Māori organisations seeking staff, health entities messaging about common Māori health problems such as gout and diabetes, and public notices from iwi bodies.

The first publication, *Te Maori News* (1992–6), started as a monthly newspaper, with five staff; over time, it became fortnightly. Explaining the paper's grassroots approach, editor Vanessa Bidois-Stephens said Māori were tired of issues being filtered through a Pākehā lens, and used fisheries issues as an example. In mainstream media, she said, a story about fishing rights was more likely to focus on the reaction of the fishing industry. For a Māori readership, the focus would be on the history and progress of fisheries-related Tiriti o Waitangi claims. Equally, she said, Māori were more likely to talk to their own, as many felt that mainstream media was too negative.[72]

By July 1993, Anaru Tumahai said circulation had risen to 7500 – a substantial tally for the time – and that the company had passed break-even point.[73] *Te Māori News* was succeeded by *Te Karere Māori News* from Dec 1999 to December 2001, *Māori News* from January to March 2002, *Te Karere News* from April 2002 to January 2004 and *Te Karere Māori News*, a magazine, to August 2005. However, at that point the enterprise folded, a victim of insufficient advertising.

### *TU MAI:* A MĀORI LIFESTYLE MAGAZINE

Glossy magazine *Tu Mai* was founded by Ata Te Kanawa in 1999; she was also its editor. The magazine, which billed itself as the first Māori 'glossy', was subtitled "an indigenous New Zealand perspective" and offered stories in English on politics, Te Tiriti o Waitangi settlements, health, business, agriculture, industry, local news, the arts, fashion, lifestyles and successful Māori in many professions. It was eye-catchingly designed in the style of news-stand magazines and targeted, in particular, professional Māori women over the age of twenty-five.

For 114 issues *Tu Mai* was a hard-copy magazine. From October 2010 to November 2013 the magazine became online only and free. Te Kanawa said that the online move became inevitable as the recession stemming from the global financial crisis of 2008 deepened and printing costs continued to rise. Readers readily switched to online, but not advertisers: "Some advertising agencies could not accept Tu Mai's Māori readership were internet-literate," Te Kanawa wrote. "I reminded one agency staff member that the internet arrived on earth at the same

Ata Te Kanawa in 2011.
NZME, AGNES GINESTET

time for all of us – not 1840 when the Treaty of Waitangi was signed. And no, Māori are definitely not lagging behind in technology."[74] Fourteen years after its launch, *Tu Mai* closed. Te Kanawa said it was difficult to keep a publishing business afloat in a recession and her business interests in the Māori high-fashion and fine art worlds had intensified; something had to give.

## *MANA* MAGAZINE

The English-language *Mana* magazine (1993–2017) launched with the subtitle "the Maori news magazine for all New Zealanders". The magazine was published by Mana Māori Media, which at the time was a news agency producing radio news in English and Māori; the journalists behind the venture were veteran journalists Derek Fox and Piripi Whaanga, both Māori, and Gary Wilson, a Pākehā with a commitment to making spaces for Māori and Pacific voices to be heard (see Chapter 5). The trio had a high-calibre stable of Māori and

The first *Mana* cover.

COURTESY OF DEREK FOX, *MANA* MAGAZINE

non-Māori journalists that at various times included Waihoroi Shortland, Rereata Makiha, Wena Harawira, Wena Tait and Caleb Maitai (Māori) and Carol Archie, Andrew Robb and Paul Bensemann (Pākehā).

*Mana* was a consciously pan-tribal magazine and celebrated Māori culture and achievement in a chatty and inclusive style. The magazine's appearance, content and cost made it "the Māori equivalent to high-end mainstream New Zealand magazines such as *North & South* and *Metro*"; the magazine represented "a growing Māori middle class".[75] Producing the first issue, said Fox, was "heady stuff ... it was just before Christmas 1992 and we had just produced this 100-page colour glossy magazine telling Māori stories: stories we'd chosen and written and told in our way – nobody got to question us or tell us what to write or how to write it – there were no gatekeepers, just us."[76]

The first cover featured three pictures: Dame Whina Cooper, a leader in the fight against land loss, "glaring through the lens and into our eyes"; an All Black idol of the time, Johnny Timu; and a gaggle of children.[77]

In the first editorial, Fox pointed out that because mainstream media didn't reflect Māori issues, New Zealanders in general were ignorant of the damage that government policies had done:

> ... we've had generations of Kiwis, including Maori, who have never suspected how good the Government has been at diddling Maori out of their property – and who have never realised the cost of that to our whole society. One effect of that ignorance is that our communities are full of people who are bored, offended or enraged by any Maori insistence that the Government should acknowledge the dodgy deals – and face up to at least a few of the debts.
>
> *Mana* can't do much about the rednecks amongst us. But our stories and images will make it easier for readers, whatever their background, to become familiar with the events, issues and personalities of importance to Maori.
>
> And that familiarity may lead to a climate where there's a natural pride in, and understanding of, New Zealand's taha Maori.[78]

Derek Fox in 1993.
NZME MARK MITCHELL

Associate editor Gary Wilson said that although *Mana* might not want to be seen to be catering to a Pākehā audience, the reality was that no Māori development could succeed without mainstream support. Therefore, *Mana* had to appeal to Pākehā as well.[79] That would be done, said Fox, by providing "a window on Māoridom for people to look through and see what we're up to. Many of our stories are never told in mainstream media and we present a uniquely Māori perspective on issues that do receive wider media attention."[80]

From issues six to twelve, *Mana* contained a reo-only insert called *Te Rito*, with many of the contributors noted orators, writers and journalists in the Māori world, among them academics Tīmoti Kāretu and Hirini Moko Mead. It is likely that finding top-flight writers in te reo was difficult. A note in issue thirteen announced that *Te Rito* had been "dropped ... just for this issue, while we work out a new approach for those pages",[81] but it never reappeared.

Overall, *Mana*'s longevity made it a reliable and consistent record of Māori life. In the magazine's 100th issue in 2011, Fox said, "There is an amazing body of work and thousands of stories; many of them in time will be seen as the first cut of the modern Māori history of this country, told and photographed as it happened."[82]

However, while celebrating the success of *Mana*, Fox had concerns about its future. It was proving financially challenging to keep the publication afloat, due to a high pass-on rate and less advertising support than he had hoped for[83] – the problems that have long beset Māori print media.

Help was at hand. Kōwhai Media, publisher *of New Zealand Geographic* magazine, bought a licence to publish *Mana*, and the next magazine was out on time.[84] However, after three years, when the licence was to be renegotiated, Kōwhai could not reach terms with Fox, who announced that he was taking the magazine back.[85] *Mana* never reappeared.

## IWI PAPERS AND MAGAZINES

In the 1980s and 1990s, momentum for change was building in the Māori world. Through the Waitangi Tribunal, iwi were negotiating and settling their historic claims against the Crown, Māori medium education was underway and te reo became an official language. The need to keep iwi informed prompted a range of tribally focused publications. In 1995, when the Ngāi Tahu magazine *Te Karaka* was launched, editor Gabrielle Huria wrote, "Why have a tribal magazine? Anei tō mātou kaupapa [this is the reason] ... We live in an information age and those who control their information will ultimately control their own destiny."[86] While some iwi papers had professional journalists at the helm, many were run by enthusiastic but under-resourced volunteers. Notable tribal publications of the era included:

- *Kahungunu* (Kahungunu iwi, bilingual monthly but with varying frequencies, 1991–5)
- *Mana Tangata* (Whanganui iwi, bilingual monthly, 1991–3)
- *Te Maunga Kōrero* (Taranaki iwi, mostly in English, 1992–3)
- *Kia Ora News* (Ngāti Raukawa, 1992–5)
- *Pikiao Pānui* (Te Rūnanga o Ngāti Pikiao, an English-language publication that was initially monthly, then fell to three times a year, 1993–2004)
- *Nga Kohinga o Ngati Porou* (bi-monthly, 2004–13).

These newspapers can be found in hard copy in some of the bigger libraries in Aotearoa. Surveying the iwi publications, Jasmine Kaa described how they changed the frame: "Iwi are more likely to cast themselves in their own stories as the upbeat protagonist, rather than the victim of state/coloniser/capitalist oppression. Communities and individuals are the agents of change, initiators of exciting new developments, drivers of their own destinies."[87]

However, the iwi papers often battled against high pass-on rates and struggled to gain enough advertising to survive; a common complaint was that advertisers didn't seem to realise that Māori bought goods and services like everyone else. The papers had to have a cover price to pay their way, but were mired in a losing battle against the free publications produced by the Māori affairs arm of government. Below, we explore several of the iwi publications that are still going.

## TE KARAKA

Among the stayers is the magazine of South Island iwi Ngāi Tahu, *Te Karaka* (1994–), which was started at the time the iwi was negotiating its claim against the Crown. The magazine is free online. The magazine's title, bestowed by Sir Tipene O'Regan, chair of the iwi trust board at the time, reflects two meanings of the word: the karaka tree, whose berries were prized as food, and 'call' or 'summon', in the Ngāi Tahu dialect, reflecting the fact that the magazine was started as an appeal to Ngāi Tahu to reconnect and support the iwi's cultural revitalisation.[88] The high-quality magazine has a pool of editorial staff and writers and an outward-looking current-affairs focus where the experiences and understanding of tribal members drive the narratives. With the subtitle "About Ngāi Tahu, About New Zealand, About You", the magazine signals its intention to speak to a national audience.[89]

## TE HOOKIOI

Waikato-Tainui's *Te Hookioi* magazine, which comes in hard-copy and digital formats, recalls its feisty nineteenth-century ancestor *Te Hokioi o Niu Tireni e Rere atu na*. Published since 1997, and in English with some reo content, it focuses on tribal governance and Kīngitanga activities. According to Waikato-Tainui communications director Jason Ake, a former journalist, "The heart of *Te Hookioi* has always been about providing a Tainui voice, but more than that, it's been about providing a Māori voice to the world."[90]

## TIHEI KAHUNGUNU

In June 2015, Ngāti Kahungunu Iwi Incorporated returned to the publishing business. It partnered with *Hawke's Bay Today*, a daily mainstream paper, to publish the first issue of *Tīhei Kahungunu*, a monthly, English-language, stand-alone insert whose stories are also available online. The publication offers success stories, marae news, photo spreads of events, opinion columns, recipes and, often, columns from the chairperson and the chief executive. In 2020, the paper ran a story in which it celebrated five years of existence: "We are over the moon about it," wrote Ruth Wong, the iwi's communications advisor. "Five years equates to 63 editions and approximately 500 stories that have been shared with the public through the *Hawke's Bay Today* paper and online media."[91]

## PRINT TODAY – IT'S ON THE INTERNET

As outlined earlier, many of the most influential iwi publications have migrated from physical newspapers to the internet. However, some of the most influential Māori interest publications have been online-only since their inception. Among these are *E-Tangata*, a free, Māori and Pacific Sunday e-zine run by a not-for-profit trust and co-edited by veteran journalism educator Gary Wilson and Tapu Misa (see Chapter 5). Launched in 2014, the high-quality e-zine provides a platform for diverse Māori and Pacific voices, with the editors publishing stories by experienced journalists as well as coaching new talent to express themselves on topics as diverse as identity, language, history, racism, the media, the arts and personality profiles.

Left: Gary Wilson, *E-Tangata* co-editor.

Centre: Tapu Misa, *E-Tangata* co-editor.

Right: Leonie Hayden, former editor of *Mana* magazine, now runs Ātea on digital news site *The Spinoff*.

SUPPLIED

For Tapu Misa, who was born in Samoa and raised in Wellington, *E-Tangata* is a space for Māori and Pacific people to control the narratives about themselves. It was among the first journalism websites in Aotearoa to sign up to PressPatron, a New Zealand crowdfunding platform launched in 2017 to support quality journalism.

Another notable online magazine is Ātea, the Māori interest section of independent website *The Spinoff*. Ātea was launched in 2017 to "build an arena of thought and debate where the indigenous perspective is the default," wrote its first editor, Leonie Hayden. She describes the relationship between Ātea and *The Spinoff* as "a fully realised Treaty partnership."[92]

# KO TE WHAKAPAPA O NGĀ PŪRONGO IRIRANGI REO MĀORI

## THE HISTORY OF MĀORI-LANGUAGE NEWS ON RADIO

## MĀORI IN EARLY RADIO

When it began in the early 1920s, New Zealand domestic radio was an amateur affair, with hobbyists playing music on the AM band. Although the state regulated the sector, it didn't take radio seriously; in 1922, an official opined that "broadcasting would have only a very short run. People would soon get tired of hearing gramophone records by wireless."[93] Ehē! The number of radio receivers grew. When private enterprise got involved, the government stepped in and regulated the field. However, rules introduced in 1923 were strict: advertising was forbidden and broadcasts were restricted to "matters of educative or entertaining character".[94] Radio was not to be used "for the dissemination of propaganda of a controversial nature".[95] Although local news was permitted, it was, by its very nature, likely to be seen as controversial, so broadcasters side-lined what twenty first century ears might recognise as news – political news in particular.[96] However, few Māori were able to listen to what passed for news, anyway; the vast majority were rural, and as rural reception was poor, few households had radios.

In 1925, a 7 p.m. 'news hour' was introduced, but this was far less important than music and drama programmes. 'News' content included items lifted from the local papers, market prices, and 'lecturettes' on health, farming, literature "and whatever other topics experts could be found to speak on."[97] These 'lecturettes' often featured Māori topics – but were usually by Pākehā talking about Māori.[98] In those early days of radio, te reo was heard largely in song, as Māori were placed in the role of unthreatening entertainers for Pākehā; tribal choirs would "present lavishly produced entertainment taking up most of an evening."[99] According to broadcaster Hēnare te Ua, such pageants perpetuated the trope of "the noble savage, the noble indigenous people type of thing

… it would be many, many years down the line before Māori could broadcast in Māori for Māori."[100]

In 1929, when the first bishop of Aotearoa, Frederick Bennett of Ngāti Whakaue, broadcast a twenty-minute talk in English, he started with a mihi in te reo but felt the need to account for it. Magazine *The Radio Record*, the forerunner of *The New Zealand Listener*, reported that "the smoothly flowing native words, perfectly enunciated, came over the air with crystal clarity and did not justify [Bennett's] humorous apology to his white listeners – 'I hope no one is cursing old-man static for what some of you have not understood. I have been greeting my Maori people.'"[101]

Still, state radio at the time had an "essentially respectful" attitude to the language – which was not always the case among the Pākehā public.[102] Although state radio was no crusader for the Māori language nor Māori generally, policy at the time was that placenames should be pronounced correctly and that broadcasters should educate their audiences. This was illustrated in 1928 when J.F. Montague, a Pākehā performer who spoke te reo, broadcast a series of programmes to improve public pronunciation of Māori words and placenames. "Some of the common mispronunciations … many of them in fact – are atrocious, and it is time something was done about it," he said.[103] Montague was succeeded in that role by a man believed to be first regular Māori radio announcer, Hāre Hongi (also known as Henry H. Stowell) of Ngāpuhi, a translator and whakapapa expert.

## POLITICAL PRESSURE LEADS TO MORE MĀORI VOICES ON AIR

As radio become increasingly popular, the lack of Māori voices didn't go unnoticed. As early as the 1930s, leaders such as Eruera Tirikātene, then the Rātana Parliamentarian for Southern Māori, complained about the poor position of Māori within the media.[104] However, it took some expertly applied political pressure to get more Māori voices on air. In 1935, members of the Rātana faith helped Michael Joseph Savage become the country's first Labour Prime Minister. However, the church's support had a price: Māori announcers on radio in the four main centres.[105] The church got what it wanted. In 1936, tenor Uramo Paora, also known as Lou Paul, was appointed in Auckland. In 1937, musician Kīngi Tāhiwi was appointed in Wellington, Te Aritaua Pītama in Christchurch and soprano Airini Grennell in Dunedin.

The quartet wasn't on air to deliver programmes in Māori or for Māori, and the opportunity to express tikanga Māori was limited. Despite the constraints, the four were trailblazers. "Each of the appointees bought with them outgoing charisma that opened their Pākehā colleagues' insight into te ao Māori, the Māori world," wrote Hēnare te Ua. "They did this with charm and inclusiveness and easily traversed the paths of biculturalism."[106] Added Rangi Matamua, "They were the pioneers of Māori broadcasting, and much is owed to their efforts in breaking down the barriers for Māori within radio."[107]

There is another name we need to add to the list of pioneer Māori voices, one that has largely been overlooked by histories of radio. Methodist minister, artist and pharmacist Ōriwa Tahupōtiki Haddon was appointed in the early days of Wellington commercial station 2ZB, which started in 1937, and, like all the commercial stations at the time, vigorously competed with the original national service for listeners. Haddon is credited with the phrase te reo irirangi, which describes Māori radio to this day. The word irirangi can be interpreted as spirit voice, or having a supernatural sound, making it an apt description of a projected, disembodied voice. Haddon, who was steeped in tikanga, collected an "almost unique fund of folk lore, history and traditions", and toured marae in order to record "Māori singers who have not become almost completely Europeanised, or Māori music that has not been spoiled by the same influence."[108] Haddon, compared to his counterparts, seems to have had more freedom to call on his culture; he became well-known for his accounts of Māori history, mythology and poetry in his twice-weekly programme *Ōriwa's Māori Session*.[109]

## AND HERE IS THE NATIONAL MĀORI NEWS

In 1937, when the Labour administration set up its own Official News Service, it was quite openly a compilation of government handouts dressed up as news items, and this would remain the case for decades to come. Listeners' reaction to the Government's 'news' was, unsurprisingly, indifference.[110] Māori, especially those aged over fifty for whom English was a second language, often found announcers spoke too fast for them to follow.[111]

News in te reo Māori for Māori didn't emerge until the years of World War II. From a Māori population of some 100,000, a total of 15,744 went to war. Of that cohort, a total of 3600 men, all volunteers, served with the Māori 28th Battalion, which was organised on tribal lines under iwi leaders.[112] Whānau left behind were desperate for news. In 1941, elders made a request through their parliamentarians for news about the Battalion in te reo, and a weekly Sunday spot at 9.20 p.m. was granted. In 1942, Wiremu Parker, a "rather stern Wellington civil servant of Ngāti Porou ancestry",[113] was plucked from the ranks of the government education department. In

How the *New Zealand Listener* advertised the service in March 1943.

ALEXANDER TURNBULL LIBRARY, WELLINGTON

## NEWS IN MAORI
### WEEKLY SERVICE BY NBS

To meet the needs of the large number of Maoris in the Dominion who listen to war news, the National Broadcastnig Service is now summarising the news once a week and broadcasting it in the Maori language. This broadcast, which is given on Sunday nights at 9.20, is made from 1YA, 2YA and 2YH. The broadcast lasts for 10 minutes, and reaches all Maoris living in the Dominion who have reasonably efficient receiving sets.

Wiremu Parker in 1969.
*NEW ZEALAND LISTENER*

Māori that was "a little stiff and English", Wiremu Parker delivered what is believed to be the first programme entirely in te reo, in 1942. The ten-minute news bulletin, prosaically titled *Weekly News Summary in Māori*, reported Battalion news and casualties.[114]

Parker, like his English-language counterparts, could read only items supplied by Government, which he translated and broadcast; it was "Pākehā news in the Māori language, meaning it was a mere transliteration of the English news services."[115] Unfortunately, we don't have recordings of those first bulletins. According to journalist and researcher Sarah Johnston, who researches radio recordings of the war years, the bulletins would have been read live-to-air and not recorded in any way, which was the case in the era. The only medium for recording sound, she says, was cutting onto blank lacquer transcription disks, which looked something like today's vinyl records. However, these were expensive and in short supply during the war years due to a scarcity of aluminium, an essential component. Even if one of the news bulletins had been recorded, she said, it could have been recorded over; once some disks were used for broadcast, they were returned to the manufacturer to be stripped and recoated with fresh lacquer: "Goodness know what treasures were lost that way."[116]

Therefore, we can't settle for sure the claim that Wiremu Parker was the voice of the *very first* edition of reo Māori news on radio. Contemporary broadcaster Leo Fowler raised some doubt. He suggested that the very first bulletin could have been read by Michael (Mick) Rotohiko Jones, at the time private secretary to the Minister Representing the Native Race. In a 1974 feature he wrote for the short-lived *Marae* magazine, edited by Whai Ngata, Leo Fowler says he asked several of those involved who read that first bulletin. "'I did,' Mick Jones told me. 'I did,' Bill Parker told me. At any rate, they alternated in those early days and then Bill Parker became the regular announcer being relieved, where necessary, by Mick Jones until he retired."[117]

Still, Parker was the best-known voice and became a celebrity. Listeners flocked to the *News in Māori*, as the broadcast became known, for his delivery as much as the information:

> At a quarter past nine on Sunday evenings, Māori homes and marae up and down the country would come to a standstill because they would be listening to Wiremu Parker doing the regular weekly Māori news bulletin. And whilst the content of bulletins was listened to avidly, particularly items pertaining to the Māori battalion – the casualty lists of course – there were also the Māori-language purists who would listen to make sure that Parker's articulation was correct, that he wasn't letting his own Ngāti Porouism intrude, where certain words which, while being acceptable on the East Coast of the North Island, would not be acceptable elsewhere …
>
> … so he had those critics, very learned academic Māori who were wont to write to him berating him that he said certain words. But generally speaking, the bulk of the listeners were mesmerised by this voice filtering through the ether, often clouded by static and

fading and hazing, and listening, avidly, because this was the news coming from a Māori about Māori to Māori.[118]

For Parker, developing the language of news in te reo was also a challenge, wrote Fowler:

> There were so many words and terms and concepts coming into use among the Pākehā for which there was no equivalent in the Māori language. Some [English] just had to be used as they were, but it became a challenge to avoid using the Pākehā word, or an obvious and crude disguising of it, but to find instead a Māori equivalent to the meaning.
>
> For submarine, for instance, Bill Parker used (in Māori of course) waka under the sea.[119] Occasionally the kaumātua would criticise, but as the years went by and Bill's linguistic ability improved, listeners took an equal delight in his resourcefulness.[120]

The bulletins created, perhaps, the first marae of the airwaves. Hēnare te Ua recalled, "It was a great big party line in which people could tune in. And whilst you might be listening in isolation, there was great feeling of community of belonging, of being part of this invisible network of people who were all listening in."[121]

However, one night in 1944, Wiremu Parker had an experience that opened the door to what we might call truly independent Māori language news broadcasts, free of government fetters – but he didn't see it coming. As te Ua recalled:

> One evening just before going on-air, the sound engineer told Bill there was a 'phone call for him from the Right Reverend Frederick Augustus Bennett, first Bishop of Aotearoa. 'Pānuitia te mea kua mate ...' [read this death notice] and the Bishop named a prominent Ngāti Kahungunu rangatira who'd died [Hori Tūpaea] and added the name of the marae where the tangi would take place.
>
> Bill quaked because the item hadn't been passed by the PM's office. Should he read the item from the Bishop, or not? He did so,

as a throwaway item at the end of the bulletin, and worried about the reaction from the Director [James Shelley].

Next morning, he presented himself to the Director and confessed to broadcasting an unauthorised item. The Director said, 'It's about time you selected your own items' and gave Bill editorial freedom.[122]

However, Parker was not given any resources or support to collect Māori news, so we can assume that he worked with what came to him from various sources. After the war, the *News in Māori* was extended from ten to eighteen minutes every Sunday, and brought forward to 6 p.m.; he would read it until 1972.[123] Over time, the topics broadened, and "in time, almost any news of Maori interest" made it to air.[124] But scripts from 1951 onwards, which exist in both Māori and English, show that the majority of information passed on was that provided by the official channels.[125] The situation in English-language radio was little better.

## MĀORI NEWS AND CURRENT AFFAIRS IN THE REGIONS

Leo Fowler, quoted above, migrated from England as a boy and grew up enjoying firm friendships with Māori.[126] In 1952, when he became station manager of Gisborne 2XG, he was welcomed by kaumātua, who told him that while 50 percent of the radio station's audience was Māori, no programmes were designed with Māori in mind.[127] Fowler made the most of being far from Wellington oversight, like many regional stations, and established a variety of content for Māori listeners. One was a magazine-style show called *Talks in Māori*. Another was a nightly radio news programme, all in te reo, of approximately ten minutes, none of whose scripts were censored. Fowler also brought many Māori into broadcasting, such as East Coast composer William Kerekere, who would develop a high profile.

Another important regional programme was a twenty-minute reo Māori current affairs magazine show, *Te Reo o Te Māori*, that started on Napier's 2YZ in 1957, hosted by Ted Nēpia, a 28th Māori Battalion

Left: Ted Nepia in 1969.

Right: Selwyn Muru in 1969.

NEW ZEALAND LISTENER

returned serviceman. The popular Saturday show was broadcast on seven other stations.[128]

Independent news on New Zealand radio became a reality in 1962, with the introduction of the autonomous, national New Zealand Broadcasting Corporation to handle radio and the newly arrived technology of television. Employees were delighted – they had long known that the 'news' they offered was inadequate.[129] In 1964, Māori news and talk shows were absorbed into the corporation's newly established, national Māori programmes section, called *Te Reo o te Māori*, in Wellington, and it had the freedom to reflect what was most important to Māori. *Te Reo o te Maori* under Nēpia became the flagship current affairs and magazine programme in te reo, broadcast nationally. Nēpia produced it until late 1974, when artist and journalist Selwyn Muru (Herewini Murupaenga) and teacher Haare Williams came on board. In May 1975, the show was renamed *Te Reo o te Pīpīwharauroa*. Others who joined the section, such as Whai Ngata, Hemana Waaka and Hāmuera Mitchell, became familiar voices. The show was renamed *Mauri*.

Notable programmes in English included *The Māori Programme*, a weekly started in 1964 under Wiremu Parker, who called it "an excellent platform on which to thrash out in panel discussions the prospects of Māori culture and language, and the problems of Māori today."[130]

*The Māori Programme* would be renamed *Te Mana Māori* and then *He Rerenga Kōrero* and continue until February 1996, a run of thirty-two years.

Another long-running show was *Te Puna Wai Korero*, a twenty-minute weekly digest initially produced by Selwyn Muru that ran from 1971 to 1997 and also highlighted issues of concern to Māori, such as disproportionate rates of Māori imprisonment and the need for Māori to be better represented in the country's institutions.

## ONE STATION FOR MĀORI AND PACIFIC PEOPLES: TE REO O AOTEAROA

An ongoing debate was the best way to set up radio to better serve Māori: as part of the established state structure, or at arm's length? Radio station *Te Reo o Aotearoa* was launched in 1978 as a unit of state-owned RNZ to serve both Māori and Pacific peoples.[131] It was initially managed by Haare Williams and hired broadcasters such as Whai Ngata and Hēnare te Ua. In its twenty years on air, the unit produced shows in te reo Māori and some Pacific languages, and also produced a range of reo Māori shows for state radio. *Te Reo o Aotearoa* went some way to making reo and tikanga Māori more visible, but it didn't fulfil the growing desire among Māori for greater autonomy in broadcasting.[132]

## RADIO AOTEAROA: A STATION BY AND FOR MĀORI

As a result, there was still considerable pressure on the government to fund a dedicated Māori-run radio station. That led, in 1988, to the creation of Irirangi Aotearoa, or Radio Aotearoa, in Auckland. It aimed for 70 percent reo Māori broadcasting, and the strategy was that, over time, the station would network to the regions and support the iwi stations.

Aotearoa Radio viewed itself as a pan-Māori station operating alongside the iwi radio stations, and broadcast news, current affairs, sport and talk programmes in English and Māori. Te reo was the primary language, with a "natural flow between Māori and English".[133] All news, weather, time checks and traffic reports were bilingual, and the station culture was guided by tikanga Māori. One of its broadcasters, musician Moana Maniapoto-Jackson, joked that the station was causing Aucklanders sleepless nights: "It was terrible, the kids especially would listen all night. People were desperately hungry for it."[134]

However, the station struggled to find both staff and interviewees with the necessary language skills, and the amount of te reo decreased over time, in contravention of an agreement that had been made for funding to continue. This led to a dispute and the station closed in 1998.

## THE GENESIS OF IWI RADIO

Iwi leaders still wanted independent Māori radio run by Māori, and they were impatient. An opportunity arose in 1983, when the Wellington Māori Language Board, called Ngā Kaiwhakapūmau i te Reo, temporarily took over the student station at the city's university for Māori Language Week, renaming it Radio Pōneke. The programming, mostly in te reo, was "amateur but gripping" and included current-affairs discussions and storytelling.[135]

The work of Ngā Kaiwhakapūmau was just beginning, and took place on several fronts. In 1985, the group, in the name of one of its leaders, Huirangi Waikerepuru, lodged a Waitangi Tribunal claim (Wai 11), asserting that the Government was obliged to protect te reo as it was a cultural taonga, or thing of value, just like tangible assets such as forests and fisheries.[136] The claim had arisen from a 1979 court ruling that Māori could not speak te reo in the courts if they spoke English. The bid succeeded. In 1987, the Māori Language Act, which made te reo an official language of New Zealand, was passed.[137] It conferred the right to speak Māori in legal proceedings and set up Te Taura Whiri i te Reo Māori, the Māori Language Commission, with a mandate to promote and preserve te reo.[138]

Ngā Kaiwhakapūmau pushed on with its radio dreams. In 1987, the group gained a temporary licence and some public funding to establish Te Reo Irirangi o Te Upoko o Te Ika, which ran for two months.[139] RNZ seconded three of its staff to help – Piripi Walker, Kura Anderson and Tama Te Huki; RNZ also provided Māori language items from its archives.[140] Positive listener feedback and fundraising saw the station become permanent in April 1988.

Huirangi Waikerepuru in 1995.

VANESSA BIDOIS

At that time, staff members without Māori language skills wrote their news in English, which was translated into Māori. Interviews were in Māori or English, depending on interviewees' abilities.[141] The station's journalists didn't dodge contentious issues, said station manager Piripi Walker: "We talk about the difficult things that once would have been dealt with on the marae: sexual abuse, domestic violence, the trauma of parents dealing with teenagers. There's a temptation on Māori radio not to do those stories, because they're too upsetting."[142]

Third birthday of Te Upoko o te Ika, features (L–R): Mike Wills, Donald (Donny) King, Henare Kingi, Piripi Walker, Erana Hemmingsen (obscured), Mere Grant (standing), Lucy Te Moana (kneeling), composer Hirini Melbourne (visiting), Philip Saffery, Henare Hetaraka (standing), Piripi Whaanga (kneeling), Murray Raihania, Kevin Hodges, Iris Te Ari Whaanga (sitting), Mahia Fuimaono (kneeling) and Huirangi Waikerepuru.

NGĀ KAIWHAKAPŪMAU I TE REO MĀORI

The example of Te Upoko was emulated by others. Other part-time and temporary stations were set up, among them Te Reo o Raukawa in Ōtaki, which went on air part-time in 1985; Tautoko Radio in Mangamuka, Northland; and Radio Ngāti Porou in Ruatōria, East Coast, followed in 1987. Next to go to air was Te Toa Takitini, for Ngāti Kahungunu, in 1988. The stations used old equipment discarded by mainstream radio stations. Lacking state funding, staff were often young volunteers, and as there was no clear career path or training, keeping them motivated was a challenge. Some of the fledgling stations relied on government-funded employment schemes to pay their staff.[143]

Journalist Piripi Whaanga described the stations as unadorned tikanga in action, unfiltered by the preoccupations of mainstream media: "Māori radio workers know little of the ethos or theories of [communications theorist Geoff] Mulgan or the Glasgow Media Research Group or research carried out in NZ universities for PhDs. What Māori do have is a view on life, a way of life, a culture and a commitment to broadcast it."[144] He added:

> Māori radio attempts to practice its tikanga (which includes Māori language), its way of doing things, on air. As with all radio, broadcasters cannot communicate something they don't possess, so they first of all need to be comfortable with themselves, to

earth themselves. Perhaps that's the biggest advantage Māori have and the most revealing, once the hands-on broadcasting skills are learned. That is putting the packaging together around the contents.

He also observed that the iwi stations possessed

> a formality that appears to be born of tradition … what is expected in ritual situations. Commonly this shows itself in interaction with others, the introductions, the formal talk and the outroductions. A lot of time is taken up establishing one's credentials, then making the links to the manuhiri (guest or guests) for the listeners and then examining the kaupapa, the reason for the guest being on air and them saying goodbyes.

There are now twenty-one iwi stations, from Te Reo Irirangi o Te Hiku o Te Ika in Te Tai Tokerau to Tahu FM in Te Wai Pounamu.[145] Umbrella body Te Whakaruruhau o Ngā Reo Irirangi Māori (the National Māori Radio Network) oversees the distribution of news bulletins, resource pooling and the production of network programmes.

## THE 'BROADCASTING ASSETS' CASE

More court action by Ngā Kaiwhakapūmau, this time alongside the pan-tribal Māori Council, secured the future of the iwi stations and laid the foundation for Māori-run television. This action, known colloquially as the Broadcasting Assets Case, came about in the 1980s when the government, bent on neoliberal economic reform, decided to deregulate broadcasting.[146] Māori saw how this would limit Indigenous access to the airwaves, and the government was accused of reneging on its obligations to te reo under Te Tiriti.[147]

The government was eventually permitted to deregulate, but only after pledging to do something concrete to safeguard Māori language and culture through broadcasting. Frequencies were reserved for Māori radio and television and the Crown laid out a timetable for developing special-purpose Māori television.[148]

At the same time, it was clear that local content needed to be funded and nurtured in a rapidly globalising world where cheap overseas content was flooding the market. In 1989, a broadcasting funding agency named New Zealand On Air (NZOA) was formed to support quality, diverse public media; it had specific duties to Māori language and culture. Four years later, an autonomous Māori language-focused broadcasting agency was split off from NZOA and named Te Māngai Pāho (TMP).[149]

In terms of radio, TMP-funded stations must be controlled by recognised Māori tribal interests, be aimed primarily at a Māori audience within a specific tribal area and promote Māori language and culture. Initially, they were required to broadcast at least ten and a half hours a day in te reo. However, in 2020, TMP decided to move away from a quota system, allowing stations to vary the hours in order to respond to the language plans devised for their audiences.[150] Output is tracked through an innovative digital interface called Kōkako, which records all the iwi stations and can tell if blocks of speech are in te reo or English.

## FUNDING MĀORI NEWS: CONSTANT COMPETITION

Since 1995, TMP has continuously funded a contract for news in te reo for the iwi stations. At the time the contract was first made available, a news agency named Mana Māori Media, directed by journalists Derek Fox, Philip Whaanga and Gary Wilson (see Chapter 2) had made the most of public funding available to this point and its experienced team provided news in English and te reo to both iwi stations and state radio. Given its track record, the company might have reasonably expected to get the iwi radio news contract.

However, Auckland iwi Ngāti Whātua owned a top-rating commercial music station, Mai FM, and, with an eye on the news contract, set up a 100 percent reo Māori station, Ruia Mai Te Ratonga Irirangi o te Motu (Ruia Mai) in May 1996. Although the station's reporting staff were, primarily, young people lacking journalism training, Ruia Mai controversially won the news contract.[151] Ruia Mai offered a lot to reo-speaking news junkies: five-minute, on-the-hour, reo Māori news and sports bulletins from 7 a.m. to 5 p.m. seven days a

The Ruia Mai team at an edition of the Māori Sports Awards. From left to right: Piripi Taylor, Simon Jackson, Ngarimu Daniels, Igor Zukina, Mere McLean Annabelle Lee-Mather, Oriini Kaipara, Helen Locke, Tina Wickliffe, Lance Kahu Rolleston and Mana Epiha.

VANESSA BIDOIS

week, as well as a daily, thirty-five-minute round-up of the day's news at 6 p.m. seven days a week. It also had a breakfast current affairs show.[152]

Initially, the iwi stations took what they wanted, but there were complaints about the quality of the language and the journalism.[153] However, Ruia Mai persevered. With TMP's support, it built the capabilities of its journalists and the service improved.[154] Ruia Mai also won several national journalism awards.[155] A number of high-profile journalists owe their start to Ruia Mai, including *The Hui* producer Annabelle Lee-Mather, Shane Taurima, head of Whakaata Māori, and *Newshub* presenter Oriini Kaipara.

The year 2004 brought more change. The news contract again came up for tender and Ruia Mai lost to Te Reo Irirangi o Waatea, an Auckland-based pan-tribal station that targets a thirty-five plus audience. Without its primary source of income, Ruia Mai closed. The closure left bitterness in its wake. Some observers felt that, given the small size of the Māori news sector, constant competition for both experienced reporters and funding was damaging to the development and maintenance of quality journalism.[156]

## MĀORI NEWS ON STATE RADIO

On state radio, Māori interest and Māori language news had a chequered history in the twenty years from 1990. Throughout this period, it relied on outside providers, the most prominent of which was Mana Māori Media, one of whose directors was Derek Fox (see Chapter 4). However, Mana and its reo Māori bulletins were to find themselves buffeted by politics, policy changes at TMP and RNZ budget crunches.

From mid-1990, Mana Māori Media provided RNZ radio with a twenty-two-minute news and current affairs package, mostly in English,[157] called *Mana News*. It had a good time slot – right after the 6 p.m. news – and was compiled in English by a bicultural team of journalists who included, at various times, Chris Wikaira, Jason Ake, Wena Tait and Caleb Maitai, and Pākehā such as Carol Archie and Gary Wilson.

The content assumed familiarity with Māori issues and terms, and sound bites were "characteristically unhurried … these might range from politicians defending policies affecting Māori to Māori people with mana who would not have had the opportunity to speak to the Pākehā world."[158] The service was high quality and the show popular. Radio New Zealand chief Sharon Crosbie described *Mana* as having done "more to alert Pākehā New Zealand to the issues and realities confronting Māori than just about anything else."[159] Years later, Derek Fox recalled the impact:

> Even if I say it myself, it was a great show and broke many new stories about Māori and kaupapa Māori. It also broke down barriers of what Māori news might sound like, introduced humour and Māori language into the news, and gave stories a chance to breathe and be told in their fullness, not reduced to a sound bite.
>
> Other news organisations were forced to listen to it because of the content. I knew people who listened as they drove home from work and despite having reached home before the show was over found they had to stay in their car until it finished.[160]

From 1990 to 1999, Mana Māori Media also provided Māori language news bulletins to RNZ. However, the glory days were not to last. *Mana*'s time slot was cut in half and then scrapped as RNZ claimed financial woes. News in te reo on the state broadcaster ended in 1999 after fifty-seven years, leaving bitterness in its wake.[161] In 2005, RNZ stepped back into Māori news by contracting Radio Waatea to supply raw material in English from which to compile four Māori interest news bulletins on weekdays. That arrangement ended seven years later, when RNZ decided to move its Māori interest news in-house.[162]

Since 2011, there has been no news in te reo Māori on the state broadcaster. However, in accordance with its 2016 charter, which requires it to "reflect New Zealand's cultural identity, including Māori language and culture",[163] the station has made visible progress on its commitments to building its capacity in reporting Māori news in English. Under its 2016 Māori strategy, Indigenous journalists have been hired, an internship for Māori graduates was instituted in 2017, and the learning of te reo – and its use on air and on its website – is encouraged. Most importantly, in 2018 it created the new role of kurahautū Māori (Māori strategy manager) to oversee progress. Māori news is no longer side-lined into a slot of its own that reporters have to scramble to fill – it is part of the RNZ's general news production, allowing staff to focus on quality above quantity.[164]

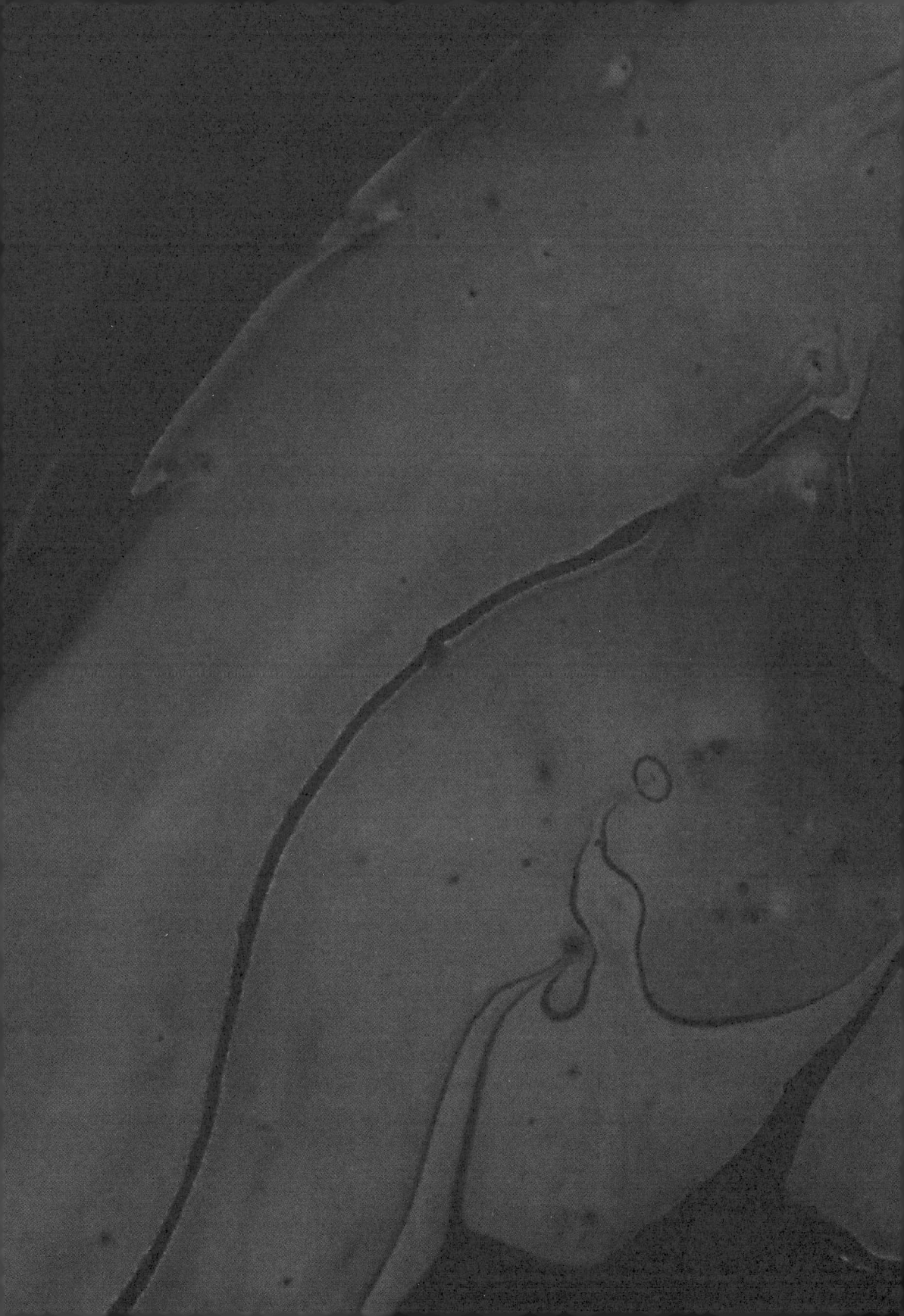

# 4

## KO TE POUAKA WHAKAATA ME TE IPURANGI

## MĀORI NEWS AND CURRENT AFFAIRS ON STATE AND COMMERCIAL

New Zealand's first television broadcast took place on the evening of 1 June 1960, in Auckland. The New Zealand Broadcasting Service's (NZBC) sole channel, AKTV-2, played *The Adventures of Robin Hood*, a live interview with a visiting British ballerina and a performance by Te Arawa entertainer Howard Morrison. In the decade that followed, Māori on screen were, like Morrison, mostly entertainers, as they had been in the early years of national radio forty years prior. As the 1960s yielded to the 1970s, the occasional programmes featuring reo and tikanga Māori beyond performance "tended to be sporadic and uncertain of the real needs they were trying to meet".[165]

However, that changed in 1974 with the English-language documentary series *Tangata Whenua*, directed by Ngāti Apa filmmaker Barry Barclay and presented by Pākehā journalist Michael King. It was ground-breaking in its reflection of Māori lives and viewpoints.[166] In *Tangata Whenua*, wrote broadcaster Tainui Stephens, Barclay developed a television language appropriate for telling Māori stories, "insisting that the camera behave with good manners. He understood how to tell a screen story that oozes respect, as much as articulate our humanity through emotional transparency and spiritual humility."[167]

Barclay later wrote the influential book *Our Own Image,* in which he defined Indigenous media as Indigenous peoples taking control of the tools of representation in order to "talk in". By this, he meant Māori talking to Māori in Māori ways and respecting tikanga Māori. This did not necessarily exclude outsiders, but no particular concessions were to be made for any lack of understanding on their part.[168]

Early television news featured an announcer reading the news to camera, essentially making it radio with pictures. But shortly after the NZBC was established in 1963, it set up a network of newsrooms to supply both radio and TV. Visual reporting entered living rooms with the Vietnam War; viewers could see the discrepancies between what official sources reported and what footage showed. Māori calls for justice were also recorded; television reporters accompanied the 1975 Land March and captured the 1978 occupation of Bastion Point.

In 1978, a 25,000-signature petition went to Parliament, calling for a dedicated Māori television unit. The NZBC started a weekly programme, *Pacific Viewpoint*, which saw "seven ethnic groups shoehorned into 15 minutes."[169] An increasing Tiriti o Waitangi consciousness was leading to small, initially tokenistic steps to recognise Māori political, cultural and social aspirations on the small screen. But it was a start.

## *KOHA* – A SIGN OF THINGS TO COME

The first regular Māori programme shown in prime time was *Koha* (1980–9), a fifteen-minute, Sunday afternoon, English-language magazine programme that explored topics ranging from Māori social problems and food preparation to tribal and natural history, weaponry, Māori art and te reo. The programme started in a 4 p.m. Sunday slot on the main channel, TV1 – a time when there were relatively few viewers – but its popularity saw it eventually moved to a prime Sunday 6.45 p.m. slot.[170] However, *Koha* was television about Māori for Pākehā, said Tainui Stephens, who started his journalism career on the show: "Our bosses were Pākehā, and they believed that Māori programmes should provide a 'window' onto the Māori world. Looking back, I take this to mean that our programmes were wanted in order to display and explain ourselves to people who were not Māori."[171]

Derek Fox, the show's first producer, agreed: The programme was "a soft, cute window on Māori society through which Pākehā people could peer."[172] Debra Reweti, who became a *Koha* reporter in 1984, said that it was difficult to craft stories in a way that catered for both Pākehā and Māori worldviews and presumed interests: "For example, a story about the opening of a whare nui in the back blocks would be difficult to make relevant to a mainstream audience, but to a Māori audience, the stories behind the hapū, the land, the carvings and the ancestor of the whare would be compelling." However, she said that Māori viewers were neither forgotten nor patronised:

In describing *Koha* as a window, the implication was the mainstream public didn't actually need to go inside, but could simply cast a curious eye over the Māori world and move on.

This view was not held by early *Koha* staff members, who sought to grab the audience in an academic headlock if necessary to ensure Māori stories were listened to and appreciated. They also felt an obligation to speak directly to Māori with an authentic voice, refusing to water down or simplify the messages for the mainstream palate.[173]

Courageous staff would put tikanga Māori first, among them reporter Selwyn Muru:

He would sometimes offer delicious poroporoaki to major figures of the Māori world who had passed on. At the time, these mihi seemed to me to be an absolutely appropriate use of television. It was also a brave thing to do. 'He kōrero aituā ka meatia nei mā te pouaka Whakaata. Kātahi rā! Haramai tētahi āhuatanga!' [There's a death notice coming through on the television. Incredible! I've never seen anything like this before] was my typical response.

To slip te reo and tikanga into shows was, added Stephens, so exciting: "It was also a subversive activity because whenever we got the language on screen we had to endure a flood of complaints from viewers. 'Tell those niggers to get their black-arse language off my TV' was one I remember from the Television New Zealand phone log."[174]

## THE BIRTH OF *TE KARERE*

The year 1982 was pivotal for Māori journalism. That year, Derek Fox was a reporter on the TVNZ current affairs show *Close-Up*. For Māori Language Week, he was asked to present a nightly two-minute news programme in Māori just before the main 6 p.m. news on TV1.

Fox ignored the brief to simply translate and present the general news of the day, and with unpaid but helpful journalist friends Whai Ngata and Purewa Biddle – but no other resources – set out to collect Māori-focused, un-subtitled news: "Each day we begged, borrowed and purloined facilities to gather, edit and transmit film stories of Māori news," he said.[175] It was stressful work, but the end result was popular where it counted, wrote an observer: "If the TV bosses thought they had done their bit for Māoridom by the end of the week, they were proved wrong. They had whetted Maori viewers' appetites for more. They had a tiger by the tail, and the tiger hasn't stopped snarling since."[176]

The bulletin raised questions among Māori and Pākehā – and, surprisingly, in mainstream media – about why such programming wasn't more regular. The then Minister of Broadcasting, Ian Shearer, told Derek Fox privately that he would take up the cudgels on behalf of a regular Māori news broadcast.[177] That broadcast was the country's first regular Māori language news programme, *Te Karere*, which started on 21 February 1983 with Derek Fox and Whai Ngata as hosts. In 2010, Ngata recalled, "Our specific aim was not really the keeping alive of the Māori language, as some people will say now. Our job was to put out the news that would be of importance to Māori but do it in the Māori language."[178]

Whai Ngata in 2007.
NZME MARK MITCHELL

The show's birth was mired in dispute about a lack of resources, on which of the two networks it should air and at what time. It eventually went to air as a four-minute show on TV2 at 5.55 p.m.[179] Fox and Ngata shared the roles of presenter, editor, reporter and producer on the show; there were no researchers, back-up staff, or a dedicated camera team. Adding to the stress, the workplace was hostile: camera crews referred to *Te Karere* jobs as the 'coon round' and mainstream reporters resented the programme's use of resources.[180]

Initially, the presentation was "straight down the barrel", reading the news in Māori with no supporting video clips.[181] Sometimes the bulletins would be little more than community news, said Tainui Stephens, "but they constituted hard news for iwi and hapū – compared to general news stories that had simply been translated into Māori".[182] Whai Ngata remembered a negative reaction to *Te Karere* from Pākehā "because a lot of people saw it as invasive, they didn't want the Māori language on their TV in their homes".[183] But for Māori, *Te Karere* was appointment viewing. One journalist wrote, "They say you can't buy a beer in the Ruatōria pub between 5.55 and 6pm. The reason is *Te Karere*, TV2's Māori language programme, which has proved highly popular with its target since starting 15 months ago … Māori meetings in Gisborne are timed to finish before 5.55 or start after 6pm."[184]

Among the early recruits to *Te Karere* were Wena Harawira and Pere Maitai. By its third year, the bulletin was ten minutes long with clips. Until 1995, *Te Karere* ran for just 42 weeks a year. At that point, the broadcasting funding agency TMP agreed to fund a year-round broadcast.

Scheduling changes have been a feature of the show's existence, drawing criticism from politicians and viewers that such shuffling is damaging. However, since 2009, the year of the show's twenty-fifth birthday, *Te Karere* has been twenty-two minutes long in a thirty-minute slot at 3.55 p.m. on weekdays. Since 2011, viewers have been able to add closed captions to the initial broadcast, and *Te Karere* stories are posted to YouTube and social media channels.[185]

*Te Karere* staff on the cover of *Tu Tangata* in 1984: (L–R) Whai Ngata, Wena Harawira, Derek Fox and Pere Maitai.

TE PUNI KŌKIRI

*Te Karere* remains the Māori world's longest-running news programme, as well as a beacon for te reo Māori. According to Derek Fox, "as a daily dose of fluent, accurate Māori, *Te Karere* has always made a priceless contribution simply towards preserving the Māori language."[186] *Te Karere* has also set the scene for te reo to be updated for a technological era. Wena Harawira, reflecting on her *Te Karere* days, said:

Scotty Morrison is the long-time host of *Te Karere*. Here, he prepares to present the show's twenty-fifth birthday edition in February 2009.

MARTIN SYKES NZME

I had used English words thrown into a Māori conversation for most of my life, because I didn't know the Māori word or there was no Māori word. *Te Karere* filled that gap. We drew on words like manu aute, to describe a satellite – the name of a traditional Māori kite. The shape resembled a satellite and it floated in the air, so it seemed appropriate to use something traditional and give it a modern twist. Rorohiko, the word for computer, literally translated to 'electric brain' to describe its functionality – roro means brain, hiko is electric.[187]

## A (BRIEF) TIME OF PLENTY

For a short time, in 1996 and 1997, there were two sources of reo Māori news on television, *Te Karere* and the services offered by a short-lived, pilot television station that was part of the government's plan to fulfil its obligations to Māori. Aotearoa Television Network was available in the evenings in Auckland and aimed to be 70 percent in Māori; it provided a seven-day, thirty-minute news show in te reo. However, the network folded in early 1997 amid allegations that the whole exercise had been doomed to fail by poor planning and underfunding on the government's part.[188]

*Te Karere* also prompted debate about the quality and style of Māori language used on air. According to Tainui Stephens, "sometimes whānau or kaumātua would berate their relations, who, while working as reporters, would use vocabulary and idioms that were not of their tribe. There was tension as early *Te Karere* reporters ... sought to find a level of Māori language comprehensible to all."[189]

Hone Kaa in 2008.
MARK MITCHELL NZME

## THORNY DEBATES ON THE SMALL SCREEN

Broadcaster and Anglican leader Hone Kaa (1941–2012) loved nothing more than a no-holds-barred debate, so he was the perfect host for two current affairs shows in TVNZ that delved into the thornier issues of public life in the 1980s. The first was current affairs panel show *Ngā Take Māori*, which ran to ten weekly episodes from November 1986 into the early months of 1987. It followed the establishment in 1986 of TVNZ's first Māori Programmes Department; *Ngā Take Māori* was described by the *New Zealand Listener* as the first fruit of efforts by TVNZ director-general Julian Mounter "to step up Māori programming as a matter of priority".[190]

The first episode of *Ngā Take Māori*, on TV1 in a prime Monday 6 p.m. slot, asked the question "He iwi kotahi tātou? Are we one people?" Hone Kaa and his panel aimed, as he said in his introduction to that first show, "to examine issues that affect Māori people. We look at problems, achievements and aspirations, and how we would like to see the wider community respond to Māori values in a bicultural society."[191] Māori mental health, Māori and trade unionism, the representation of Māori in the media and the performance of the government's Department of Māori Affairs were among the topics debated. Kaa was not afraid of raising dust and putting hard questions to panellists; he enjoyed verbal combat.[192] Although the show was aimed at Māori, it assumed no prior knowledge or tikanga or reo on the part of its listeners and was thus accessible to non-Māori as well. It was a bilingual show, with all commentary, whatever the language, subtitled in the other; the *Listener* noted that this was the first regularly scheduled programme to be broadcast in Māori with English subtitles.[193]

However, by March 1987, *Ngā Take Māori* was airing at 10 p.m. on Sundays, which Kaa said showed TVNZ's lack of commitment to Māori programmes. At the many hui he attended around the country, added Kaa, the programme garnered widespread applause for its content, but intense criticism for its late-night slot.[194] Still, Hone Kaa was back on TV1 in late 1987 with a Sunday night current-affairs programme, *Te Kupenga* (1987–8), in which he and a guest debated thorny race-related issues. Also produced by TVNZ's Māori Programmes Department, the nine-episode, half-hour show started in a 9.30 p.m. slot, but jumped all around the schedule, and even went a fortnight without screening at all. But the biggest problem, it appeared, was finding commentators to go head-to-head with the formidable Hone Kaa. He said:

> Those who speak strongly against the kind of stand that we take are reluctant to front up to articulate Māoris. It seems they find it much more comfortable to sit back and take shots, rather than face the people they need to face. I find that very sad because unless you bring things out in the open, it sits there like a cancer.[195]

### WAKA HUIA

An influential exhibition of Māori art that toured that United States led to the birth, in 1987, of *Waka Huia*, an archival programme whose primary aim is to preserve the reo and mātauranga of kaumātua. *Te Māori* toured the United States from 1984 to 1986 before returning to New Zealand for a nationwide tour in 1987. Many kaumātua travelled with the exhibition in the US. This prompted Whai Ngata and fellow TVNZ producer Erie Leonard to reflect on the consequences if a plane-load of returning elders fell out of the sky, taking their cultural knowledge with them.[196]

The Māori Affairs Department, the Ministry of Education and TVNZ agreed to fund a team of eight to start the reo-only, hour-long programme. The first two interviewees were towering leaders of their time: Sir Hēmi Henare, the Ngāpuhi leader and ex-Colonel of the 28th Maori Battalion, and Dame Mira Szászy, the former President of the influential Māori Women's Welfare League. In 2014, when TVNZ decided to outsource all of its Māori and Pacific programming except news show *Te Karere*, production of *Waka Huia* went to independent company Scottie Productions.[197]

### A LONG-STAYER: *MARAE*

*Marae* was introduced in 1990 as a catch-all title for a collection of Māori and Pacific-oriented programming on Sunday mornings. It included *Waka Huia* and a ten-minute slot called *Panui*, hosted by the head of Māori programming, Ernie Leonard, that critiqued mainstream media coverage of Māori affairs. At the time, he said, "It's not our intention to come out with a baseball bat and bang the media over the head with it, but there are many instances of bad journalism."¹⁹⁸ Watching *Pānui* today, the growing confidence of Māori within the state broadcaster is clear. In its analysis of mainstream media coverage of Māori issues, Ernie Leonard occasionally adopts a mildly exasperated tone, but the show also praises fair and balanced coverage of Māori issues in mainstream media.

*Marae* eventually became the name for an hour-long magazine programme that started with ten minutes of news, then moved onto English-language current affairs and magazine content. It eventually became a current affairs and magazine show. *Marae* was produced in-house until the end of 2014, when, as with *Waka Huia*, production was outsourced.¹⁹⁹ *Marae* is now in the hands of independent company Pango Productions but is still state funded.

## WHAKAATA MĀORI'S NEWS AND CURRENT AFFAIRS

After years of political wrangling and extensive planning, Māori Television Service (MTS) was born in March 2004 to great excitement in te ao Māori. The station is a statutory corporation under the Māori Television Service Act 2003, its function to make a significant contribution to the revitalisation of Māori language and culture through accessible, relevant and effective programming. There are two channels available both live-to-air and online: Whakaata Māori, which is bilingual and provides a range of shows from news and current affairs to documentaries, children's programming and entertainment shows, and Te Reo, which is 100 percent in te reo. In practice, Te Reo runs a lot of the content from the main channel, but without subtitles.

News and current affairs have been a mainstay of the output of Whakaata Māori. Its first news story was about the channel's launch, which was easily the biggest news in the Māori world that day, a Sunday. Its reo Māori news show *Te Kāea* went to air at 8 p.m. that night. Although the bulletin on a normal day was to be thirty minutes, the launch-day broadcast was an hour. News editor Te Anga Nathan had spent just a month working with his seven "cub reporters", six of whom had never worked in television before, and they had to hit the ground running.[200] Tina Wickliffe was the old hand on the team, and said of the show and its staff: "We were the bilingual, inquisitive, unapologetic, contemporary face of Māori media. We were nothing like our slow-lane TVNZ cousins who were constantly being knee-capped by their Pākehā masters. Or so we imagined, despite barely measuring a blip in the ratings."[201]

A blip in the ratings, perhaps, but the differences from mainstream, English-language news were immediately apparent to outsiders. Jim Tully, head of Canterbury University's journalism school, said that the stories seemed long-winded compared to mainstream news, but this wasn't a bad thing. "Items are refreshingly longer and so are soundbites. There's an opportunity for people to express their views in a more leisurely and relaxed way."[202]

The fact that the news was being produced by a wholly Māori outfit – rather than being part of a mainstream broadcaster, as is *Te Karere* – piqued academic interest. Research four years later that compared *Te Kāea* with mainstream television news found that *Te Kāea* had less advertising and no international items. Politics, then crime stories, dominated both MTS and mainstream news. However, *Te Kāea* had little on accidents and disasters, no personality or celebrity stories, and gave proportionally more time to education, environment and Māori–Pākehā relations than did mainstream news. MTS gave on-air sources significantly more time than mainstream channels. All the channels featured members of the public, but *Te Kāea* used more non-elite sources – that is, people without any particular public leadership role or status.[203]

The news programme's current affairs sibling was a weekly current affairs show, *Te Hēteri*. It was a half-hour bilingual programme that covered local and international events, hosted by veteran journalist Wena Harawira. Later, in 2007, the current affairs slot was rebranded *Native Affairs*. In its nine years on air, *Native Affairs* developed a reputation for polished, incisive current affairs with reporters who were unafraid to challenge the Māori establishment (see Chapter 9 for an analysis of one of its more controversial investigations).

Veteran journalist Wena Harawira interviews Prime Minister Jacinda Ardern as part of Māori Television's 2021 Anzac Day coverage.
WHAKAATA MĀORI

During MTS's first decade, two panel shows delivered current affairs talk shows in te reo. *Te Tēpu* (2006–14) was helmed initially by Waihoroi Shortland, then later Hone Kaa and Chris Winitana.[204] Its successor was *Paepae* (2015), which featured Chris Winitana and his son Tūpoutahi Winitana talking with commentators from a broader age range.[205] This was an interesting show not just for the intergenerational format, which often prompted spirited father-and-son discussions, but because both used traditional weaponry in their mihi to viewers such as patu and taiaha, breaking the standard television format of presenter behind a desk.

MTS has also experimented with creative, bilingual approaches to news and current affairs. *Paepae* was replaced by *Kawe Kōrero*, which ran from 2016 to 2018. A trio of MTS journalists discussed the news circulating on social media, with interviewees brought into the studio using video chat applications. The journalists spoke only te reo Māori between each other on screen, but the show was allowed up to two interviews per show in English to ensure newsmakers were not excluded. The show was also packaged as a podcast (see Chapter 10). Another bilingual effort was *Rereātea – Midday News Bytes* (2015–8). This online-only show was a noon, bilingual rundown of the headlines to come on *Te Kāea*. It was hosted by a two-person team, switching between te reo and English, and varied in length from three to ten minutes depending on the news available. Occasionally *Rereātea* broadcast live from the field; two examples of this were the All Blacks' homecoming after they won the 2015 Rugby World Cup and activities at Waitangi in the days leading up to Waitangi Day 2015.

### TE AO MĀORI NEWS

A surprise came in November 2018, when Whakaata Māori announced it was scrapping its four news programmes, evening news show *Te Kāea* and *Native Affairs*, *Kawe Kōrero* and web-only *Rereātea* for a digital-first approach to news under a single brand name. The latter three ceased at the end of 2018, with *Te Kāea* continuing until February, when all the station's news offerings came under the single brand *Te Ao Māori News*. News is pushed out on various digital platforms during the day with an evening wrap on television hosted by one presenter. Deputy chief executive Shane Taurima, a journalist by profession, told RNZ the move would be cost-effective, sustainable and enable more reporters to work out in the field:

> We produce content for platforms not for specific programmes … we tell the story as we know it, on the best, most suitable and most instant platform. There is an emphasis on our reporters to be out and about in our communities and at all the different and important Māori occasions throughout the motu. The result will mean more Māori news content.[206]

A digital-first approach allows for experimenting and flexibility, and the station took advantage of that when Aotearoa suffered its first COVID-19 lockdown in early 2020. It launched a breakfast news and current affairs show, *Te Ao Tapatahi*, to keep viewers abreast of COVID-19-related developments. Longer interviews and stories are in English, with news bulletins delivered in te reo. MTS's current affairs offering is represented by *Te Ao with Moana* (2019–), a current affairs show hosted by Moana Maniapoto that examines national and international stories through a Māori lens. Her son, former *Marae* reporter Hikurangi Kimiora Jackson, produces the show.

Moana Maniapoto.
WHAKAATA MĀORI

## MĀORI INTEREST NEWS AND CURRENT AFFAIRS ELSEWHERE

**The Hui, Newshub (2016–):** *The Hui*, a half-hour Māori current affairs, arts and culture programme, first aired in April 2016 on Three and streams on social media. It bills itself as Māori current affairs for all New Zealanders. *The Hui* is produced by Annabelle Lee-Mather and presented by Mihingarangi Forbes, both of whom previously worked for Whakaata Māori show *Native Affairs*.

**Re: (2017–):** Re: is TVNZ's rangatahi-focused online news and current affairs platform. It makes high-quality videos, articles and podcasts exploring the issues that matter most to young people, and has a particularly strong section titled Te Ao Māori. Staff are mostly rangatahi.

*The Hui* staff, 2021: (L–R) Ruwani Perera, John Boynton, Annabelle Lee-Mather, Mihingarangi Forbes, D'Angelo Martin and Sarah Hall.

GREAT SOUTHERN TELEVISION

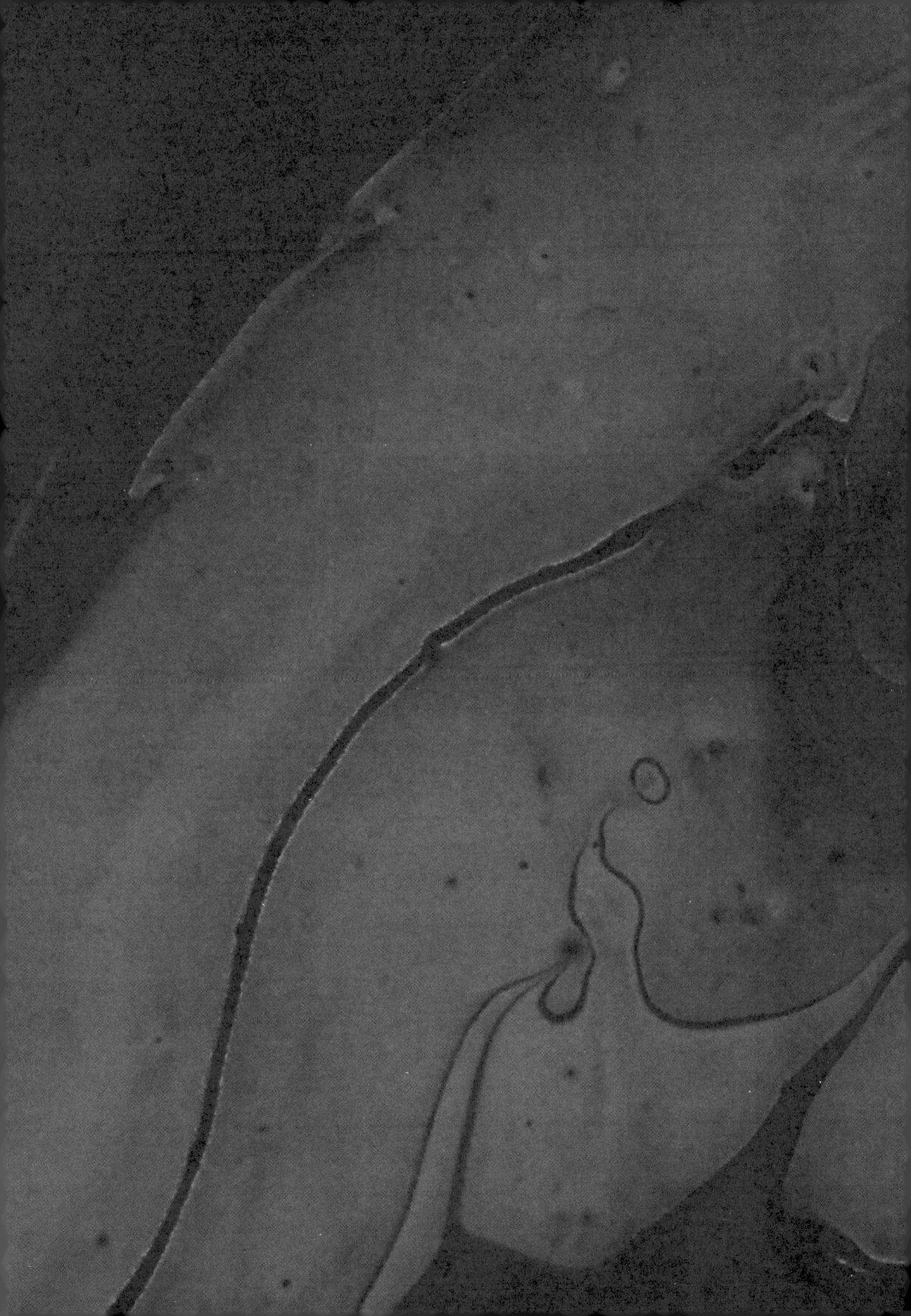

# 5

## HE WHAKANGUNGU KAIKAWEKŌRERO

## MĀORI JOURNALISM TRAINING – MANY PATHS TO THE NEWSROOM

In the first half of the twentieth century, there was little formal institutional journalism education in New Zealand; young people with aptitude were hired as cadets on newspapers, learning about the business on the job. Very few were Māori. However, several Māori reporters who started their careers on English-language newspapers in the post-war years became prominent. Among them were Māori Battalion veteran Harry Dansey, who started as a cadet with the *Hawera Star* after World War II;[207] and George Koea, who was a cadet at the *Taranaki Herald* from 1947 and later became its editor.[208] Another journalist of the era, Whai Ngata, estimated that when he started on the *Auckland Star* in 1968, there were fewer than five Māori journalists in the entire country.[209]

From the 1960s, programmes focused on practical skills were launched in polytechnics and universities, with various levels of industry oversight and input into what was taught.[210] What I did as a school-leaver in the late 1980s was typical: a six-month crash course at a polytechnic on the basics of print journalism, then a cadetship at a daily newspaper, which involved being dropped in the deep end. However, the rise of the internet in the new millennium turned the news business on its head. Legacy media – the separate siloes of radio, television and print – struggled to adapt to the flight online of their precious advertising revenue. As smart phones became more accessible, anyone could become their own broadcaster. Enrolments in journalism training slumped, and several training programmes collapsed. At the time of writing, there are five institutions, two polytechnics and three universities, that offer formal journalism qualifications. These range from sub-degree certificates and diplomas to three-year degrees with a journalism specialism, and one-year postgraduate diplomas.

KIA HIWA RĀ! MĀORI JOURNALISM IN AOTEAROA NEW ZEALAND

# HOW I BECAME A JOURNALIST

Shannon Haunui-Thompson interviews John Whaanga, lead negotiator for the 2016 Te Wairoa Treaty settlement.

ATAKOHU MIDDLETON

# SHANNON HAUNUI-THOMPSON

I did media studies at school and loved it, so I decided to apply for journalism courses. The course at Auckland University of Technology was my top pick and I was lucky enough to get in.

Through AUT I met a few people who were working part-time at TVNZ, listening to police scanners. So I started at TVNZ listening to police scanners at night. For any breaking stories, I was the person to wake people up. Then I went to a part-time job in the TV3 newsroom, first of all in the news library, logging the news bulletins, which was a great learning experience.

My first full-time job, at TV3, with a real proper contract, was in the year 2000 and I was the assistant assignments editor for the Wellington newsroom. I'm now at Radio New Zealand

The Māori population of Aotearoa New Zealand is 16 percent, and research suggests that journalism schools attract Māori students in slightly lesser proportions. From 2012 to 2017, across all the journalism schools, the proportion of students of Māori ethnicity was 12 percent, with Europeans totalling 80 percent and Asian, Pacific Island and other ethnicities making up the remainder.[211] However, there is considerable Māori attrition between training and newsroom; in 2016, the news media workforce tallied just 7.9 percent Māori.[212]

Several factors may be contributing to the low number of formally trained Māori in news work. Journalism has been subject to 'qualification creep'; the courses that deliver the most focused journalism training are now, mostly, either degree programmes or post-graduate diplomas, requiring university entrance and a commitment of time and money that might not be appealing or possible. Although Māori participation in tertiary education has risen in recent years, just 16 percent of Māori under the age of twenty-five participate in study at level 4 (post-school) and above, compared to 23 percent of the total population.[213] Additionally, the journalism programmes available prepare students for mainstream media, which, historically, many Māori have perceived as hostile to tangata whenua aspirations. Although mainstream media reporting of Māori issues is improving, a perception of prejudice lingers.[214]

Research by journalism teacher Bernie Whelan into the courses available at present identified a significant barrier to Māori enrolment: a lack of bicultural consciousness in journalism courses, which he defined as an understanding of the legal, political and cultural relationship between Māori and other citizens based on Te Tiriti o Waitangi. At the time he did the study, there were no educators who were culturally Māori and information related to biculturalism was generally found in theory courses. "Neither educators nor their students are required to engage with te ao Māori, the Māori world, in an applied way," he wrote. A further hindrance[215] was that journalism skills such as news gathering, story production and publishing are often conceived as relatively neutral in their application among the current crop of journalism programmes, rather than culturally based.

While some journalists have come through formal tertiary training, Māori paths to journalism as a career have been many and varied, and have often relied on organisations and individuals with an agenda to improve the diversity of newsrooms. Below, we look at some of the currents that have carried Māori into journalism.

## TVNZ CREATES A TALENT POOL

The first reo Māori news bulletin, *Te Karere*, started in 1983 on state broadcaster Television New Zealand (see Chapter 4) and initially relied on fluent reo speakers who had trained in English-language journalism. Founder Derek Fox, who had started at the broadcaster in 1967 as a university graduate, tapped the unpaid labour of fellow reporters Whai Ngata and Purewa Biddle, who were both working for Radio New Zealand. However, as *Te Karere* started to grow, the severe shortage of trained reo-speaking journalists necessitated finding fluent speakers and training them on the job. Many of the initial reporters on *Te Karere* were from Ngāi Tūhoe. As an example, the first three women hired for the show, Wena Harawira, Tini Molyneux and Hinerangi Goodman, are all Tūhoe.

Historically, due to the iwi's isolation in the rugged eastern North Island, it was the last to feel the effects of colonisation and was able to protect, to a certain extent, the intergenerational transmission of language.[216] The 2013 Census found that overall, 37 percent of Tūhoe could "hold a conversation about everyday things in te reo Māori" compared to 18 percent of the country's total population of Māori descent.[217] Today, compared to other tribes, Ngāi Tūhoe still has the highest proportion of Māori speakers[218] and Tūhoe people remain well-represented in journalism.

Also among the reporting team on *Te Karere* in the 1980s were John Tahuparae, Hone Edwards, Moari Stafford, Pierre Lyndon, Waihoroi Shortland, Rereata Makiha and Tawini Rangihau.

TVNZ training courses were notable for their success in ushering more Māori into news. As an example, in September–November 1986, TVNZ and Auckland Technical Institute (ATI; now Auckland University of Technology) partnered to train seven young people, both

**KIA HIWA RĀ!** MĀORI JOURNALISM IN AOTEAROA NEW ZEALAND

# HOW I BECAME A JOURNALIST

# HONE EDWARDS, TELEVISION PRODUCER

*Te Karere* had just started and Derek Fox interviewed me during a Māori student protest at Auckland University about establishing a marae there. He approached me to go and join the *Te Karere* team after my final exams to get work experience in the newsroom. At that point I decided to focus on a post-graduate journalism course at the University of Canterbury. When I completed the course, Derek Fox hauled me back into *Te Karere* because of my language skills and newly obtained diploma.

Hone Edwards hosted *Marae* in the 1990s.

Tini Molyneux early in her journalism career.

NZME

Hinerangi Goodman in 2016 as she retired from *Te Karere*.

BEN FRASER, NZME

bilingual and monolingual, in a range of television skills in preparation for the launch in 1987 of TVNZ's Māori Programmes Department. Training was overseen by TVNZ staffers Whai Ngata, Ernie Leonard and Pere Maitai. Of those students, four had just completed the Waiariki journalism certificate, discussed later in this chapter: Iulia Leilua, Fiona Murchie, Eliza Bidois and Bradford Haami. The other students were Erana Reedy, Temuera Morrison and the late George Stirling. ATI taught the students a wide range of roles in television storytelling and production, and they were all employed by TVNZ the following February. It was an effective launch pad for them all.

Another notable programme emerged after TVNZ's Māori Programmes Department was created in 1987. Early in 1989, the department oversaw a one-off, eight-week journalism course for reo speakers, the aim to recruit them primarily into *Te Karere*. The eight students had varied work backgrounds, including the army, the Māori Land Court and Māori language teaching. Afterwards, most of them signed up to *Te Karere* and made journalism a long-term career. Of those students, Arana Taumata became the executive producer of *Te Karere* and now holds the executive news role at Whakaata Māori. Wena Tait spent a year at *Te Karere* before moving into radio; she is now manager of iwi radio station Awa FM. Martin Rakuraku spent nineteen years on *Te Karere*, retiring in 2008. Joe Glen worked for *Te Karere* from 1989 to 2005 and then, after a two-year break, re-joined until 2011. The late Rau Kapa worked for *Te Karere* and then *Te Kāea*.

## INTERVENTION: 'TASTER' COURSES FOR RANGATAHI

In 1980, former *Auckland Star* journalist Gary Wilson, a Pākehā, became executive training officer of New Zealand Journalists Training Board, the industry-led organisation that at the time oversaw on-the-job print training. One of his first tasks was a survey of the workforce, and he was concerned to find that fewer than 2 percent of working journalists in Aotearoa New Zealand were of Pacific Island or Māori heritage.[219] Already troubled about the perpetuation of racial prejudice in and through news media, Gary Wilson decided to create a more diverse pipeline to provide a broader range of perspectives in newsrooms. With the "huge co-operation" of the government departments for Māori and Pacific Island affairs, strong support from various Māori and Pacific Island leaders and voluntary help from like-minded journalists,[220] he set up five-day introductory print journalism programmes for Māori and Pacific school-leavers, with the first in Wellington in 1980. The tasters ran for most of the decade in, mainly, Auckland, Rotorua, Wellington and Christchurch, and prepared students for print-oriented mainstream journalism training, principally the six-month certificate programmes then available at Auckland and Wellington polytechnics.

The many journalist helpers on the taster courses included newspaper editors Michael Forbes and Judy McGregor, magazine editors Piripi Whaanga and John Wood, television critic Barry Shaw, journalist-turned-historian Michael King, journalists Chris Winitana, Raewyn MacKenzie, David Young, Maurice Dick and Mata Mihinui, television broadcasters Brian Edwards, Olly Olsen and Ric Carlyon, and radio broadcaster Bruce Broadhead. A story in *Tu Tangata* reported that students in a course in Wellington in 1982 had sessions on basic journalism skills, scouted for news items, conducted interviews and wrote stories, visited editors and reporters at RNZ and TVNZ, and had a go at interviewing on camera.[221] Overall, the programmes gave an estimated 300 young Māori and Pacific Islanders a taste of print journalism and broadcasting, with more than fifty of these going into further training and then professional journalism. As Gary Wilson remarked, "It wasn't a bad haul considering how poor the fishing had been before."[222]

Among these early students were *E-Tangata* editor Tapu Misa, who trained at Wellington Polytechnic before taking up her first job at the *New Zealand Herald*; Gary Wilson has long called her, affectionately, 'Example Number One'. Others included Sonya Haggie, who attended ATI before taking up a job at the *Waikato Times*, and Sefita Hao'uli, who went to ATI and then *Sunday News*. However, Wilson also saw some talented students being rejected by the polytechnics and suspected racism. He arranged what he called 'booster courses' of two or three weeks for those who had been knocked back to ensure they were too well prepared to fail. However, he eventually concluded that the mainstream programmes "weren't much good at developing Maori and Pacific Island talent"[223]; it was time for a new approach.

Among his allies at the time were Piripi Whaanga, then editor of *Tu Tangata* magazine, the magazine of the Department of Māori Affairs. In 1983, Whaanga "cobbled together"[224], as he put it, money from a variety of funders to run a six-week programme out of the Havana Motor Lodge in Rotorua under the auspices of Waiariki Community College. Its dozen students contributed to an issue of *Tu Tangata*. "The premise was get them published," Whaanga told me in an interview. "That was Gary's thing, get them published anywhere, and then they would know they were journalists."[225] The experiment also showed observers, among them Waiariki Community College head Malcom Murchie, a reo-speaking Pākehā, that there was plenty of potential for a longer programme.

Taster courses were also run under Māori Access (MACCESS) schemes that had been set up to provide employment and vocational training for the long-term unemployed and others disadvantaged by what was, at the time, a shrinking labour market. One was run by Auckland Black Power leader Abraham Wharewaka, whose work trust Tatau te Iwi gained MACCESS funding to hire eight trainees for a newspaper, *Te Iwi o Aotearoa*. In Tauranga, a newspaper called *Te Kohanga o te Tui* ran to four issues in 1988 and 1989; it was produced by MACCESS trainees on a six-month journalism and community newspaper production training module at Bay of Plenty Polytechnic, Tauranga.

## THE WAIARIKI JOURNALISM SCHOOL

In 1985, Gary Wilson and his volunteers were instrumental in starting up a long-running and successful six-month journalism programme aimed primarily at Māori at Waiariki Community College (now Toi Ohomai Institute of Technology). They had solid support from principal Malcolm Murchie as well as iwi leader Maanu Paul, who chaired the programme's advisory committee. The model was the sixth-month Certificate in Journalism at ATI, with students studying competency-based unit standards required by the industry-led National Diploma in Journalism. The point of difference at Waiariki was its focus on training students to look at current events in terms of their importance to and their impact upon Māori; some students were bilingual. In 1986, a similar school aimed at Pacific young people was set up at Manukau Technical Institute in Auckland.

Among Waiariki graduates of the 1980s and early-to-mid 1990s who are still well-known in Māori media are Maramena Roderick, Eruera Lee-Morgan, Kirsty Babington, Justine Murray, Iulia Leilua, Laurence Wharerau, Te Anga Nathan, Semiramis Holland, Damiane Rikihana, Jodi Ihaka and Lynette Amoroa.

KIA HIWA RĀ! MĀORI JOURNALISM IN AOTEAROA NEW ZEALAND

# HOW I BECAME A JOURNALIST

# KIRSTY BABINGTON, TELEVISION REPORTER

I was part of those two-week holiday courses run by Gary Wilson, Derek Fox and Piripi Whaanga, which gave me the bug. My mum was a teacher and I was lucky enough to have been brought up reading, and I loved writing, so journalism was a good fit for me, although I was dreadfully shy for many, many years. I trained at Waiariki in 1989.

When we began in journalism, the only time Māori were in the media was either as criminals or 'radicals'. There was no attempt to get the Māori viewpoint across. We felt it was our duty to create awareness around Māori issues and to start telling our stories not only to ourselves but to the mainstream New Zealand in a bid towards understanding. We were made aware of the power of the media to shape viewpoints and I wanted to do my part in changing the racist, complacent New Zealand we lived in.

Telling Māori stories was my sole purpose of becoming a journalist – not the profile, not the career path, and I saw it as my way of contributing to the struggle.

---

Kirsty Babington.
WHAKAATA MĀORI

**KIA HIWA RĀ!** MĀORI JOURNALISM IN AOTEAROA NEW ZEALAND

# HOW I GOT INTO JOURNALISM

Iulia Leilua.
SUPPLIED

HE WHAKANGUNGU KAIKAWEKŌRERO: MĀORI JOURNALISM TRAINING – MANY PATHS TO THE NEWSROOM

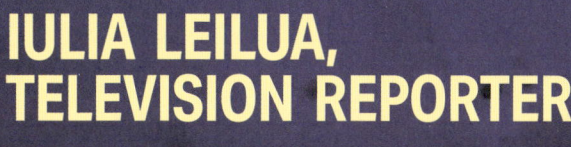

# IULIA LEILUA, TELEVISION REPORTER

I did my 7th form at Taumarunui High School after four years at St Joseph's Māori Girls' College. It was a culture shock and I didn't handle the transition very well.

I was about to give up half way through the year and went to the careers teacher, Mr Pete Wikaira – his son Chris is a former journalist and now a public relations consultant in Wellington. Mr Wikaira knew I was doing well in English and Māori and told me about these Māori journalism courses during the school holidays that I could attend to see if it was my vocation.

I went to the introductory and booster courses and found my calling among talented Māori storytellers.

**KIA HIWA RĀ!** MĀORI JOURNALISM IN AOTEAROA NEW ZEALAND

# HOW I BECAME A JOURNALIST

# IRENA SMITH

My mother tells the story of how we watched *Te Karere* at home every day while I was growing up. I would see Tini Molyneux and tell my mum, 'I'm going to be her one day and I'm going to work for *Te Karere*.' Once I got to high school, I realised I had good skills in speaking and speeches and things like that, and te reo Māori was really my main skill, especially as I was a second language-learner for English.

I went to the Waiariki journalism school straight after high school. I started at *Te Karere* in 2003. Then I went to Māori Television – I wanted to be a part of it. I think most Māori journalists wanted to be a part of this kaupapa. I was there for the kaupapa of te reo Māori and it was like a Māori thing that was for us, and that was ours, and you wanted to go over there and give what you could to it. I was there for four and a half years, then I came back to *Te Karere*.

Irena Smith.
JAE FREW

Māori already established in journalism were strong supporters of Waiariki. Among the programme's early advisors and journalism tutors were Piripi Whaanga, Chris Winitana, Waihoroi Shortland and Rawiri Wright. The latter, who trained in Auckland and later worked the *Taranaki Herald* and the *Evening Post*, headed the journalism school from 1989 to 1994. At the time, he said that he saw his role as imparting technical skills and enlightenment – as well as preparing students for the barriers and prejudices they would face working in mainstream media.[226] However, by 1997, the resourcing and quality of teaching on the journalism programme was causing concern. A relaunch of the primary journalism qualification as a two-year diploma was beset with difficulties to the extent that the influential Māori journalists' association, Kawea Te Rongo, withdrew its support; the industry peak body, the New Zealand Journalists Training Organisation, considered doing the same.

In 2002, former newspaper editor Annabel Schuler was recruited to guide change. Annabel, now living in Nelson and working for the Southern Institute of Technology as a dissertation supervisor, devised a more appropriate, print-focused journalism programme with the oversight of a stakeholder group whose leaders, at various times, were Kawea te Rongo journalists Chris Wikaira and Wena Harawira. She recalled that that in discussion with stakeholders, "it became clear if the Waiariki journalism programme was to live up to its kaupapa, it should include those elements of te ao Māori that were not included in other journalism programmes at diploma level".[227]

The result was the launch of the eighteen-month, print-oriented Diploma in Bicultural journalism, which incorporated the practical, unit standard-based elements of the National Diploma in Journalism such as interviewing and writing, but aimed to go further, training both Māori and non-Māori who wanted to be effective journalists in a bicultural Aotearoa. Students learned how to work in Māori environments and some basic language skills and underwent study of Te Tiriti o Waitangi and tikanga. They spent a good deal of time on the polytechnic's marae, Tangatarua.

Annabel Schuler recalls that top journalists such as Maramena Roderick and Kim Webby answered her call to deliver some of the courses. Eventually, satisfied with progress, Kawea Te Rongo pledged its support. The demand for graduates was strong, and at the time, said Schuler, the programme took two annual intakes of around seventeen people. However, in a paper delivered to the Journalism Education Association of New Zealand in 2003, Schuler revealed the difficulties in keeping a Māori-focused journalism programme going. Acquiring and keeping staff was difficult. Ideally, she said, training "should be led by Maori journalists, but they are still few and far between and in such high demand that they can find better-paid positions in the media, Parliament and public relations". In addition, student attrition was high: "We have to supply significant pastoral care, and we have to empower the students to take on what can be a crusading role."[228]

The ways in which Galtung and Ruge-style news values (see Chapter 6) were routinely interpreted in mainstream media presented students and tutors with a dilemma. "On one hand," said Schuler, "they are being taught all the usual values of negativity, accessibility, and unexpectedness, but on the other they can see great stories in the philosophies of self-determination and solidarity." A canvass of past and present students showed that "not one of them felt they would walk away from facts, balance and good ethical standards but they felt empowered to take on the gatekeepers and advocate for people, culture and the minority when it was news."[229]

By the late 2000s, print journalism in Aotearoa New Zealand, as overseas, was in difficulty due to the impact of digital media and this had negative downstream effects on journalism schools. It was no secret that journalism was poorly paid, stressful and held in low regard by the public, making it unappealing to young people, and journalism-school enrolment numbers started falling. Waiariki was not immune, Schuler said: enrolments were sliding, and students had more options as other journalism schools started embracing diversity. She left Waiariki in 2010. The journalism programme became year-long in 2011, partly to combat difficulties getting students to complete the final six months, according to David Scadden, a senior leader at the time.[230]

(L–R) Gary Wilson, Maanu Paul, Malcolm Murchie and Waihoroi Shortland, who were involved in running the Waiariki journalism school, and early graduates Damiane Rikihana and Lawrence Wharerau were reunited at the 2011 Waiariki journalism hui.

NZME

In July 2011, a hui at Tangatarua brought together more than 100 past and present Waiariki graduates, tutors and key figures in Māori media. At the event, delegates applauded the progress that had been made, but a clear message from newsroom leaders was that the shortage of staff with both journalism and reo skills was chronic; many roles in Māori language media were left empty or taken up by people with te reo only.[231]

The event was Waiariki's last dance. In 2013, faced with declining enrolments, the programme was suspended[232] and has not been revived. Keith Ikin, a senior leader at Waiariki at the time, suggested that young people no longer saw journalism as a worthwhile career:

> We closed it because we spent two years trying to encourage young Māori to come in to do the programme and they weren't interested. And they were telling us 'Look, you know, if I want to access an audience, I can pick up my phone and I can actually have an audience straight away. I don't need to go and work for a broadcaster, I don't have to work in radio, work in television.' And so there's a real … challenge, I think, for this industry to win back hearts and minds of young Māori.[233]

There was also a structural problem, according to Scadden: the programme was still tied to the national journalism framework, which had become outdated due to the rapid pace of change. The framework no longer exists and there is no longer a national industry body on journalism training. However, both Schuler and Scadden said the closure of the Waiariki journalism programme wasn't a failure – on the contrary. By then, individual journalism schools around the country were becoming more focused on diversity; Schuler said, "the Waiariki bicultural programme had made its point, served its purpose and others had caught up".[234]

Graduates of Waiariki since 2000 include TVNZ reporter Maiki Sherman; *New Zealand Herald* reporter Alanah Eriksen; Marcus Kennedy, executive producer Sky Sport Live; former MTS reporter Heeni Brown; former *Te Karere* reporter Irena Smith; former *Bay of Plenty Times* head of news Sonya Bateson; *Matamata Chronicle* editor Katrina Tanirau; and the late Anzac Pikia, a *Te Karere* reporter. Graduates from this era who started in journalism and moved to communications include former *New Zealand Herald* reporter James Ihaka and former Rotorua *Daily Post* reporter Megan Lacey.

## THE KURA KAUPAPA GENERATION

The failure of the Waiariki journalism school raised concern that closure of the only institution to prioritise journalism through a Māori lens could have a negative impact on the talent pipeline to newsrooms.[235] However, a new stream of talent was becoming available. The first fruits of Māori language education – the graduates of kōhanga reo and kura kaupapa – were finishing secondary school in the 1990s, and newly established iwi radio stations were providing them with opportunities.

People educated in te reo Māori since the 1980s have enjoyed a radically different upbringing to that of their parents; it is now possible to pursue an education grounded in te reo and tikanga Māori from pre-school to degree level. This has led to bicultural, bilingual young people secure in their identity[236] and it is perhaps little surprise that this group has found Māori media an attractive path. To be educated in te reo Māori means to inhabit an environment that values oral dexterity, public speaking and public performance; from an early age, children learn to give their pepeha in public and lead karakia, and the two most

# HOW I BECAME A JOURNALIST

## KEREAMA WRIGHT

Growing up, *Te Karere* was the only Māori programme on TV. It was the only programme my father would let us watch. So Martin Rakuraku, Tini Molyneux, Hinerangi Goodman – they were our TV stars because that was the only programme we watched, because ko te tūāpapa ko te reo Māori, ko to whakarauora i te reo Māori (the reason was the revitalisation of our language). And so I feel like I'm now the one with the paddle, and I'm the one paddling this waka, and I need to paddle it properly kia au ki tōna ūnga (so it gets where it needs to go). And I feel that there is a responsibility on us to educate our viewers. It's not about only informing; it's about educating and it's about introducing new words.

Kereama Wright.
WHAKAATA MĀORI

hotly contested competitions in reo Māori secondary schools are the Manu Kōrero speech competition, which started in 1965, and national kapa haka championships, held at primary and secondary level. Those in this generation are, wrote political scientist Aroha Mead, "active, intelligent, enthusiastic, inclusive, articulate young Māori, groomed to succeed in whatever they choose".[237]

As an example, brothers Kereama and Manawa Wright were educated in te reo and both followed their father Rawiri into journalism. Kereama Wright said that telling stories from a Māori viewpoint "came natural to us because we were brought up in the Māori immersion education system. Listening to stories and eventually telling stories plays a large part in that type of education system."[238] Sisters Heeni and Harata Brown were also both educated in te reo Māori and both went into journalism, Heeni via Waiariki journalism school and Harata via South Seas Film and Television School.[239]

Iwi radio often took on bilingual high-school students who wanted to learn about broadcasting, and many of them took media jobs after they left school. Iwi radio remains an important training ground for the current generation of practising journalists, more than thirty years later.[240] Of the iwi-run stations, perhaps the most important for developing news skills in young people with and without formal journalism training was Ruia Mai (see Chapter 3), which held the iwi radio news contract from May 1996 to June 2004. Ruia Mai took on young reo speakers who were mentored by pioneers in iwi radio such as Kingi Taurua, Wiremu Huta-Martin and Pere Maitai.[241]

# HOW I BECAME A JOURNALIST

## DEAN NATHAN

My background was in the public service – ten years in the Māori Land Court, the Māori Affairs department, and I did some oral history research for Muriwhenua. When that ended, I was on the dole for a couple of weeks and my lady said, "Hey, here's three hundred bucks, jump on the bus, get a haircut and a job, go to Auckland."

My mate Te Rangihau Gilbert, who was a TV presenter at the time for *Waka Huia*, rang up and said, "Come and write news at Ruia Mai! Come and write news in Māori for radio." I said, "Mate, I find it difficult to put a sentence together in Māori. I can understand it" – because I had been transcribing a lot of interviews in Māori for Muriwhenua claims research – but he said, "Mate, it's better than being on the dole." And I was highly motivated to get off that, so I was down there. I worked with a lot of people who are now the Scotty Morrisons and the Eruera Morgans.

# HOW I BECAME A JOURNALIST

## GLORIA TAUMAUNU

I started out as a Ruia Mai newsroom cadet at fourteen with Tāmati Waaka, Reikura Morgan and Amomai Pihama – the three of us girls were all still at Te Kura Kaupapa Māori o Hoani Waititi Marae. The four of us translated and presented the hourly bulletins in the weekends throughout our school years and went full-time when we finished school. I've come to love the mahi: our style of story-telling and our type of story.

# ANNABELLE LEE-MATHER

I knew I wanted to work in the media, but I wasn't sure what specifically I wanted to do or how to go about doing it. At school, I made short films and mockumentaries and filmed our parties, but I didn't really think about journalism because it didn't really seem like an option that was open to a young Māori girl. At uni, lecturers would often comment that I wrote my essays like articles (it wasn't a compliment) and that's when I started to think that maybe I could be a journalist.

I lucked into my job at radio station Ruia Mai through a family connection and once I started I became completely enthralled by journalism, but more importantly, Ruia Mai hot-housed my reo. I learnt more in one year there than I had during my entire high school and uni reo studies. Mei kore ake a Ruia Mai!

**KIA HIWA RĀ!** MĀORI JOURNALISM IN AOTEAROA NEW ZEALAND

# HOW TE REO TOOK ME TO THE NEWS BUSINESS

# JULIAN WILCOX

I was kūare about te reo Māori until I went to boarding school Te Aute and started learning there. The reason that te reo is so important to me now is because I always felt that I'd started behind the eight-ball. Dad was a fluent speaker, Mum was brought up in Ōhinemutu in a Māori community, but I was brought up in Upper Hutt so I had no idea.

So you get to Te Aute and there are all these Ngāti Porou boys and Coasties who know their whakapapa, and you feel like you're behind all the time. I started working at Radio Kahungunu in 7th form, on the drive show, and then I went to Te Ūpoko o te Ika in Wellington.

**KIA HIWA RĀI** MĀORI JOURNALISM IN AOTEAROA NEW ZEALAND

# HOW I BECAME A JOURNALIST

# ORIINI KAIPARA

What motivated me to become a journalist? The simple answer is my mum and my tamariki. I was a teenager and had two babies at the time – both under two years of age – and my mum gave me no choice but to go out and do something with my life. I chanced upon an ad for South Seas Film and Television School in the *Western Leader*, a west Auckland paper, and said, "I'll go there then." I applied the next day, and within a week I was accepted, then offered a full scholarship. That too became my motivation, my opportunity.

I went to Ruia Mai in 2003, the year after I finished film school, and that's pretty much where I got thrown in the deep end and trained on the job. In saying that, at that time it was a great team, we had a really strong team, so Shane Taurima, Ngahuia Wade, Tina Wickliffe, Annabelle Lee, Roihana Nuri, Ngarimu Daniels (Matahiki now). It was a good crash course, learning with all of them and from them. One of the most important lessons I learned was how to identify a Māori news story, and how to maintain my point of difference as a Māori reporter – not following the status quo or the mainstream way.

Oriini Kaipara.
STUFF

# WHAT MOTIVATED ME TO BECOME A JOURNALIST

## MIHINGARANGI FORBES

My great-great-grandparents owned a printing press and published the *White Ribbon* for the Women's Christian Temperance Movement. My great-great-grandmother, Jeanie Lovell-Smith, was the editor, so it must be in my veins. From very early I was exposed to protest and the fight for equality through my mum, who was heavily involved in everything from anti-apartheid to women against pornography, equal rights for workers, unions, political parties and much more.

Mum says I used to record myself on a tape deck reading the news, so I guess I had my eye on journalism before I even knew what it was. I wanted to be a journalist when I was at school, but I didn't rate my writing and I had an unfriendly English teacher who was uninspiring. I fought at school for equality for the Māori performing arts group and our te reo Māori whānau, so I got offside with teachers and school leaders.

Then in my last two years, a young teacher arrived at school, Irene Pewhairangi, and she was instrumental and inspirational. She helped me find my te reo Māori journey and pushed me in the right direction. That was Waikato Polytech and Te Ataarangi under the leadership of Kataraina Mataira, Petiwaea Manawaiti, Boy Rangihau, Ringiringi and Okeroa Manawaiti and many more reo exponents. It was an enlightening experience and one of the best things I ever did. From there, I was offered an internship at TVNZ from the editor of *Te Karere*, who was the son of one of my tutors.

# WHY I BECAME A JOURNALIST

## JUSTINE MURRAY

I guess the main reason is that I always wanted to tell stories. That's really the gist of it. When I was young I would make up stories and tell stories as a kid. Fast forward to college and I still had the same passion.

I did the Waiariki journalism course in the mid-1990s, when I was nineteen, and for that did a few weeks of work experience at Moana Radio in Tauranga, then known as Moana AM. … Later, the reporter at Moana, the late Richard Knight, moved on to the *New Zealand Herald*, and I took over his role. I moved up the ladder, from news, to drive show, writing ads, and then the breakfast show.

However, taking on young people with reo skills but no formal training has posed its own challenges. The flow of new Māori and biculturally competent non-Māori dried up after Waiariki closed in 2013. The very next year, TVNZ's Māori and Pacific programming departments, which had been a reliable source of training for a generation of reporters, also closed. Suddenly, young people with reo skills but no journalism training were being funnelled into reo Māori newsrooms. However, once they got there, training was piecemeal and sidelined in the rush to fill bulletins every day. The skills deficit was often apparent, and has led to criticism that Māori news does not always display the depth and rigour required.[242]

## QUALIFICATIONS THROUGH IWI RADIO

As the iwi network proliferated in the 1990s, it became clear that staff needed training. In 2002, the stations' umbrella body, Te Whakaruruhau o Ngā Reo Irirangi, and the New Zealand Qualifications Authority, the Crown entity in charge of assessment and qualifications, developed an on-the-job qualifications pathway for reo Māori media. Over the past two decades, the qualifications available to iwi radio staff and the providers have varied. For many years, the New Zealand Radio Training School in Auckland, part of the Wellington-based Whitireia Institute of Technology, trained iwi radio staff, though not all the qualifications on offer over that period included journalism. After Whitireia was restructured in 2020, the radio training school and its staff, headed by former radio executive Larry Summerville, transferred to the Manukau campus of Te Whare Wānanga o Awanuiārangi. The school, whose Māori moniker is Te Kura Pāpāho o te Motu, offers the year-long, entry-level New Zealand Diploma in Radio Broadcasting. Training includes news writing, news reading and live-cross skills.

## BESPOKE BUT SHORT-TERM SOLUTIONS

New pathways into journalism have arisen in recent years, with Māori among those able to take advantage of scholarships for tertiary journalism courses and/or workplace internships that major media outlets have offered at various times. However, there was little aimed

Raewyn Rasch, New Zealand On Air's first head of journalism.
SUPPLIED

specifically and regularly at Māori until 2017, when RNZ launched its annual RNZ Hēnare te Ua Māori Journalism Internship to foster Māori journalism. The twelve-month role is awarded annually to a Māori tertiary graduate.

The biggest journalism training opportunities for Māori have come about as a result of the COVID-19 epidemic. When the virus hit Aotearoa in March 2020, legacy media had been struggling for some time to find sustainable long-term business models; some nimble, subscription-based start-ups such as Newsroom and BusinessDesk had started showing the way. At the time, Māori news outlets such as iwi radio, long underfunded compared to their state counterparts, were in a holding pattern as work continued on a wholesale restructure of the Māori media sector that had started in 2018. After the country's first lockdown in early 2020, which saw advertising plummet, around 600 journalism jobs disappeared[243] and the government stepped in with short-term funding for mainstream and Māori media alike.

In terms of Māori journalism training, the biggest impact has come from the Public Interest Journalism Fund, a $55 million, three-year programme announced in February 2021 to support the media's contribution to a healthy democracy. It is administered by broadcasting funding agency New Zealand on Air under the management of its first head of journalism, former television reporter Raewyn Rasch, who is Māori.[244] Millions of dollars in funding have been directed to training, a large portion of that to develop Māori journalists. That emphasis, said Raewyn Rasch, was a deliberate response to the lack of Māori representation in newsrooms.[245]

Among other initiatives is a $2 million training programme called Te Rito, a collaboration between Whakaata Māori, Newshub, NZME and Pacific Media Network and eleven other media organisations that is training twenty-five new journalists from Māori, Pacific and other communities traditionally under-represented in media. Ten of that number are fluent speakers of te reo and based at Whakaata Māori. Veteran journalists Annabelle Lee-Mather and Mihingarangi Forbes are behind a training scheme called Kōmiromiro that delivers online workshops on Māori public interest journalism for iwi radio staff. Elsewhere, Māori language media outlets and the Māori-issues departments of various mainstream news operations have benefitted from money to hire Māori reporters, among them stuff.co.nz, TVNZ and Three. Although these programmes are short-term, they promise to plug the skills shortage that has plagued Māori journalism over the past decade.

# KO TE ĀHUATANGA O TE MAHI

## ANALYSING NEWS VALUES AND THE MĀORI PERSPECTIVE

## THE MĀORI PERSPECTIVE

Journalism is a cultural resource and is culturally contextualised – that is, the priorities of journalists and the stories they tell are influenced by the shared outlooks, norms and beliefs of the societies they live in. Māori journalism, in general, reflects the Anglo-American journalistic tradition – informational, independent reporting that monitors power[246] – but privileges a Māori perspective on an issue.[247]

The dictionary definition of perspective is "a mental view of the relative importance of things";[248] the way we are raised and our experiences influences our view of what we deem important. Māori who live in a Māori way – who are committed to language and culture, rather than monolingual, monocultural and assimilated – are "necessarily bicultural", moving between worlds.[249] However, we can't say that all Māori share the same life experiences or worldview: "Today, Māori worldviews are the product of the various original worldviews, overlaid by a variety of post-European colonial experiences, Christianity, literacy, the impact of new technologies and economy, the Treaty of Waitangi, the 'Māori renaissance' and not least, the influence of the media."[250]

Still, it's useful to describe the outlooks and perspectives that are most strongly associated with a Māori worldview, as below.

| Key indicators to understanding a Māori worldview | |
|---|---|
| Tribal identity | The importance of a sense of place and belonging through genealogical ties. |
| Land and landscape | The recognition by the people of the need for respect for the harmony and balance of the land and the resources it provides. |
| Spirituality | Based on a spiritual view of and response to the natural world. |
| Elders | Elders serve as a critical link to the past in the present context to ensure cultural practices and tribal knowledge remain intact for future generations. |
| Language | The recognition that the language contains so many cultural indicators that enrich one's identity. |

| | |
|---|---|
| Culture | The importance of culturally-determined ways of thinking, behaving, communicating and living as indigenous people. |
| Diversity | The celebration of tribal identity and a rejection of non-indigenous labels and definitions that homogenise Māori people. |
| Kinship structure | Based on a collaborative/shared power system within social hierarchies where cultural concepts manage people's behaviour and their relationships with each other and their environment. |
| Self-determination | The recognition of the rights of indigenous peoples to live as indigenous people. To be healthy, Māori people need access to learning their language; to education and qualifications and quality learning environments; to employment and a high standard of living; to have their culture valued in relation to Te Tiriti o Waitangi; to live as Māori and as global citizens; and to be active participants in determining their own future. |
| Concept of time | Māori look to the past as a guide for the present and future. |
| Cultural knowledge | Cultural knowledge is viewed in a holistic framework with all aspects interrelated. It enables one to function with a degree of comfort in Māori contexts and to understand what is going on within that context. Hence, the connection between cultural concepts and a Māori world-view. |
| Reciprocity | Based on the view that mutual respect is the cornerstone of human relationships and between humans and their environment. |

SOURCE: KA'AI T., & HIGGINS, R. (2004). TE AO MĀORI: MĀORI WORLD-VIEW. IN T. KA'AI, J. MOORFIELD, M. REILLY & S. MOSLEY (EDS.), *KI TE WHAIAO* (PP. 13–25). PEARSON EDUCATION NEW ZEALAND, REPRINTED WITH PERMISSION.

Next, we explore how these principles intersect with the news values that guide journalists' work.

## NEWS VALUES

News is a social construct, with journalists creating and curating news stories according to the cultural values most familiar to them.[251] In a country whose dominant culture was shaped by a colonising narrative that Māori were inferior, mainstream media have often marginalised and misrepresented Māori, with many Pākehā journalists unaware of the ways in which their monoculturalism intersects with their framing of Māori. In 1986, a time of hostility in the media towards Māori, journalist Philip Tremewan wrote, "Many Pakeha don't understand their own conditioning. They're so monocultural that they don't realise they have a culture and that the values of that culture at the core of their work are culturally based, not some universal, divinely ordained law."[252]

Journalists are socialised by an editorial pecking order into reproducing the values of their newsroom, which in turn reproduces the values of the dominant culture.[253] The values reporters reproduce are viewed as an expression of collective common sense rather than a set of ideological values that might be damaging to certain sectors of society.

There has been a great deal written about racism in mainstream media – see authors such as Judy McGregor, Ranginui Walker, the research group Kupu Taea and others – so we won't go into that issue here. As discussed earlier, Māori language journalism arose to give space to Māori voices, and journalism by, for and about Māori generally follows the structural, technical and storytelling conventions of the Anglo-American model. Māori language reporting also applies the news values of that model. However, the difference in Māori journalism is that over these standard news values is laid a filter informed by Māori history, experiences of colonisation, contemporary identities and aspirations for the future, and these factors determine the resources and importance given to a story.

If we amalgamate the most important research in this area, particularly that of Norwegians Johan Galtung and Mari Holmboe Ruge; Tony Harcup and Deirdre O'Neill, based in England; and New Zealand journalist Judy McGregor,[254] we end up with a list of general news values as listed below, in no particular order. These principles of news storytelling apply, broadly, in all developed democracies.

- **Exclusivity:** Stories generated by, or available first to, the news organisation as a result of interviews, letters, investigations, surveys, polls, and so on.
- **Bad news:** Stories with particularly negative overtones such as death, injury, defeat and loss.
- **Conflict:** Stories concerning conflict such as controversies, arguments, splits, strikes, fights, insurrections and warfare.
- **Surprise:** Stories that have an element of surprise, contrast and/or the unusual about them.

- **Audio-visuals:** Stories that have arresting photographs, video, audio and/or that can be illustrated with infographics.
- **Shareability:** Stories that are thought likely to generate sharing and comments via social media.
- **Entertainment:** Soft stories concerning sex, showbusiness, sport, lighter human interest or animals, or offering opportunities for humorous treatment, witty headlines or lists.
- **Drama:** Stories concerning an unfolding drama such as escapes, accidents, searches, sieges, rescues, battles or court cases.
- **Follow-up:** Stories about subjects already in the news.
- **The power elite**: Stories concerning powerful individuals, organisations, institutions or companies.
- **Relevance:** Stories about groups or nations perceived to be influential with, or culturally or historically familiar to, the audience.
- **Magnitude:** Stories perceived as sufficiently significant in the large numbers of people involved or in potential impact or involving a degree of extreme behaviour or extreme occurrence.
- **Celebrity:** Stories concerning people who are already famous.
- **Good news:** Stories with particularly positive overtones such as recoveries, breakthroughs, cures, wins and celebrations.
- **News organisation's agenda:** Stories that set or fit the news organisation's own agenda, whether ideological, commercial or as part of a specific campaign.
- **Emotion:** Stories that arouse emotional responses.
- **Celebrification of the journalist**, with reporters becoming the personality and central actor in the news story.

News values that relate to the production process have a bearing on which stories are pursued:[255]

- **Values in the news text** itself, such as clarity and brevity.
- **Values in the news process**, such as a story that will meet its deadline.

It's important to point out that all the above criteria can be contested as other considerations come into play, among them resources, time and the subjective influence reporters bring to bear. However, to put these values in context, we'll look at three stories to show how they reflect news values through a Māori lens. We'll also discuss some of the practical production issues that influenced each one.

## STORY 1: MURDER ACCUSED ACQUITTED

This story aired on *Te Karere* on 20 October 2016.[256] Peata Melbourne reported the outcome of a court case in Brisbane, Australia, in which Australian man Gable Tostee was acquitted of the murder or manslaughter of Māori woman Warriena Wright. The pair had met through the dating app Tinder while she was visiting the Gold Coast from Aotearoa. Hours after the pair met face to face, she fell from the balcony of Tostee's fourteenth-floor apartment and died.

Peata used footage shot the previous afternoon by Australia-based staff of TVNZ's flagship news programme, *1 News*, as the parties emerged from the courthouse. To this, she coupled file footage of the scene of the death, pictures the pair took of themselves together and social media images. In terms of structure and editing, this was a typical television news story, with a reporter voice-over linking its elements. The presenter was Scotty Morrison.

> Presenter: "Kāore a Gable Tostee i kōhuru i a Warriena Wright. Koirā te whakatau a te rōpū tekau mā rua i whakawā i te whakapae kōhuru i utaina atu ki runga i a Tostee. Engari i roto i te kōti te kaumingomingotanga e āwhiowhio ana i te whakapātaritari i ngā roia wawao i te kaiwhakawā nā te mea i te tuhi kōrero tētahi o te rōpū tekau mā rua ki runga Kōtui Pāpori. Nei rā a Peata Melbourne."

Screenshot, *Te Karere*.
TVNZ

*Subtitles: Gable Tostee has been found not guilty of murdering Warriena Wright. But the verdict did not come without court room confusion. Prior to the verdict the defence team asked for the jury to be discharged because of a breach of information on social media. Here's Peata Melbourne.*

Reporter: "Ka mutu te rā tuawhā o ngā ngārahutanga, i puta mai a Gable Tostee i te kōti hai tangata kore hara."

*Subtitles: After four days of deliberation, Gable Tostee emerged from the court a free man.*

Screenshot, *Te Karere*.
TVNZ

Grab, unnamed defence lawyer: "Mr Tostee is very happy with the result. He's relieved this matter is now behind him and he's looking forward to moving on with his life."

Screenshot, *Te Karere*.
TVNZ

Reporter: "Kāre ia i hara, engari he aituā tonu mō te whānau o Warriena Wright."

*Subtitles: No crime committed, but a tragedy for Warriena Wright's whānau. (Note that the word whānau was not translated.)*

Screenshot, *Te Karere*.
TVNZ

Grab, unnamed Wright family spokesperson: "As you may appreciate, Warriena Wright's family are still coming to terms with

Screenshot, *Te Karere.*
TVNZ

the loss of their daughter and their sister, as well as enduring the anguish of being present here for this trial this last two weeks."

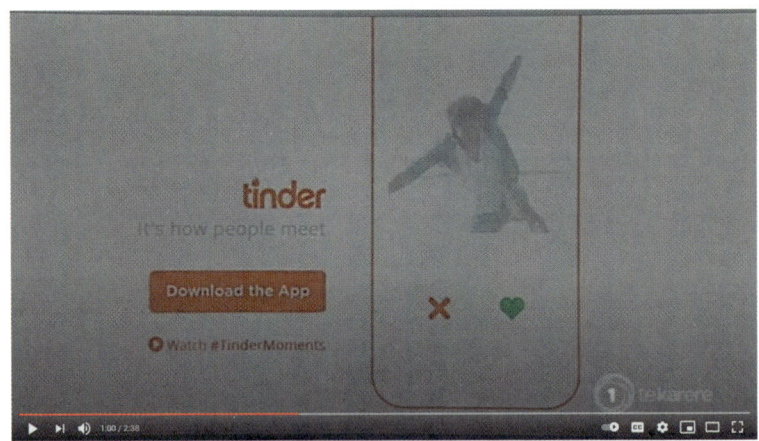

Screenshot, *Te Karere.*
TVNZ

Reporter: "I whai aroha a Wright i tētahi tāne tauhou i runga i a Tinder. I haere ia ki te Takutai Kōura mō tētahi mārenatanga. Ki reira ia tūtaki ai ā-kanohi nei a Tostee mō te wā tuatahi. Ko tōna tūmanako he pō tūtaki tāne noa iho, engari kē, he pō tūtaki i a Hine-nui-te-pō."

Subtitles: *Turning to Tinder for some fun with a man she'd never met, Wright was in Gold Coast for a wedding and met up with Tostee for the first time. What was supposed to be a night out with a man ended up being the night she met her death.*

Screenshot, *Te Karere.*
TVNZ

Grab: unnamed man doing a haka for Wright at the place she died.

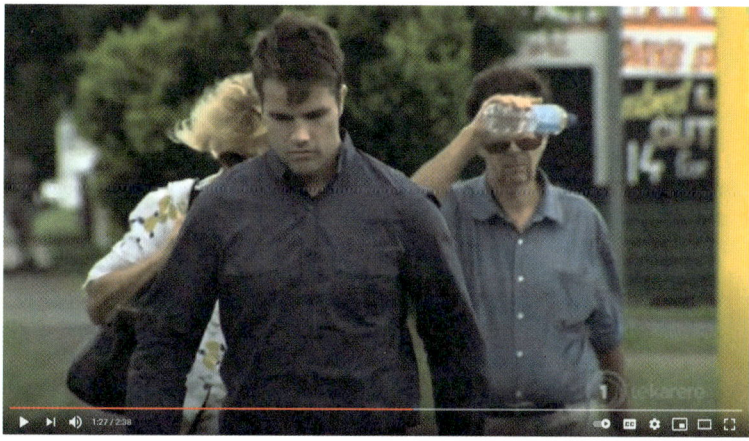

Screenshot, *Te Karere.*
TVNZ

Reporter: "Kua mauhere a Tostee i ngā rā ki muri me tana kaha ki te whakairi kōrero ki runga i āna whārangi ipurangi me te pahupahu mō te maha o ngā wahine kua moea e ia. Koinei hoki tāna whai muri i tana wetekanga i te whare herehere."

Subtitles: Tostee has previously served time in prison and is a prolific social mediarite who has boasted online about sleeping with hundreds of women, and posting this shortly after his release.

Screenshot, *Te Karere*.

TVNZ

Screenshot, *Te Karere*.

TVNZ

Reporter: "Heoi ehara tēnei ure paratī i te kaikōhuru."

*Subtitles: But the self-proclaimed playboy is no murderer.*

Screenshot, *Te Karere*.
TVNZ

Gable Tostee audio: "I swear to God I didn't push her or anything, I just chucked her out on the balcony and shut the door 'cos she was beating me up."

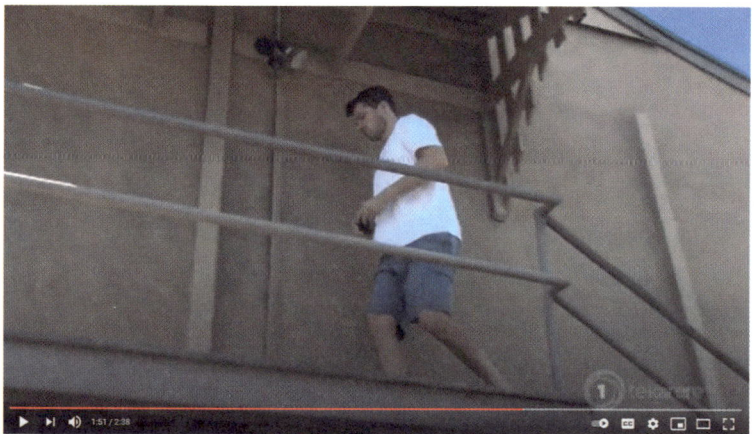

Screenshot, *Te Karere*.
TVNZ

Reporter: "He momo mate rongo kua pāngia hoki ki a ia, me tana whakapae kua tāhaetia ana rawa e tētehi i ngā rā ki muri. Nā whai anō ngā kāmera i waho i tōna whare me ana mahi hopu reo i runga i tana wāea. I kitea te mana o aua hopukanga i te kōti."

Subtitles: *Tostee also suffers from a form of autism who [sic] says he had been robbed previously. He set up security cameras and habitually recorded audio conversations on his phone. Those recordings proving vital in court.*

Screenshot, *Te Karere*.
TVNZ

Audio from the fatal night. Gable Tostee: "Who the [beep] do you think you are?" Warriena Wright: "No, no, no!"

Screenshot, *Te Karere*.
TVNZ

Reporter: "I ngā miniti tata i mua i te whakataunga, i huraina te kōrero i te whakairi kōrero mō te kēhi ki runga Instagram e tētahi o te hunga whakawā. I tono ngā rōia o Tostee kia whakakore i te whakawātanga, kia whakawātea hoki i te hunga whakawā, engari i whakahētia tā rātou tono e te kaiwhakawā. Kāre i hara a Tostee."

*Subtitles: Moments before the verdict was due to be announced, it emerged that a juror had posted messages of [sic] the case on Instagram. Tostee's defence demanded that the trial be aborted and the jury discharged, an application rejected by the judge.*

Screenshot, *Te Karere*.
TVNZ

Reporter: "Engari i te mutunga iho, ko te oranga o tētehi i mutu, ko te orangatonutanga o ētehi atu i turaki. Peata Melbourne, *Te Karere*."

Subtitles: The jury found Tostee not guilty after one life ended, and many more ruined.

## News values in this story

Warriena Wright's death and ensuing events were widely reported. The news values were multiple, among them **drama**, **bad news** and **relevance**. The latter was particularly important as so many people use social media like Tinder to meet strangers for casual sex, making this story a cautionary tale for the digital age. The story also had good **audio-visualness**, as the media had a lot to choose from: photos the pair took of themselves, Tostee's recordings and footage of him outside the courtroom. There was also **follow-up**, as the media had followed the case from Warriena Wright's death to acquittal, a period of more than two years; and, **surprise**, as it was not obvious that Gable Tostee would be cleared.

For *Te Karere*, the most important single news value that justified the story was **relevance**, and that was cultural. Peata Melbourne said that when *Te Karere* found out that the victim had Māori heritage, its reporters had a reason to follow up. However, they were unable to find out Warriena Wright's iwi, a fact that viewers would want to know.

Said Peata Melbourne, "That's Māori enough, I think, that she's got Māori whakapapa." Still, as she embarked on the story, Peata Melbourne said this reason needed to be made clear: "We've mentioned it [Wright's whakapapa] before and we'll probably mention it again … we can't assume that everyone's been following this case and [may be] wondering why *Te Karere* is following a murder trial of an Aussie boy." In the event, there was no explicit mention in the final story of Warriena Wright being Māori, which may have been an oversight under time pressure. However, her family was described in the English subtitles as her whānau, a signpost to her whakapapa.

*Te Karere* is part of the TVNZ newsroom and is able to tap into the resources of the flagship show *1 News*. *Te Karere* repurposed pictures, audio and graphics that had been used on *1 News* the previous night, which meant that the story was able to be turned around quickly and in-house. There were no photos or videos of Warriena Wright in settings that emphasised her Māori heritage; it is possible she wasn't raised to be culturally Māori. However, *Te Karere* included pictures that would increase the story's visual appeal in a Māori sense: file footage of a man performing a haka at the place she died. Earlier that day, a news editor had instructed Peata Melbourne "to put the Māori spin on it … get that haka".

### Writing scripts in two languages

Like all reo Māori television reporters, Peata Melbourne writes her scripts in both English and Māori. The added workload is necessary, she said, as subtitlers can't be expected to understand the context of a story as thoroughly as the reporter. English scripts are sent to subtitlers for input. *Te Karere* goes to air at 3.55 p.m., so its reporters and subtitlers work under immense time pressure; this explains the transfer of minor typing and grammar errors from the original script to the subtitles.

Typically, Peata writes her first script in the language of her grabs: "It flows better for me as a writer to write in whatever language my talent is speaking in." But that isn't a hard and fast rule, she said; for this story, a straightforward account of a verdict, she wrote the script in Māori first and then in English. She used the same format for both languages – active sentences in an inverted pyramid.

Peata Melbourne.
WHAKAATA MĀORI

*Te Karere* reporters write their introductions for the presenter in English only, with translation left to the presenter, and this was the case here. Executive producer Arana Taumata says that each presenter has their own mita, or way of speaking, which includes dialect, intonation and pronunciation; the English-only approach to introductions reduces the risk of something being lost in translation.

Peata Melbourne, who is Tūhoe, enlarged on this by saying that there was a difference between people like her who speak the straightforward conversational Māori of their childhoods – she grew up speaking te reo at home but was educated in English – and colleagues whose style of language had been shaped by tertiary study. "I think there's a massive difference between the conversational Māori I hear back [home] from my family versus the academic Māori that I hear [at work]," she said. Peata Melbourne aims to keep her reo Māori scripts "simple, so a 12-year-old can understand". Like the majority of reporters who participated in this book, she doesn't translate commonly used Māori words in her English translations: "Mainstream is now using these words, so I leave them."

### Handling the gulf in worldviews

Journalists working in te reo often make references to the cosmological, given the primacy of the creation story. However, given the difficulty of translating between worldviews and the space constraints of subtitles, references to the esoteric are usually not translated into English. To explore this, let's return to a paragraph from the Gable Tostee story:

> Reporter: "I whai aroha a Wright i tētehi tāne tauhou i runga i a Tinder. I haere ia ki te Takutai Kōura mō tētahi māreenatanga. Ki reira ia tūtaki ai a kanohi nei a Tostee mō te wā tuatahi. Ko tōna tūmanako he pō tūtaki tāne noa iho, engari kē, <u>he pō tūtaki i a Hine-nui-te-pō.</u>"
>
> Subtitles: *Turning to Tinder for some fun with a man she'd never met, Wright was in Gold Coast for a wedding and met up with Tostee for the first time. What was supposed to be a night out with a man ended up being the night <u>she met her death.</u>*

The phrase "the night she met her death" could be translated factually as "te pō i mate ai ia" [the night she died]. But in her reo script, Peata wrote "he pō tūtaki i a Hine-nui-te-pō", or "the night she met Hine-nui-te pō", the goddess of death. The allusion is elegant and unobtrusive, but not translated. Peata doesn't translate metaphors into English, assuming the primary audience for subtitles is non-Māori and/or monolingual:

> There's no need to literally translate what I say – Māori talk figuratively a lot, and that's how I talk in Māori too. But Pākehā don't, so I translate it to capture the meaning. With this particular example, I wrote it in Māori first and it was a play on words … she embodies the concept of death, and I assume reo Māori speakers will already know this. I don't assume the same of non-Māori speakers.

However, figures of speech grounded in common understandings of human behaviour rather than cosmology can, in some cases, translate well from Māori into English, as in this paragraph about Tostee:

> Heoi ehara tēnei ure paratī i te kaikōhuru.
>
> Subtitles: *But the self-proclaimed playboy is no murderer.*

The Māori equivalent for playboy combines the word for penis (ure) and spurt up or scatter (paratī).

## STORY 2: MINISTER LOOKS TO COOKS OVER LAND SALES TO FOREIGNERS

Auckland-based Radio Waatea produces news bulletins and current affairs interviews for the wider iwi network. Due to limited newsroom funding, most stories in the news bulletin, *Waatea News*, are drawn from the previous night's episode of *Manako*, a Sunday to Thursday night, live, 7 p.m.–8 p.m. current affairs discussion show featuring high-profile commentators, politicians and community leaders. Interviewees are able to speak at length with very little interruption.

To create news stories, Waatea's Māori language reporters mine as much as possible from *Manako*, so their stories tend to focus on these newsmakers' opinions and ideas; there is little resource to develop stories further. If there is no usable audio from *Manako*, Waatea staff write a reader – a news story without audio, read by the presenter. Staff also develop news stories from phone interviews and media releases and write Māori language news from English-language news interviews.

The following story, written and presented by Tumamao Harawira, was a typical example of the way in which news is culled from the previous night's *Manako*. The Minister for Māori Development, Te Ururoa Flavell, had discussed his activities in an interview that ran for eleven minutes. The news story gleaned from it was forty-two seconds long and aired in the 11 a.m. bulletin on Monday, 20 March 2017; it is no longer online.

The context was that the New Zealand Government had given American billionaire Peter Thiel citizenship for his investments in local companies, although he had not lived in the country and had no intention of doing so, thereby circumventing immigration law. He then bought large tracts of sensitive rural land. The government was accused of selling citizenship to the wealthy, reflecting longstanding and widespread concern, particularly among Māori, that wealthy foreigners were alienating New Zealanders from their land. The controversy was widely covered in mainstream media.

This was a standard radio text – short, active sentences in the present tense followed by a quote.

Presenter: "Kei te rere te whakawhiu ki runga i te Kāwanatanga mōna i whakaāetia ki te urunga mai a Peter Thiel, tangata whai rawa o Amerika, ki konei ki Aotearoa noho ai."

*Subtitles: The Government is being heavily criticised for allowing wealthy American Peter Thiel to gain citizenship here.*

Presenter: "E ai ki te Minita Whakawhanake Māori, a Te Ururoa Flavell, me whai pea tātou i te tauira o ngā Kuki Airani mō te hunga e āhei ana ki te hoko whenua."

*Subtitles: According to Māori Development Minister Te Ururoa Flavell, we should probably be following the example of the Cook Islands on who is able to purchase land.*

Audio, Te Ururoa Flavell: "… i ētehi tikanga pēnei i ērā i roto i te Moana Nui-a-Kiwa. Kua rongo ake au i te āhuatanga o ngā whakahaere i ngā Kuki Airani. Ko tā rātou kāwanatanga, ko te whakatau tētahi kōrero e mea ana kāore e taea e wai rānei te hoko i te whenua ki tangata kē, ki iwi kē, ki a wai ake i tua atu o te Kuki Airani. He māmā noa ake te rīhi engari kaua ki te hoko."

*Subtitles: … practices like those in the Pacific Islands. I've heard about the way it's managed by the Cook Islands. Their government, the law says no one is able to sell land to people from elsewhere, from outside the Cook Islands. It's easy enough to lease out land, but not to sell.*

Presenter: "Ko te reo tērā o Te Ururoa Flavell."

*Subtitles: That's Te Ururoa Flavell.*

### News values in this story

This story aired a fact that listeners might not know: In the Cook Islands, foreigners can lease land, but not own it. The Minister suggested Aotearoa New Zealand should look to the Cook Islands' example and ban land sales to foreigners. This reflects the news value of the **power elite**, the idea that the things powerful people say are automatically seen as more valuable than the opinion of an ordinary citizen. In addition, this Minister, like many other Māori MPs, made himself readily available to Māori media, so earned good coverage.

Another important news value was **relevance**, in that the story was about people and a country culturally familiar to listeners, and here relevance operated on linked cultural, geographical and ideological levels. The Cook Islands, four hours' flight from Aotearoa New Zealand, is self-governing but part of the Realm of New Zealand, and its people carry New Zealand passports and use New Zealand currency. Ethnic Cook Islanders are Māori, and their languages come from the same language family as te reo Māori. The story essentially asked the question: 'The Cooks are part of our political and cultural family and they've done it, so why don't we?'

### Soundbites

One notable aspect of this story was that the grab of Flavell came to twenty-six seconds, nearly double the length of a mainstream radio quote of about fifteen seconds.[257] Quotes in Māori media tend to be more lengthy than those in mainstream,[258] and there are generally two reasons for this. Due to the structure of te reo, saying something in Māori takes longer than the equivalent in English – up to one and a half times longer.[259] In addition, tikanga values listening and allowing everyone to have their say without interruption, and this is clearly heard on *Manako*, the show from which the soundbite was lifted. Although *Manako* is about current affairs, it takes a conversational, non-confrontational tone; interviewees are not hurried and hosts interrupt infrequently. This style tends to militate against short soundbites for news.

## STORY 3: IWI GETS $100M TREATY SETTLEMENT

This story was posted on the website of Radio New Zealand National, the state-funded radio broadcaster.[260] It delivers all its news in English but has a dedicated Māori issues news team to report Māori interest stories in a way all listeners can understand. This story, by

# Govt sorry for taking iwi's land

9:02 pm on 26 November 2016

Share this

**Shannon Haunui-Thompson**, in Wairoa
@SHaunui  shannon.haunui-thompson@rnz.co.nz

The Government has apologised for stealing land from iwi as it signed a Treaty settlement with Ngati Kahungūnu ki Te Wairoa today.

Pauline Tangiora and Rose Pere. Photo: RNZ / Shannon Haunui-Thompson

Hundreds gathered at Takitimu Marae to celebrate the signing and hear the Crown's apology.

The iwi and hapū of Wairoa have worked on their treaty settlement for more than 30 years. It is the fifth largest Treaty of Waitangi settlement to date and includes a $100 million payment.

Treaty Negotiations Minister Chris Finlayson spoke about the Crown's role in taking, by force, land from Ngati Kahungūnu ki Te Wairoa and apologised for the Crown's role in the iwi's loss of land.

Iwi members young and old lay down the challenge with a haka. Photo: RNZ / Shannon Haunui-Thompson

Screenshots, RNZ website.
RNZ

Mr Finlayson said he regretted the destructive and demoralising effect the confiscation had on the Ngati Kahungunu ki Te Wairoa hapū.

"The Crown can never fully compensate for the wrongs of the past, but this settlement provides the people of Te Wairoa with the foundation for a stronger cultural and economic future," he said.

Mr Finlayson said intense military campaigns against Te Wairoa led to socio-economic deprivation, which still existed.

The iwi and hapū of Te Wairoa have worked on their treaty settlement for more than 30 years. Photo: RNZ / Shannon Haunui-Thompson

Pauline Tangiora was one of the first people to start the settlement more than 30 years ago.

"It's a great relief that the job has finished for our rohe, we now pass it on to the next stage and hopefully they'll settle for the benefit of the beneficiaries in peace and harmony."

The newly-established Post-Settlement Governance Entity, Tatau Tatau o Te Wairoa Trust, has two years to formulate a business and social plan for the settlement money.

The full pōwhiri welcomes Mr Finlayson onto the marae grounds. Photo: RNZ / Shannon Haunui-Thompson

During the whaikōrero today, Kiingitanga advisor Rahui Papa said the Crown needed to stand by its apology.

It was to redress a grievance from a Crown attack on the iwi on Christmas Day, 1865, which resulted in loss of life and property.

The iwi and hapū of Te Rohe o Te Wairoa includes seven iwi and hapū covering northern Hawke's Bay, southern Gisborne, the township of Wairoa, Lake Waikaremoana and the Mahia peninsula.

Screenshots, RNZ website.

RNZ

Shannon Haunui-Thompson, documents a Treaty of Waitangi settlement ceremony earlier that day during which the Government apologised for past wrongs and presented redress of cash and shares.[261] The story privileged a Māori perspective and was published on the evening of Saturday 26 November 2017. This is a typical example of a Treaty settlement story, written in the inverted pyramid style.

### News values in this story

The most prominent news value in operation from a Māori perspective is **good news**. After three decades of work by the tribe to prove its claim, the wrongs done in the nineteenth century were acknowledged and compensated, and the Government and iwi came together in reconciliation. Another value was **magnitude**. The $100 million settlement promised to have a significant impact on the economic, cultural and social wellbeing of a relatively poor and isolated tribe of some 34,000 people. **Relevance** was another value in operation. Given the interconnected nature of Māori life, many people not directly involved with the settlement itself would have blood or marriage links to the tribe and would benefit from its post-settlement activities. Almost all tribes were affected by war and land loss in the 1800s, and many suffered disastrous dispossession. Iwi whose claims remain unresolved are intensely interested in other tribes' progress.

**The power elite** is another value present. Here, the elite people were government ministers and the iwi leaders to whom they apologised. However, the pictures showed which group was most important in this paradigm: Māori leaders rather than Crown officials. From a (Māori) news selection point of view, Crown officials are present at all settlement ceremonies; there is nothing visually new in that. However, the ceremonial activity of the local people at that time and place is unique.

This story was also an example of **follow-up**. The iwi had spent thirty years working towards settlement, and as resolution neared, RNZ had done several reports. In addition, the story had great **clarity**: the Crown was welcomed with ceremony, admitted it stole land from iwi, apologised and paid compensation. This story also bore a critical news value for the digital age – **audio-visuals**, with four appealing on-the-scene pictures – and **shareability**. The reporter tweeted photographs taken from her seat during the pōwhiri, posting two in the first hour.

## The use of te reo Māori in English-language reporting

The story featured Māori words and ideas that are part of New Zealand English and widely understood.[262] The increasing normalisation of Māori language and culture[263] is underlined by the fact that certain issues and concepts from te reo Māori are no longer glossed or described in English-language media.[264] Six Māori words stand alone in this story; these are among the most common Māori words and phrases in New Zealand English.[265] Shannon Haunui-Thompson didn't translate them because "they are commonly used words, not just by Māori, but by Pākehā".[266] However, in general, if she used a word that she felt may not be understood, she translated it in the text. Examples included pakanga (battle) and tumuaki (head of an institution).

Shannon Haunui-Thompson consciously uses macrons in Māori words. She relies on the guide to orthography produced by Te Taura Whiri i te Reo Māori, the Māori Language Commission: it is her "most reliable reference".[267] However, one word in her story was spelled without a macron, and that's 'Kiingitanga', the King Movement. The administrative arm of Waikato-Tainui and the closely linked Kiingitanga have conspicuously not adopted the macron,[268] and appear to be the only Māori organisations to eschew it. In doing the same, she was demonstrating respect for the tribe's mana motuhake – its independence and its way of doing things: "It's an acknowledgement of them and how they have chosen to spell that word."[269]

# KO TE REO KIA RERE

## MĀORI JOURNALISTS AS AGENTS OF LANGUAGE REVITALISATION

## THE CONSTRAINTS FACING MĀORI LANGUAGE JOURNALISTS

As earlier outlined, much Māori language and Māori interest journalism is state funded as a result of Tiriti o Waitangi claims. The remit of news funder TMP, an independent government agency, is to promote Māori language and culture through the provision of funding for Māori initiatives in music, radio, television and new media. TMP bulk-funds Whakaata Māori, which produces its news and current affairs in-house, and funds TVNZ's *Te Karere*, which re-applies for funding every year. Radio Waatea, the urban, pan-tribal station in Auckland, has held TMP's three-year news and current affairs contract continuously since 2004. The twenty-one iwi stations funded by TMP are not obliged to take Waatea's news and current affairs service, but all twenty-one take some or all the output.

However, TMP policy is silent on what constitutes quality news and current affairs. It is not charged with assessing the quality of the journalism it funds; the problematic assumption is made that news staff will be appropriately qualified. Māori language journalists are framed, then, primarily as agents of language revitalisation; their newsgathering is a by-product of a national agenda to create a languagescape where te reo Māori is heard in a wide variety of domains. Once upon a time, TMP could rely on outside groups training Māori speakers in journalism and funnelling them into reo Māori media over time. But those days are gone, and the pipeline of people has reduced to a trickle (see Chapter 5).

Reporters are under constant pressure to find a rare creature – a subject expert who also speaks te reo well. Irena Smith said, "It's always got to be in the forefront of your mind, because at the end of the day, that's our point of difference … we are here to uphold reo Māori over and above everything else. That's our job, as Māori news … we're here to revitalise the language and keep it alive."[270]

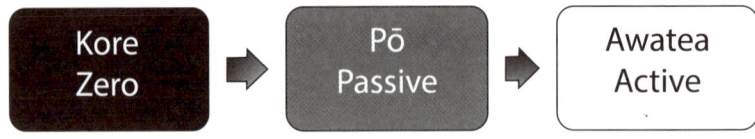

The ZePA model, showing the attitudes of people to te reo. Proposals for Māori language shows must demonstrate how they propose to move consumers to the right.

SOURCE: HIGGINS, R., & REWI, P. (2014). ZEPA: RIGHT-SHIFTING: REORIENTATION TOWARDS NORMALISATION. IN R. HIGGINS, P. REWI, & V. OLSEN-REEDER (EDS.), *THE VALUE OF THE MĀORI LANGUAGE TE HUA O TE REO MĀORI* (VOL. 2, PP. 7–32). HUIA AND NGĀ PAE O TE MĀRAMATANGA, P.25.

To receive TMP funding, all shows, including news and current affairs programmes, must provide a language plan that aligns with the agency's funding and policy framework, itself informed by a language revitalisation model called ZePA.[271] This model acronymises three positions on the Māori language continuum, reflecting the attitudinal and psychological stance people hold towards it: Kore, or zero interest; pō, or passive engagement; and awatea, or active use.

Language plans must demonstrate how a show will help "right-shift" people along the continuum.[272] *Te Karere*, Whakaata Māori news, *Waatea News* and *Manako* serve consumers who are active users of te reo or want to be, which requires their shows to be 70–100 percent in te reo and at a level "that permits the presenter and participants to express simple and complex ideas on diverse topics in a wide range of social domains".[273] The extent of variation between episodes may be only plus or minus 5 percent, and this is assessed. Language quality is also assessed, with consultants marking shows for pronunciation, vocabulary, grammar, euphony (an appealing sound), captions and strategic consistency, described as the production's identifiable contribution to revitalisation.

Several veteran reporters said that the reo Māori imperative gave them the incentive to maintain networks of strong speakers. However, as Hone Edwards pointed out, news goals and language revitalisation goals sat together uneasily: "Where you have a remit around revitalising the language, that clashes with the reality of newsgathering."[274]

That reality is that around 50,000 adults, or 10.6 percent of the Māori population, claim to "speak te reo Māori very well or well; that is, they could speak about almost anything or many things in Māori".[275] From a reporter's perspective, some of these people are newsmakers, so subject expertise and language talent often come in one person. However, a far larger number of Māori adults – 257,500 (55 percent) – have "some" ability; "that is, they are able to speak more than a few words or phrases in the language". Their ability to express themselves is far less certain.

TMP documentation does not have any expectations around the quality of Māori language in those being interviewed for Māori news.[276] The agency recognises that many people integral to news stories are monolingual and there are various dynamics in play that journalists can't control, such as the language interviewees choose to use and how comfortable they feel in front of a reporter. Journalists, then, have to rely on their judgment.

This prompts a range of issues and dilemmas that we can sum up as questions: Do you go for the subject expert who speaks no Māori so has to be interviewed in English, or the fluent speaker who has less knowledge of the issue? If people say they want to be interviewed in te reo but what they say isn't intelligible enough, do you ask them to repeat their sentiments in English and risk embarrassing them? Do you ask interviewees at the start to be interviewed in both languages, and then choose the better version? And if you opt for this, how do you ensure you maintain your subject's mana and their confidence?

Or, from another perspective, how far do you push people to use their imperfect reo? How many grammatical errors are acceptable? What about a competent Māori speaker who won't speak Māori on air for fear of error? If someone asks for help to formulate what they want to say, do you help, and for how long?

In practice, journalists take a stance noted by revitalisation experts Rawinia Higgins and Poia Rewi, who developed the ZePA model. The journalists in this book hold, in general, what the pair term a "liberal and/or compromising" attitude: they are not fixated on linguistic accuracy and take the position that a spoken language is a living language. Such liberal compromisers, wrote Higgins and Rewi, "place value on the language merely being spoken – syntactic and lexical errors are not a priority – nor do they highlight or impress upon the speaker in a manner that compels the speaker to shy away from speaking".[277] Reporters understood the nature of the 'reo journey' – the phrase commonly used to describe the ups, downs and wavering confidence levels that face adult learners of te reo – and accepted that being on television could increase interviewee anxiety. They were realistic about what they might be able to get from interviewees, and there was an absence of judgment.

Among the news shows, *Manako* faces the biggest challenge; it has to produce nearly five hours of live reo a week. Television news reporters on *Te Karere* and *Te Kāea* often do interviews in English, but these can be kept short and the reo quotient redressed through voiceovers and pieces to camera. *Waatea News* has some flexibility; if a story has no reo Māori grabs, the presenter can paraphrase the English in a read-only report.

## STRIKING A BALANCE BETWEEN GOOD LANGUAGE AND QUALITY INFORMATION

In the early days of the first Māori language television news bulletin, *Te Karere*, news was read to camera and there was minimal video, so a

Arana Taumata.
JAE FREW

100 percent reo quotient was easily maintained. In the early 2000s, when reporter Dean Nathan was working at *Te Karere*, English was "staunchly kept to a bare minimum," he said. "We were urged to constantly expand and develop our contacts of Māori speakers on all issues."

However, the policy was later relaxed, and the current TMP requirement is that the two television news shows are at least 70 percent in te reo. This can be seen as problematic in that it might reduce the incentive for newsmakers with some reo skills to improve. However, according to Arana Taumata, *Te Karere* executive producer at the time of writing, allowing more English in news shows was a practical evolution that better balanced subject expertise and language, and led to better news stories as people were not excluded. Greater use of English also helped the show's mission of attracting viewers: "It's important to draw non-reo-speakers in," he said. "We don't want these people to think they can't watch *Te Karere* because they don't have the reo."[278]

The daily weighing-up journalists do between quality reo and quality information is "not ideal," said Oriini Kaipara, "but that's how things are."[279] It appears that Whakaata Māori, in particular, has grappled with where to draw the line on the proportion of reo in news shows. For example, in the early years of MTS, any English in a news story was voiced over in te reo by the reporter. Annabelle Lee-Mather was among the cohort who did so, and said that the move, since discontinued, was the outcome of considerable discussion about what to do when the show aimed to be 95 percent Māori but newsmakers were often monolingual. She believed that voice-overs sent the wrong message: "Our people can actually speak English … it felt condescending to viewers, and whakaiti [belittling] of our talent. To me, it drew attention to the fact that they couldn't speak Māori and they needed some little young upstart reporter like me to talk over them."[280]

When news chat show *Kawe Kōrero* was launched (see Chapter 4), it had an aspirational aim to be 100 percent in te reo. However, said producer Hone Edwards, it quickly became clear that "nine times out of 10", the newsmakers didn't speak Māori, and amassing talent for interviews five days a week was "an impossible task"[281] for a team of four, not all of whom were fluent speakers themselves. He negotiated with his managers to be allowed a maximum of two interviews in English in each bulletin.

Reporters generally aimed for subject experts, knowing that if they spoke in English, other parts of the story would redress the balance. Reporter Kereama Wright said:

> I prioritise the right person to speak about that kaupapa. If there is someone who can deliver the same strong message in Māori, then I'll go for the Māori person. But if I had to choose out of the right person and the Māori speaker who doesn't really know about the kaupapa, then I'll be speaking to the English speaker.[282]

Oriini Kaipara gave an example of how she would script and edit an English interview to increase the amount of Māori:

> If the grabs are all in English, I'll cut them right down and paraphrase the rest of their grab into a voiceover, which is all in te reo. So, while my 1.30 min story has English-only grabs, at least 70% of it will be in te reo – that includes the presenter intro, my voiceovers and maybe a piece to camera.[283]

Although TMP sets a 70 percent lower limit for *Te Karere*, the show aims for an 80/20 ratio. The show is twenty-two minutes and thirty seconds, which allows four to five minutes of interviewees speaking in English. All other elements – presenter introductions, voice-overs and pieces to camera – are in Māori. Arana Taumata said that he did spot checks when he felt the proportion might be slipping, but has not yet found it breaching the lower limit.

Arana Taumata advises reporters to be transparent about the information they are seeking to help subjects prepare their vocabulary for a reo Māori interview. However, the success of this depends on the complexity of the topic:

> There have been cases where talent, in an attempt to stay true to te reo and *Te Karere*, insist on doing the interview in te reo. Generally, this is cool; through preparation and keeping it simple,

we can usually get a couple of sound grabs in te reo and build the story around that. If it's a particularly complicated, technical story and the talent is a learner or intermediate, then we might suggest doing an English interview.[284]

## NEGOTIATING LANGUAGE

Research for this book showed that on first contacting strangers on the phone, the majority of journalists greeted people with common openers such as 'kia ora' or 'tēnā koe'; the response often gave the cue to continue in either English or Māori. If people responded in Māori, said Wepiha Te Kanawa, an MTS reporter at the time of writing, their fluency quickly became apparent. He adapted to what he heard: "I'll know if they can speak Māori within the first 10 seconds … I can hear if it's a native tongue, also if it's a second-language learner, so I base it on that. If they can speak Māori, I'll continue that whole conversation in te reo Māori."[285]

On meeting face to face, male Māori journalists usually gave a hongi to other Māori men, and Māori men expected that; in my observation, the hongi is the standard greeting among Māori men in any situation, and it is often accompanied by a handshake with the right hand and the left hand placed on the shoulder or upper arm of the other. However, non-Māori often got a handshake only, with the reporters sticking to the gesture they knew would be understood by the interviewee. Male reporters tended to shake women's hands and kiss them on the cheek, and male interviewees tended to do the same.

Women infrequently did a hongi with other women, usually opting for a handshake and/or kiss. For Irena Smith, the hongi is associated "with more formal occasions, so it's not an everyday thing". She was among several women who said they took their cue from the person they were meeting: "I just take my lead off the talent. I stick my hand out first … mostly I just kiss them, though, rather than hongi, but then, you can tell if they're going in for a hongi, so you go in for the hongi too."[286]

To Hinerangi Goodman, a *Te Karere* reporter at the time of writing, some sort of touch was important to show sincerity: "[Ko] te mea nui, kua pā. Ko te ihi ko te wehi o te tinana kei te rere, nō reira, he rite anō.

[The main thing is that there's contact. The life force of the body is shared so it's the same thing (whether one does a hongi or kiss)]."[287]

Fieldwork showed that if reporters had already been speaking English to someone and were ready to interview, they would usually ask: "Do you speak Māori?" If they had been speaking Māori, they would generally offer a choice: "Reo Māori, reo Pākehā rānei?" [Māori or English?] As *Marae* producer Tini Molyneux observed, "Some people speak te reo but can't actually articulate themselves as well in te reo as they would in English, and there are some people that are more articulate in te reo Māori than they are in English."[288]

MTS reporter Taroi Black encouraged people to use their reo, whatever the standard. He reasoned that with use came improvement:

> If they are capable to speak te reo Māori, then you go with it. Here and there, they're going to have a few errors, they're not going to be grammatically correct in their reo. But I'm not all about a speaker who's grammatically correct; I'm about a person who knows how to speak enough in te reo and having the confidence to actually utilise the language … the more you speak it, the better you become.[289]

## SUPPORTING LEARNERS

For many people learning a new language, anxiety and apprehension can cause a lack of confidence and a reluctance to speak.[290] This can be compounded among Māori, who may feel whakamā, or shame, self-doubt and embarrassment, and also grief that they don't speak their heritage language or have an imperfect grasp of it.[291] This mix of emotions can strike very painfully at one's mana, sense of identity and self-esteem. This can be acute for those in middle-age and above, who comprise both the urbanised generation that didn't have access to Māori language education as well as the generations before them who were punished for speaking Māori at school.[292] *The Hui* producer Annabelle Lee-Mather said she never presumed people spoke te reo:

Annabelle Lee-Mather.
SUPPLIED

> Because my mum couldn't speak Māori and my grandmothers couldn't speak Māori, and I know first-hand the whakamā they would experience when people presumed that they did and would launch into a te reo Māori conversation with them ... so I never want to make anybody else feel – what's the word – whakamā or wanting. That's tikanga too, being mindful that not all of our people have been lucky enough to learn te reo Māori and that is just as much a part of our story.[293]

In the research for this book, it became clear that the language revitalisation imperative encouraged journalists to step beyond the usual definition of journalist. Kereama Wright, for example, saw his role as cultural ally as well as journalist:

> The thought of speaking Māori on television is daunting. It's about confidence-building. You're not just there to get the story, you're there to empower someone to deliver the message in their native tongue. And I love it. I'm a product of second language-learning parents, and I can see the importance of it. So we'll sit there for half an hour sometimes and practice the kōrero. Or

Kereama Wright.
SUPPLIED BY WHAKAATA MĀORI

sometimes we'll write it. It happens quite often. Often it's just repetition, repeating the answer until they get confident enough, and we'll take a number of takes.[294]

Reporters recognise that people on their reo journey may be the highly fluent speakers of the future, so it is important to maintain their confidence. Research has documented the journeys of people who learnt te reo later in life and became experts, among them broadcasters Julian Wilcox and Scotty Morrison and educator Hana O'Regan.

However, there were limits to how long journalists could spend helping people with grabs. Oriini Kaipara, for example, gives people three practices before she suggests a switch to English. Irena Smith encourages people to speak Māori to see how they go. If she feels that their ability to communicate clearly might be marginal, she asks them to comment in English as well. It can feel awkward to ask for interviews in both languages, Irena Smith said, but she reminded people that clarity was critical:

> I just cut to the chase and say, 'Can we do this in English as well, just to give us an option on whether we use your interview in te reo

or English?' and ... I say, 'I think you will be able to explain yourself more clearly in English' to try to ... make them feel a bit better about the fact that we're just here to get the story, and we need to get the story in the most clear and succinct way. 'It would help you, and it would make you look better on TV, if you say that in the language that is most comfortable to you.'[295]

Asked how people reacted, she said, "They're usually okay with that. They see that we are probably the best people who can help them in that situation, and they're always conscious of how they look on TV anyway."[296]

Radio journalist Ana Tapiata spent six years until 2010 producing a five-minute RNZ programme called *He Rourou*, which captured people informally discussing various topics in te reo. Her strategy with those less fluent was to keep her questions narrow: "I would focus the interview quite intensely ... so that they knew what they had to focus on and not worry about going anywhere else." Many of her less-fluent interviewees were, however, subject experts, and including them was a respectful nod to that expertise: "It had to do with enhancing mana."[297] Ana would ensure that a fluent speaker was recorded as well, even if that person was further removed from the issue, to ensure top-quality reo was also present.

Tumamao Harawira is aware that live interviews are "nerve-wracking" for learners, and his strategy is to keep his language simple. "*Manako* is not in the business of subjecting an already uncertain talent pool, a pool that is the future of the language, I might add, to an environment that is not conducive for them." Bernie O'Donnell, the news manager of Radio Waatea at the time of interview, said he might offer to pre-record an interview and edit it. "The pressure is taken off them. I suppose the biggest problem for our speakers is to admit that they are not up there and once you broach that, they seem a little bit relieved."[298]

When preparing scripts, television reporters type out grabs verbatim. However, when translating grabs into English for subtitling, they tidy errors of expression. Below is an example from an interview

Dean Nathan.
SUPPLIED

Dean Nathan did with a police officer who worked with young people, and on that day was at high school to watch a touring anti-bullying play. This is the grab used in the story, and the subtitles:

> Officer: "Mō tenei wā āe e kite katoa ngā hara ki runga i te rorohiko, te whakaweti ki runga i te Pukamata pea te ipurangi me rorohiko ā ko au e haere mai nei ki te tautoko i a rātou me ngā kura katoa."
>
> *Reporter's interpretation and subtitles: At the moment we are (seeing) all types of negative stuff happening online, including cyberbullying, and my role here is to support this initiative amongst all schools.*[299]

While the verbs and nouns most critical to meaning are there, such as bully (whakaweti), support (tautoko), computer (rorohiko), internet (ipurangi) and Facebook (Pukamata), the surrounding grammar is imprecise. However, the officer was confident enough to use what he had, and the message was clear: he wanted to visibly back the community's anti-bullying efforts.

In the film, as reporter and officer were exchanging farewells, the latter, uncertain he had explained himself well, said, "I hope that was alright." Nathan replied, "It was cool, bro." As the pair shook hands, Nathan switched to Māori, saying, "I rongo au i te wairua o tō kōrero, e hoa. [I felt the spirit/essence of what you were saying, my friend]."[300] In his words of encouragement, he was displaying manaakitanga and care for the officer's feelings as a learner of te reo.

Nathan said later that he probably wouldn't have used such a grab from an ordinary member of the public; he might have asked for English instead. But he wanted to include the officer in his story as he had personal and positional mana, and was a role model for using the reo he had: "I don't think I would have accepted that comment from many, if any, others. But in this case I ... took into account the important role that he plays in our community and allowed him the opportunity to comment. Plus he's a good guy."

People's language skills generally improved over time, he said, and this eventually benefited reporters: "I recall having to edit one particular talent to pieces to get a grab appropriate for news. But in the years to come, this person became one of the most outspoken Māori leaders of their generation and a go-to talent for Māori and mainstream news media alike."[301]

The pressure is less for Māori-focused shows funded under TMP rubrics requiring a lesser amount of reo. For example, TVNZ's weekly current affairs show *Marae* has to produce a show that is 30–70 percent in te reo. Producer Tini Molyneux aims for a 50/50 English–Māori show, but "sometimes we have our whole bulletin in te reo Māori, subtitled."[302]

## AN ETHICAL ISSUE?

We could argue that it is unethical for a journalist to help any subject work out what they want to say or tidy up their language; indeed, it would be rare for such an issue to arise among English-language journalists in Aotearoa New Zealand. However, in the reo Māori reporting world, the intersection of the limited pool of speakers, manaaki tangata and the funding regime engenders a different perspective. The consensus is that telling people what to think is clearly unethical but helping them translate their own ideas into Māori is acceptable for clarity and to maintain their mana.

Oriini Kaipara emphasises that Māori journalists have to take on the role of coach at times "whether we like it or not. Our job is not to teach people how to speak Māori, but to help people communicate effectively in te reo by showing manaakitanga." Annabelle Lee-Mather reflected a sentiment common in revitalisation circles when she said that all reo Māori speakers had a duty to provide language support to those who sought it from them. "As journalists, that includes us, and we need to be extra mindful that we give that support in a way that empowers the talent to tell their story in their own words."[303]

A common refrain in the revitalisation movement is "one generation to lose a language, three to get it back", a paraphrasing of the words of American linguist Joshua Fishman,[304] whose work on reversing language shift has been influential in Aotearoa New Zealand. Reporters and others who are role models for language know that they are playing a long game; it will take some generations before te reo Māori moves beyond its current status, described by TMP as "somewhere between definitely endangered and severely endangered".[305]

Live studio panels are a particular challenge for those who are not fully fluent, and this can lead to newsroom compromises. In 2014, it emerged that *Te Karere* gave all in-studio guests their questions in advance; it wanted to help people who were less fluent to prepare, but to be fair, had to extend the courtesy to all panellists. This insight, however, emerged in a roundabout way after rival broadcaster TV3 alleged that staff of TVNZ's Māori and Pacific programmes unit had used TVNZ resources to carry out activities in support of the Labour Party, which was then the Opposition in Parliament. TVNZ's subsequent investigation found that, while staff had used company resources to campaign for Labour, there was no evidence of bias towards the party in their programmes. Giving questions in advance did not constitute bias because the circumstances of the bulletin's production – that is, the shortage of fluent speakers – were unique and created "severe constraints".[306]

## DEBATE: CLARITY OF TE REO VERSUS EXTENSION OF THE LANGUAGE

Since the early 2000s, native speakers, who are an older age group, have periodically complained that the language used on reo Māori television news uses too many unfamiliar words and is incomprehensible to them.[307] Broadcasters defend themselves by pointing out that these words come from two sources, both legitimate. One is Te Taura Whiri i te Reo Māori, whose role includes coining words (see some of them later in this chapter). The other is the influential 1844 dictionary by H.W. Williams from which journalists are re-introducing words that have fallen into disuse.[308] Much of the latter has been driven by the many broadcasters who attended the elite Māori language school Te Panekiretanga o te Reo Māori, the Institute of Excellence in the Māori Language; collectively, these graduates have had considerable influence on the language heard on air. The school ran from 2004 to 2019 under academics Tīmoti Kāretu, Te Wharehuia Milroy and Pou Temara; its aim was to produce "graduates who are excellent in the Māori language, who are equally proficient in the English language and are able to perform the customary practices of their marae to the highest level".[309]

## MEASURING THE QUALITY AND QUANTITY OF TE REO IN NEWS

Concerns are also periodically raised about the quality of language in reo Māori television news programmes. In 2010, academics Pou Temara and Rangi Matamua described the language of some *Te Karere* and MTS reporters as "simply diabolical", adding that some journalists weren't making enough effort to fix entrenched errors and improve their language.[310] Language quality was also raised in a 2009 review of the law that established Māori television. The review noted that the Act didn't define what was meant by quality, noting the "inadequate language proficiency of some on-air presenters" and "recurring grammatical mistakes by some journalists and narrators". Some of the language patterns reflected English-language constructions and Pākehā worldviews, which risked diluting the "Māoriness" of the language: "To lose these insights into our singular Māori thought processes would be a tragedy."[311] In response, TMP commissioned a language assessment framework to clearly define the standards broadcasters must reach. The framework is prescriptive, suggesting the following areas are problematic areas across reo Māori broadcasting: the incorrect use of stress in multi-syllabic words; errors in negation; and following the English word order of subject-verb-object rather than the Māori patterning. Importantly, the framework encourages reporters to use their mita or dialectal variation of te reo.[312]

Reo Māori news shows are selected randomly for assessment of the quality and quantity of language. Newsroom leaders said that they welcomed the perspective outside assessments provided; while producers were the front line in error-checking, the nature of news meant that errors sometimes got to air. Both Whakaata Māori and *Te Karere* news heads described their journalists as passionate about te reo; many of them attended high-level language classes in their own time, and some were also language teachers, graduates of Te Panekiretanga o te Reo, and/or licensed as interpreters by Te Taura Whiri i te Reo Māori. One reporter said she and her colleagues were too busy with newswork to worry about the assessments: "Of course we are open to criticism and getting it right, but to be honest, we are so busy trying to find stories, and get the stories out, we don't have time."[313]

However, Māori language news appears to be living up to TMP's expectations. In September 2018, the agency's assessments showed that both Waatea News and *Manako* got top scores of 5/5, or "matatau/ excellent". Both earned the commentary "excellent quality of Māori from experienced fluent speakers and broadcasters". On a five-point scale, *Te Karere* and MTS news both rated 4/5, described as "Tino pai – very good". To give a flavour of the feedback dispensed, one of the television commentaries noted that a particular broadcaster "still uses interesting words" – the suggestion being that these are old but rarely heard words the reporter has chosen to reintroduce – and added that context did not always enable listeners to grasp the meaning of these words. Both television news assessors noted that language abilities varied from reporter to reporter.

It is pertinent to note that both assessors also made value judgments, one neutral and one negative, about perceptions of "good reporting" and a "good reporter", although this is technically outside TMP's remit and thus the assessors' scope. The assessor for *Te Karere* wrote, "It is about good reporting as much as anything", suggesting that it was difficult to separate out language skills from journalistic ability. The assessor for MTS news wrote, "In general, I feel it is the craft of journalism that is questionable, because [being] a good reo speaker doesn't necessarily qualify you as a good reporter."[314]

We could argue that the preparation a journalist is able to do and their capacities – which includes whether they have been formally trained – has a bearing on the quality of the language they use. The assessor's role is to judge the final product in terms of language, not information. However, we could argue that an assessor is also a member of the public and, like any consumer, will have an opinion on how well reo Māori news fulfils its purpose as a news vehicle. The gap between what Māori language news is funded for and what journalism is expected to do risks becoming wider when considered in light of holes in the pipeline of trained journalists.

Whakaata Māori news and *Te Karere* must be, bulletin by bulletin, 70–100 percent in te reo; the quantity of spoken dialogue is measured by a language consultant watching selected episodes with a stopwatch. The target is that 90 percent of samples meet the 70–100 percent threshold. The two 100 percent reo Māori news shows on Waatea, *Waatea News* and *Manako*, are rated digitally. All the TMP-funded iwi radio stations stream their content through a web-based language-recognition system called Kōkako that identifies whether te reo or English is being spoken or sung; real-time, comparative data is provided on a web-based dashboard.[315] The quality assessor alerts TMP to any quantity issues.

This slice of the dashboard shows Radio Waatea's tally from midnight to 3 p.m. on Thursday 30 May and Friday 31 May 2019. The timeline runs from midnight on the left, with te reo the red blocks

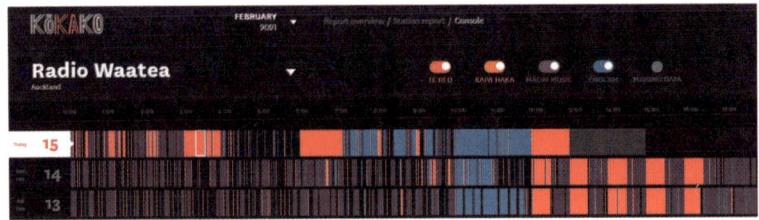

The Kōkako dashboard collects and analyses real-time data about English and Māori language use from the iwi stations' broadcasts.

SOURCE: DRAGONFLY DATA SCIENCE

and the English blue. The system also captures what Māori language songs are playing, also in red. Clicking on the bands plays the content. At the time of writing, Kōkako correctly identifies te reo 90 percent of the time.

## EXPANDING THE PĀTAKA KŌRERO THROUGH NEWS

Māori journalists are important disseminators of language developed for new concepts and ideas, and words heard on reo Māori news can quickly fall into common use. Journalists feel a responsibility to expand their own vocabularies, among their strategies querying new language they hear in colleagues' work, tapping mentors and friends, using dictionaries to replace vocabulary they felt they overused, attending high-level immersion courses and adopting new words developed by Te Taura Whiri i te Reo Māori. As an example, below are five words the organisation has released in recent years:

- Karihika ngakinga: revenge porn, made from karihika (pornographic) and ngakinga (reprisal).

- Hōtaka ā-tono: TV On Demand, from hōtaka (programme) and tono (command).

- Kurutene kore: gluten-free, made from transliteration of gluten and kore (none).

- Mana matua: parental controls on technology, made from mana (to have authority) and matua (parent).

- Hītini: phishing, from hī (to fish, raise up) and tini (many).

However, newsrooms are occasionally ahead of Te Taura Whiri i te Reo Māori. *Te Karere* staff came up with the word tāhine, which means non-specific gender or transgender; it combines the words tāne and wahine in a natural-sounding way. A Google search for tāhine in Aotearoa New Zealand finds more than 1000 mentions, mostly on sites for transgender health and wellbeing services, showing that the rainbow community has embraced the word, and on news sites and social media. However, journalists don't coin words lightly. Scotty Morrison, the show's primary presenter and language advisor, says that *Te Karere* has a protocol about coining new words. Staff meet to discuss the issue, with the reasoning and the decision about a new word logged "to protect our integrity and the integrity of the process … if we put a word out on air, it's amazing how many people will hear that word and will start to use it. So we need to be accurate."[316]

## CASE STUDY: MĀORI OR ENGLISH?

Journalists working in te reo often check with each other about the fluency of people they are thinking of interviewing. In this case study, reporter Peata Melbourne is doing a story about a foreign oil company's exploratory drilling in a remote part of the country and plans to interview the area's member of Parliament. This politician, Manu, describes himself as a conversational speaker of te reo rather than fluent, but Melbourne is not entirely sure about the level of his reo. As a reporter, she needs to secure Māori language interviews as much as possible. However, she also needs clear information from her subjects, and this is her top priority.

Left: Harata Brown.
JAE FREW

Right: Peata Melbourne.
WHAKAATA MĀORI

From her desk, Melbourne looks across to producer Harata Brown and asks: "Shall we get Manu in Māori or English?" She knows that Brown comes from the same tribal area as Manu and knows him well enough to make a judgment. As Melbourne asks the question, she is frowning slightly, displaying uncertainty; she later said that at that point, she felt "50/50" on using te reo for the interview. Brown replies, "Māori. He's ... getting better in Māori."

Melbourne is quick to reply, saying "Is he?" with the same doubtful face. Brown sees and hears the doubt and responds with a firm "Yeah." Then she clarifies exactly what she means by this, saying, "I reckon he can give you punchy grabs in Māori." Here, she cuts to the heart of the matter – can Manu provide the pithy but illuminating soundbites that reporters need? She believes he can.

Grabs communicate opinions, ideas and feelings rather than facts, and television reporters often build their stories around them. Brown is suggesting that, although the MP might not be able to give a word-perfect, lengthy interview about the complexities of the issue, he can probably come up with short, interesting soundbites. Melbourne's doubtful expression is replaced by a smile and "Oh, okay, let's go for Māori then." She has adjusted upwards her opinion of Manu's reo skills. She is turning away from Brown when the latter quips, "He's been practising."

Brown later told me she had known Manu since she was a teenage radio announcer on iwi radio in her home region, and over the years she had often seen him in the community. She knew he had been practising his reo as she had seen him not long before this interaction, and Manu had told her that he was making concerted efforts.

Melbourne rang Manu to clarify a few points with him in English. The interview was to be an ear-piece interview, with the reporter at her desk on her mobile phone and Manu in his office, also wearing an earpiece and sitting in front of a camera operator. When the camera was ready, Melbourne switched into te reo and the interview ran for six minutes. To end her conversation with Manu, she said, "Okay, choice, ka pai [great], thank you!" As Brown had predicted, Manu provided two clear grabs.

Speaking later, Melbourne said she sometimes asked the question "English or Māori?" about fluent or native speakers. But in these cases, she said, she wanted to know if the speaker could express herself or himself succinctly: "There are some people who can speak a lot of Māori but can't necessarily get a concept across well in te reo Māori." Grammatical accuracy and a natural syntax, she added, are less important than a subject's ability to make a point in such a way that soundbites can be lifted. "We're not there judging their grammar," she said. "We are just going, 'Can they get their idea across?'"[317]

# TIHEI MAURI ORA!

8

## ELEMENTS OF WHAIKŌRERO IN NEWS

There are two registers of te reo Māori: te reo ōpaki, everyday language with its shortcuts and idioms, and te reo ōkawa, the formal register, which includes whaikōrero, or public oratory. Māori language reporters are acutely aware that they are role models and agents of language revitalisation, and, like their nineteenth-century forebears, they weave into news reports various elements of whaikōrero, such as whakataukī, metaphors, allusions to pūrākau and references to spiritual concepts.

To show how they make these adaptations, in this chapter we'll explore what was said during a week's worth of Māori language broadcasting in September 2017. The shows are *Te Karere* (TVNZ); the news service on Whakaata Māori, named *Te Kāea* at the time of writing; and two shows on Radio Waatea: its hourly news bulletin, *Waatea News*, and *Manako*, an hour-long current affairs show.[318]

Whai means to follow and kōrero to speak, reflecting the expectation that speakers build on each other's commentary – something like a news story laying out various points of view. Whaikōrero showcase one's eloquence and cultural knowledge and generally follow a three-part structure. Te tau (opening) indicates that a formal speech is coming. In te kaupapa (main body), the speaker greets the dead and the living before moving to the take (discussion of the issue at hand). The final portion, te whakamutunga (ending), ends with a waiata tautoko, or song in support, started by the speaker or their entourage. The diagram below outlines how most whaikōrero are structured, but there are variants. That said, greetings to the dead, greetings to the living and a central topic are the essential components.[319]

## WHAKAARAARA IN THE NEWS

The tau (opening) often begins with a whakaaraara, a short, sharp utterance defined as a "chant, to keep the watch awake, or give the alarm in time of war".[320] These chants, handed down through the generations,

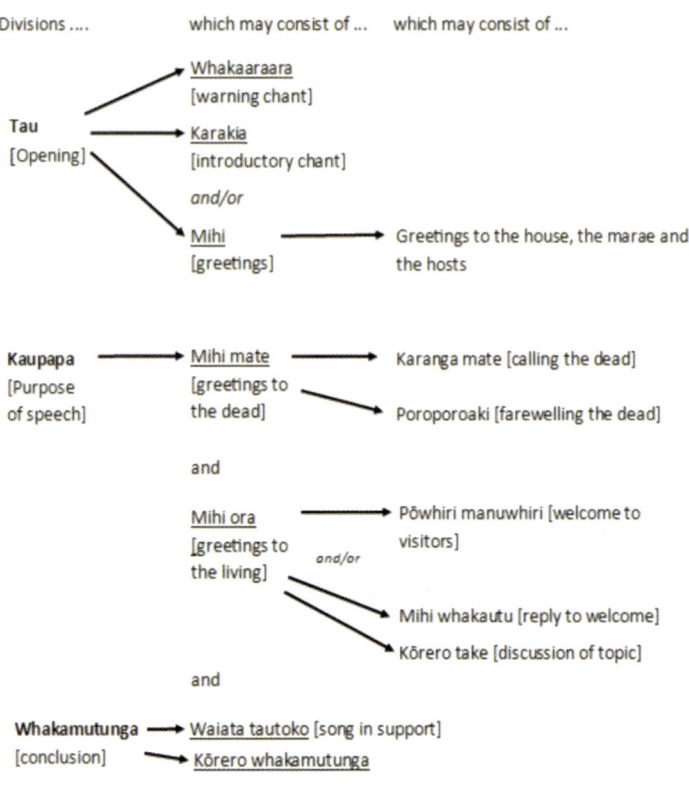

The structure of whaikōrero.

BASED ON MAHUTA, R. T. (1974). 'WHAIKOORERO: A STUDY OF FORMAL MĀORI SPEECH'. UNPUBLISHED MA THESIS, UNIVERSITY OF AUCKLAND

have become a colourful, evocative way to announce an intention to speak. Commonly heard today is the ancient phrase "Kia hiwa rā!" Te Rangi Hīroa (Sir Peter Buck), an anthropologist, military leader and doctor, recorded it as below:

Kia hiwa ra e tenei tuku
Kia hiwa ra e tera tuku
Kei apurua koe ki te toto.

[O hither terrace, be on the alert
O yonder terrace, be on the alert
Lest ye be smothered in blood.][321]

A whakaaraara in the context of oratory often ends with the phrase "Tīhei mauri ora!", which means "the sneeze of life" and serves to say, "here I am", "let there be life" or "I speak". The phrase refers to the origins of humans; Tāne breathed life into the first woman, who sneezed. A speaker uttering these words, said academic Poia Rewi, "is establishing this particular setting as tapu, embedding it with all the sanctity, formality, spirituality and revere of the Māori world".[322]

*Te Karere*, *Te Kāea* and *Manako* regularly use whakaaraara to open. Short and crisply delivered, they are clearly a call to attention. On *Manako*, Tumamao Harawira said:

> Kia hiwa rā, kia hiwa rā!
> Kia hiwa rā ki tēnei tuku, kia hiwa rā ki tērā tuku
> Kia tū, kia aho, kia mataara!
>
> [Be alert, be alert!
> Be alert on this terrace, be alert on that terrace.
> Stand up, be awake, be wary!]

He then added:

> Tīhei mauri ora.
>
> [Let there be life/I speak.]

Harawira said that it was natural for him to structure his radio openings as if he were about to deliver a real whaikōrero. In news, as on the marae, the whakaaraara was important to "grab the listener's ear".[323]

*Manako* and *Waatea News* are monolingual shows, but news programmes on TVNZ and Whakaata Māori are subtitled in English. The translations, however, aren't literal. Translations of Māori concepts into English can seem stilted due to the gulf between the worldviews that each language encodes, so news and current affairs show in te reo don't translate phrases that are esoteric or rooted in tikanga, such as whakaaraara. Producer Arana Taumata said, "In my opinion, what sounds fine, beautiful and natural in te reo Māori can be kind of cheesy and floury when translated into English. We try and protect our language by avoiding literal translations, but default to a generic translation."

In addition, subtitles designed to be read at a glance are not the place to explain complex concepts. Taumata explained, "The captioners' usual brief is to provide a summary, a synopsis of what's being expressed, not a word-for-word translation, as there is not enough time to do that."

Whakaata Māori news opened with whakaaraara six nights out of seven. The call "Kia hiwa!" was used twice, the phrase "Kia mataara" three times and "E tūtakarerewa mai" once. All call on hearers to be alert; all were translated as "welcome" or "greetings". Presenter Piripi Taylor said that presenters usually scripted their own greetings and links, and had some autonomy:

Piripi Taylor.
WHAKAATA MĀORI

Kei tēnā kai-whakapaoho, kei tēnā kai-whakataki tōna ake mana me āna ake whakaritenga. Ko tāku, he ū ki ngā tikanga Māori e mōhio nei au, ka nanaiore kia mahia, kia hāpaingia i roto i aku mahi pāpāho, i runga hoki i te arohanui ki taku Māoritanga, otirā ki te reo Māori.

[Each broadcaster and presenter has a certain amount of freedom to do things his/her way. For me, it's about adhering to the tikanga Māori that I know to actively encourage and support its use in my broadcasting duties, all of which stem from a deep affection for my Māori culture and the Māori language as well.]

*Te Karere* usually opens with the lines "Kia ora e te iwi. E haere ake nei i *Te Karere.*" This translates as "Greetings to all; coming up on *Te Karere*" and is subtitled "Coming up on Te Karere". The assumption is that monolingual viewers will know what "kia ora" means, as it is part of New Zealand English.[324]

## KARAKIA

Karakia can be interpreted as incantations, spells, charms, offertories, ritual words, rites, pleas, invocations and recitations. In daily life, they invoke spiritual guidance and protection from atua and/or ancestors and are an important element in safeguarding spiritual and bodily health. In ritual, they "are a means of participation, of becoming one, with the atua and the ancestors and with events of the past in the eternal present of ritual".[325]

A tauparapara is a formulaic type of karakia and can be used as well as, or instead of, the call to attention. Tauparapara are composed for a variety of outcomes, from chants to help move a canoe across land to chants that assist in learning genealogy; they also invoke the tapu of whaikōrero.

Eruera Lee-Morgan hosted *Manako* on two nights. The show is, he says, "formal; te reo ōkawa and the formalities of a marae still apply … Marae have traditionally been our means to communicate messages, formally, and it has a formal language … and rituals that go with it." He wove in as much ritual as he felt the format allowed, choosing words

Eruera Lee-Morgan.
SUPPLIED

that were appropriate for the night's interviews. One night, he chanted a portion of a well-known tauparapara:

> Ko te hōkai nuku, ko te hōkai rangi, ko te hōkai nā tō tupuna a Tāne-nui-a-rangi puta ai ko te ira tangata, ki te whaiao, ki te ao mārama. Tihei wā mauri ora.
>
> [I retrace the sacred footsteps that journeyed about the earth and journeyed about the heavens; the journey of Tāne-nui-ā-rangi, from which came human life and the world of light. There was life/I speak.]

This refers to the journey of Tāne to the heavens in search of knowledge and te ira tangata, the human aspect. Tāne reached his goal and, on his return, created the first woman. Below is the incantation as it is usually heard, with the portions Lee-Morgan used underlined:

Tēnei au, tēnei au, te hōkai nei o taku tapuwae
Ko te hōkai nuku, ko te hōkai rangi
Ko te hōkai a tō tupuna a Tāne-nui-a-rangi

This is the journey of sacred footsteps
Journeyed about the earth, journeyed about the heavens,
the journey of your ancestral god Tāne-nui-a-rangi

Ka pikitia ai ki te rangi tūhāhā ki Te Tihi-o-Manono

Who ascended into the heavens to Te Tihi-o- Manono
(a citadel in the twelfth heaven)

Ka rokohina atu rā ko te matua-kore anake
Ka tīkina mai ngā kete o te wānanga

Where he found the parentless source
From there he retrieved the baskets of knowledge

Ko te kete tuauri
Ko te kete tuatea
Ko te kete aronui
Ka tiritiria ka poupoua

The basket of peace, love and goodness
The basket of warfare, agriculture and building
The basket of literature, philosophy and ritual
These were distributed and implanted about the earth

Ka puta mai iho ko te ira tangata
Ki te whaiao, ki te ao mārama
Tihei mauri ora!

From which came human life
Growing from dim light to full light
There was life!

The whole incantation takes at least thirty seconds and the shortened version thirteen seconds. The full version is well known and, even when shortened, casts one's mind to the spiritual realm.

*Te Kāea* also made use of portions of tauparapara, but less frequently. Piripi Taylor opened one bulletin with "Ko *Te Kāea* tēnei e ōi atu nei", which translates as "This is *Te Kāea* calling to you". It's a modification of "oioi te pō, oioi te ao", which translates as "the world of the dead and the world of the living cry out". His words were translated as "Welcome to *Te Kāea.*"

The rituals of whaikōrero in a formal marae setting invoke the gods and ancestors and create tapu spaces. To invoke tapu necessitates its later neutralisation by the return of participants to a state of noa, or the everyday. So what happens when ancient, sacred speech such as karakia is taken out of the rituals of encounter and used in another setting, such as a radio or television broadcast? Is tapu invoked by the use of karakia, and does that mean whakanoa, or a neutralisation, is required? The place of sacred speech in Māori news media hasn't been overtly addressed by those working in the field. The answer lies in the multiplicity of ways Māori live in the twenty-first century and the adaptive flexibility of tikanga, and we'll look at this later in the chapter.

## MIHI: GREETINGS

Mihi often extol "the virtues of the opposite party".[326] Mihi are a core component of any formal exchange and, depending on context, may also be made to the primal parents Ranginui and Papatūānuku; the Christian God; the monarch of the Kīngitanga; the marae hosting the event; and its whare nui. Common phrases include "Nau mai, haere mai!" (Welcome, welcome!) and "Tēnā koutou, tēnā koutou, tēnā koutou katoa" (Once, twice, thrice, I acknowledge you all).

In news, opening mihi often frame viewers as honoured guests. The speaker might take a straightforward approach, as in this opening to *Waatea News*:

> Tēnā koutou katoa e ngā iwi o Aotearoa. Nau mai, whakatau mai ki ngā pitopito o te wā.
>
> [I greet you all, the tribes of Aotearoa. Welcome to the news.]

They may use a metaphor or simile that positively compares the audience to people of standing, from *Te Kāea* and *Te Karere* respectively:

> E rau rangatira mā huri noa, tēnā koutou katoa
> (subtitled as Good evening).
>
> [To you, the many chiefs throughout the country, greetings.]
>
> E ngā ihorei tītī e ngā ihorei tātā, tēnā koutou katoa
> (subtitled Tēnā koutou katoa and welcome to *Te Karere*).
>
> [Chiefs from near and far, I greet you.]

Mihi may flatter by comparing people to elements of the natural world, such as rivers, birds and trees. These are kupu whakarite; the English approximation is metaphor.[327] On *Manako*, Eruera Lee-Morgan used the flow of streams into larger bodies of water as a metaphor for people coming together to talk. He said:

> Tēnā rā koutou kei ngā tai e whā o te motu, ā, kua whakawhāiti mai ki te pūtahitanga o te kōrero, ki te kōmititanga mō ngā whakaaro ...
>
> [I acknowledge the four tides of the country that have gathered together at the confluence of discussion, at the convergence of ideas ...]

Listeners were also likened to a type of precious greenstone, the semi-transparent whatu tongarerewa. This was the opening of a *Waatea News* bulletin:

> Kei ngā whatu tongarerewa o te ao reo Māori, tēnā koutou katoa.
>
> [The greenstone treasures of the reo-speaking world, I greet you all.]

With just 10.6 percent of Māori able to speak te reo Māori for everyday purposes,[328] these listeners are indeed valuable.

*Te Karere* greeted viewers with "E aku huia kaimanawa, tēnā koutou katoa", or "My huia birds that consume my heart, I acknowledge you", subtitled as "Tēnā koutou katoa and welcome to *Te Karere*". The huia, now extinct, had tail feathers that were prized as headwear denoting high rank. Here, viewers were again ennobled.

Such language, says producer Arana Taumata, adds daily variety to the show. "If we used a standard 'kia ora' at the beginning of each show, it would very quickly become a bland greeting". The many and varied metaphors to call on "shows the richness of te reo Māori and is a neat and dynamic way of engaging with the viewer".

Mountains featured in four of the seven mihi to *Te Kāea* viewers. Mountains feature heavily in Māori imagery, their physical presence inspiring a range of emotions. Most tribes have a maunga tapu, or sacred mountain, that forms a pillar of individual and collective identity alongside a local body of water and that tribe's ancestral canoe. In formal settings, people introduce themselves by these landmarks, starting with one's mountain.

Presenter Piripi Taylor often invokes mountains as, he says, they have mana. The translations below can't do the sentiments justice, but the attitude they convey is one of respect for the tribes of the land, here metaphorically identified as mountains:

Kei ngā maunga whakamana, tēnā koutou katoa

(Subtitle: Good evening).
[Prestigious mountains, I greet you.]

E ngā maunga whakahī huri noa, rarau mai rā.

(Subtitle: Good evening).
[Proud mountains of this land, welcome.]

Kei ngā maunga kōrero huri noa, tēnā rā koutou katoa

(Subtitle: Welcome).
[Speaking mountains of the land, I greet you.]

### MIHI MATE, MIHI ORA: FAREWELLS TO THE DEAD, GREETINGS TO THE LIVING

During formal events, speakers summon the dead and farewell them. Formulaic phrases to address the dead include:

Haere, haere, haere.

[Go.]

Haere ki Hawaiki nui, ki Hawaiki roa, ki Hawaiki pāmaomao,
ki te Hono-i-Wairua.

[Go to the ancient homeland of Hawaiki.]

Hawaiki is the homeland from which the ancestors migrated, believed to be in East Polynesia.

To summon the dead requires an explicit return to life with a mihi ora, or acknowledgement of the living, in order to separate the two domains. In whaikōrero, the below is a common pairing:

Ka āpiti hono, tātai hono, te hunga mate ki te hunga mate.

[The lines are joined, allow the dead to rest with the dead.]

Ka āpiti hono, tātai hono, te hunga ora ki te hunga ora.

[The lines are joined, allow the living to remain with the living.]

The phrase "āpiti hono, tātai hono", or "the lines are joined" comes from a weaving chant. Here, it is used to mean that "All of the rites of the ancestors are brought out because of the final stitch by death. Just as the weaving and stitching of thread bring together a cloth in which each thread and stitch is part of the whole, so the living and the dead are together part of a whole that is the tribe."[329]

The tikanga of acknowledging the dead and returning the focus to the living is reflected in Māori news in several ways, generally with a truncated version of the formulae heard in whaikōrero. In opening *Manako*, host Eruera Lee-Morgan acknowledged the grief of the living, then described the journey of the dead to the spirit world before offering a farewell:

Tēnā hoki koutou e tangi mai nā i ō tātou tini aituā kua whai rā i te
tira haere o Maruiwi kua heke ki Te Reinga ki te nia i te matoru o te
pō. Haere, takoto, okioki.

[I acknowledge all of you mourning our deceased who have
followed Maruiwi [an ancient tribe] to Cape Reinga [the Northland
cape where spirits leap to the underworld] to pierce the darkness
of the night. Farewell, lay in peace, rest in solitude.]

He then separated the dead and the living, using three kupu whakarite in a row – all symbols of vigorous life – to return listeners' thoughts to the living world:

Tēnā koutou kei ngā kākā waha nui, kei ngā tōtara haemata,
kei ngā manu honenga o te pae ...

[I acknowledge you, the animated voices of the kākā birds, the
vigorous tōtara trees, the melodious songbirds of the altar ...]

A tōtara is a sturdy hardwood tree often referred to as a rākau rangatira, or chiefly tree, and appears frequently in oratory; we'll discuss its use as metaphor shortly.

On another occasion, Eruera invoked the dead and the living through the atua of each realm: Hine-nui-te-pō, the goddess of death, and Tāne.

Whakatau hā ō tātou tini aituā ki a Hine-nui-te-pō, whakatau hā
tātou ko te hunga ora ki a Tāne-te-waiora.

[Welcome our numerous deceased dwelling in the realm of
the goddess of death, Hine-nui-te-pō. Welcome us, the living,
in the realm of Tāne-te-waiora.]

This same week, there was a notable death, that of former All Black rugby star and farmer Sir Colin Meads. Known as Pinetree for his stature, Meads, who was Pākehā, died of cancer aged eighty-one. He was revered by Māori and Pākehā alike for his rugby prowess and charitable work and had two funerals: the first at a marae in his hometown of Te Kuiti, and the second at a local events centre.

*Te Kāea, Te Karere, Waatea News* and *Manako* all covered Meads' death. The reporters involved said while there were no rules or

Rapaera Tawhai.
JAE FREW

prohibitions about the language they used in reporting death, they felt that it was important to adhere to cultural norms around separating the living and the dead. *Manako* presenter Tumamao Harawira believed this was particularly important for his listeners, many of whom were older, adhered strongly to tikanga and expected demarcation.

We turn first to *Te Karere*. After the story about Meads ended, presenter Rapaera Tawhai maintained separation by spontaneously saying:

> Nā, hoki mai ki te hunga ora. Ki ngā take tōrangapū …
>
> [Now, we return to the living. To politics …]

He inserted the line "just used to make sure there was a transition between a story about the dead and then a story about the living … it wasn't scripted – it just felt right to say it."

A later *Te Karere* bulletin ran a story about Meads' tangi at the marae. After the report ended, presenter Irena Smith addressed Meads directly with:

> Moe mai rā, e te tōtara haemata.
>
> [Sleep well, strong-growing tōtara.]

Her words were not subtitled. About the mihi, Smith said, "That wasn't scripted or written on the autocue to say, but I said it off-the-cuff as a sign of respect and mihi to someone who was widely respected … it's personally from me, as the presenter; it's my personal acknowledgement to Sir Colin Meads." She chose the tōtara tree metaphor "because it suited the man – he was a big man who did big things." Smith is conscious of audience expectations; the mihi served "to finalise a story about a death before moving onto a story about the living".

*Te Karere* presenter Scotty Morrison is also the show's language and tikanga advisor and said that presenters have discretion on the linguistic devices they employ. One's individual sense of what is appropriate at a particular time and place informs decision-making, he says: "You'll have presenters who will adhere more to tikanga than others, be more conscious of tikanga than others."

*Waatea News* didn't use any formal mihi mate in its news bulletins; it has the greatest time pressure of the shows discussed here. However, like *Te Kāea*, *Waatea News* used various metaphors in talking about Meads. Given his stature and nickname, it was no surprise that journalists reached for a tōtara tree metaphor. Here are two examples from *Waatea News*:

> He tōtara nui kua hinga i te wao nui a Tāne, ā, ko te ihorei i te ao whutupōro, a Colin Meads.
>
> [A great tōtara has fallen in Tāne's great forest – Colin Meads, a star in the rugby world; or, less literally, A figurehead has died – rugby star Colin Meads.]

Irena Smith reports on the death of All Black star Colin Meads.

TVNZ

In this next example, the phrase has been adapted, but its origin is clear:

> Tēnā koutou e ngā iwi o te motu. Ko Eru Morgan tēnei me ngā rangona kōrero a Waatea. E mahuta ake nei, kua hinga tētehi o ngā tōtara haemata o te ao whutupāoro.
>
> [Greetings, tribes of the country. This is Eru Morgan with the *Waatea News* bulletin. Coming up, one of the tōtara of the world of rugby has passed away; or, less literally, ... one of the stars of the football world has died.]

In a *Waatea News* story later that week, presenter Tumamao Harawira used two metaphors to discuss Meads. He compared him to a kōtuku, or white heron, whose scarcity gave rise to the phrase "He kōtuku rerenga tahi" or "A white heron of a single flight" – meaning a person who is one of a kind, or a talent rarely seen. Harawira also invoked the prized kōtuku feathers, or piki kōtuku:

> He kōtuku rerenga tahi a Tā Colin Meads i ōna rā. Koirā tā Wairangi Kopu whai muri mai i te hinganga o tēnei ō ngā tino piki kōtuku i roto o Aotearoa.
>
> [Sir Colin Meads was one of a kind in his time. That's according to Wairangi Kopu, following the death of one of New Zealand's greatest treasures.]

Tumamao Harawira.
WHAKAATA MĀORI

As death often prompts orators to be highly eloquent, so Harawira used expressive language to report notable deaths: "Poetical … as opposed to just the normal, everyday language that you use in news bulletins".

### INTERVIEWEES ADDRESSING THE DEAD

It's not unusual for *Manako* interviewees to deliver a farewell directly to the deceased. On the day Colin Meads died, host Tumamao Harawira and Henare Kingi, a radio broadcaster now in his eighties, discussed the sportsman's life. At the end of their conversation, Harawira prompted Kingi to share his memories of Meads with these words:

> Hei whakakapi ake i tā tāua kōrero, e te matua, kia kōrero poto tāua mō te hinganga o Colin Meads i te rā tonu nei. Kia mōteatea tonu te ngākau.

> [To round off our chat, uncle, let's talk briefly about the death of Colin Meads today. Our hearts are grieving.]

Kingi shared his memories of Meads for a few minutes, then segued into a poroporoaki or farewell address:

> E kara, e Colin, haere rā. Ko koe tēnei kua mahue mai te ao hou nei i a koe. Ka hoki atu koe ki tōu nei kaihanga. Nā reira, haere, e kara, haere, haere, haere.
>
> [Dear friend, Colin, farewell. You have left this world. You are returning to your creator. So, my friend, farewell, farewell, farewell.]

## KŌRERO TAKE: THE MAIN TOPIC AND THE PLACE OF PROVERBS

The kōrero take is the section where the 'news' is dispensed and opinions aired. Speakers can approach their topic in many stylistic ways, perhaps calling on proverbs, songs or haka. English-language journalists are taught to equate proverbs with worn-out, hackneyed phrases that people "dismiss … rather cavalierly as clichés of not great depth or literary merit".[330] However, Māori speakers don't share this view about whakataukī (sayings whose provenance isn't known) and whakatauākī (sayings by an identified individual); stories and ancestral sayings carry weight.

Whakataukī are "short, highly informative, expressive and memorable"[331] and in an oral society, are a vital way to memorise and pass on knowledge. Apparent simplicity hides great depth:

> While they often appear to be simply recording observations about nature, they are in fact talking about human beings and their interactions. They operate through analogy … for this purpose, they call on a rich repertoire of metaphors which evoke vivid mental images and lend themselves to visual expression. A large number of these metaphors are drawn from the world of nature, but they also include the things humans make (ropes, cloaks, houses, canoes).[332]

Whakataukī also link past and present, particularly timeless quotes about human nature and endeavour. In addition, as Joan Metge and Shane Jones note, whakataukī "sound *good*. They are characterised by musical cadences, pronounced rhythms, and the contrast of flowing with staccato phrases. They make much use of repetition, opposition and balance. They exploit the possibilities of onomatopoeia."[333]

Figures of speech are useful shortcuts for journalists. To Eruera Lee-Morgan, they are "scene-setters … one little metaphor can tell the whole story, especially if you know the context". For example, he wrote a story about a general election special that Whakaata Māori was preparing. Wanting to express the Māori equivalent of "many hands make light work," he alluded to this well-known saying:

> Mā whero, mā pango, ka oti ai te mahi.
>
> [By red and black the work is finished.][334]

Red refers to kōkōwai, a mixture of shark oil and red ochre that was smeared on the body of a chief. Rank-and-file manual workers looked black by comparison.[335] Lee-Morgan recontextualised the proverb to say that the broadcast's success would depend on many people from all levels of the organisation working as one. The phrase "by red and black the work is finished" became "by red and black, the live broadcast will succeed".

> E takatū ana a Whakaata Māori ki te whakahaere hōtaka motuhake e pā ana ki te Kōwhiringa Pōti ā-Motu. Hei tā Oriini Kaipara, kaiwhakataki o te hōtaka, mā whero, mā pango e tutuki ai te whakapaohotanga arorangi nei.
>
> [Māori Television is preparing itself to produce a special broadcast for the night of the General Election. According to presenter Oriini Kaipara, with everyone pitching in, the live broadcast will go well.]

In journalism as in whaikōrero, orators exploit the fact that whakataukī are not fixed: "The art of using whakataukī involves applying them in new contexts."[336] On *Waatea News*, Tumamao Harawira opened a story about the opening of Whakaata Māori's new headquarters by refreshing a whakataukī first recorded in writing in 1857:

> Ka mate kāinga tahi, ka ora kāinga rua.
>
> [One dwelling is overrun, but the second is secure.][337]

The various interpretations all boil down to having two ways to achieve something. In earlier times, one interpretation was the need to have two plantations in case one failed, and another the necessity for a second dwelling-place that could serve as refuge. The English equivalent is "having two strings to your bow".

In this case, the lease on Māori Television's expensive inner-Auckland building was expiring, and the company's leaders wanted to move to a more cost-effective home. This was the full opening of the news story:

> Ka mate kāinga tahi, ka ora kāinga rua. He rangi nui āpōpō ka tū mō ngā kaihāpai o te kaupapa o Whakaata Māori. Āpōpō whakatuwheratia ai te whare hou o Whakaata Māori ki Tāmaki ki te Tonga.
>
> [Their first home has outlived its usefulness, but another home is ready. It's a big day tomorrow for the staff of Māori Television – their new home in south Auckland will be opened.]

In journalistic terms, the whakataukī was used as a drop or delayed intro – the key point was not plainly stated in the first sentence, coming in the second. While Harawira acknowledged that using a saying as a drop intro didn't get listeners straight to the point, the revitalisation funding model underpinning Māori language news influenced how he spoke. "The news bulletin is about the language just as much, if not more, than the actual story. So it's about having that real eloquent style about writing the language … the things that our eloquent speakers use."

A *Waatea News* story about an election candidate opened with a saying that advised preparing soil well in order for subsequent plantings to flourish. The story, by Eruera Lee-Morgan, said:

> Mā te ngakingaki ā mua, ka tōtō ā muri. Koinei te whakahau a Nanaia Mahuta, mema Māori mō te tūru o Hauraki-Waikato. Hei tā Nanaia mā te whakatakoto tika i te tūāpapa o te Rōpū Reipa, e pai ai ngā mahi ā muri nei.

> [Cultivate the ground first, and your plantings will flourish later. That's the assertion of Nanaia Mahuta, Māori MP for the Hauraki-Waikato seat. According to Nanaia, if Labour lays a good foundation, it will win the election.]

Having delivered the proverb as a drop intro, he clarified its meaning by adding, "if Labour lays a good foundation, it will win the election". He added: "You can never assume what your audience knows and what they don't know. So I qualify, or validate it, with that other brief little explanation as well."

## WHAKAMUTUNGA: CONCLUSION

Whaikōrero are followed by a waiata tautoko, a traditional song delivered by the speaker and their group to show solidarity and to lift tapu from the speaker. Orators choose one appropriate to the occasion, as songs contain and transmit ideologies, philosophies and viewpoints. Their waiata over, a speaker will usually utter a few sentences to end, perhaps as brief as "Tēnā koutou, ka huri", which translates as "I acknowledge you all, I turn/sit". Although the waiata has not transferred into news, Māori current affairs shows have various ways of bidding farewell.

Most of them use, as a minimum, "Tēnā koutou katoa". For example, *Waatea News* usually ends with the presenter identifying himself or herself if that hasn't already occurred, then delivering a short mihi. The latter is most often "Kia ora" or "Tēnā koutou katoa", which can be translated as "Thank you" or "I acknowledge you".

*Manako* presenter Eruera Lee-Morgan doesn't script his farewells, letting the mood of the show lead him. One night, he employed an extended metaphor, describing the night's interviews as the contents of a woven flax basket that was being returned to its peg in the whare nui:

> Heoi anō rā, kua pau te wāhi ki ahau, koinei ahau ka whakairi ake te kete kōrero o Manako ki te pātū, ki te pakitara o tō tātou whare kōrero. Mai i te pou irirangi o Waatea, tēnā koutou, tēnā koutou, tēnā tātou katoa.
>
> [Well, I'm out of time, so I'm about to suspend on the wall of our house the basket of conversations until next time. From Radio Waatea, many thanks to you all.]

Lee-Morgan's own spirituality is rooted in Māori cosmology and in the past he would draw on the imagery of that world to close *Manako*. However, after a listener complaint that he wasn't recognising "the whole wairua tapu", or range of sacred and spiritual beliefs, he started including an acknowledgement of Christianity as well. Covering the spectrum, he added, required "a strategic choice of words". This was one of his farewells in the sample week:

> Heoi anō kua pau te wāhi ki a tātou o Manako mō tēnei pō, heoi anō rā kia tau ngā manaakitanga o te runga rawa, te wāhi ngaro ki runga i a koutou katoa. Noho ora mai.
>
> [Well, that's it – my time's up for another evening. May the care of God and those who have gone beyond be bestowed upon you all. Stay well.]

In Māori thought, te wāhi ngaro means, depending on context, the hidden realm, the world of gods and spirits, divine intervention and the heavens. In the survey week, *Te Kāea* invoked te wāhi ngaro six days out of seven:

> Ngā manaakitanga o te wāhi ngaro ki te tī, ki te tā, tēnā rā koutou katoa. (Subtitled as Thanks for joining us, good evening.)
>
> [May one and all enjoy the care of those in the hidden realm.]

The Christian God, or te runga rawa, was invoked once:

> Ngā manaakitanga o te runga rawa ki te tī, ki te tā, tēnā rā koutou katoa. (Subtitled as Thanks for joining us, good evening.)
>
> [The care of God over everyone. I acknowledge you all.]

*Te Karere* used a variety of sign-offs in the survey week. One was a simple "Kia ora tātou katoa", subtitled as such. Another was "Kia tau te manaakitanga o te wāhi ngaro ki a koutou katoa", which was not subtitled; it means "May the care of the hidden realm rest upon you all."

One night, listeners heard a more unusual farewell – a whakataukī that has become a signature *Te Karere* sign-off and has spread beyond the show. The proverb demonstrates the power of reo Māori journalism to influence language use. The sign-off had two parts, neither of which were subtitled. The first part was straightforward:

> Kia haumaru te noho ki tō koutou kāinga maha.
>
> [May you all be safe in your many home areas.]

However, the second half was distinctly Māori:

> Turou parea, turou Hawaiki.
>
> [Let the ancient homeland of Hawaiki glisten in your mind's eye for eternity.]

Most Māori and East Polynesian traditions refer to migration from Hawaiki. The mythical homeland features frequently in songs, proverbs and genealogies. The meaning of the phrase, said *Te Karere* presenter

Scotty Morrison, was "never forget your origins, where you come from and use that as power for you as you stride into your future". It was, he said, a phrase commonly used by tohunga on the migratory waka as they left for Aotearoa New Zealand. He has popularised it by translating it as "May the Force be with you" – the phrase that defines the *Star Wars* movie franchise.

## TAKING KARAKIA TO NEWS SETTINGS

The rituals of whaikōrero in a formal marae setting invoke the gods and ancestors and create tapu spaces. We need to explore, then, what happens when ancient, sacred speech such as karakia are taken out of the rituals of encounter and used in another setting, such as a radio or television broadcast.

In formal ceremonies, once tapu is called forth by karanga and karakia, we exist in that state of tapu until it is neutralised by the hongi, exchange of breath and shared food, which serve to "decommission participants".[338] In these settings, karakia are a powerful way to call the tapu and the mana of our atua and our tūpuna to us; the formulaic nature of karakia ensures that we are speaking as they spoke: "This is a oneness with the living, but also with all those who have gone before them, and a oneness which extends right back into te kore, the 'nothingness' of the beginning of creation."[339] Academic Meihana Durie wrote that such ritual allowed one to "enter safely into atua-specific domains and activities with an enhanced sense of sensory awareness and preparedness".[340]

Pre-contact, everyone adhered to rituals, processes and protocols, as survival meant maintaining good faith with the atua of the various domains that sustained life. According to academic Te Ahukaramū Charles Royal, "Māori lived in and around a very tapu culture … in the past there was a very strong belief that if you infringe a tikanga or a kawa [fixed ritual] that you would face a very strong retribution of some kind".[341]

The most important rituals of life, such as death, exhumation and the lifting of tapu, were overseen by men trained in the priestly arts and their chants were seen to have great power. However, every person had a stock of karakia for everyday life, for example, to help heal wounds or broken limbs; appease Tangaroa, god of the sea, for the first fish caught; and ensure success in hunting and gardening.

We now live in a world where society – and survival – is no longer predicated on tapu and noa and the mechanisms of social and individual control they fostered. Royal says, "I don't think people are beholden to the tapu system any more … attitudes and ideas about cause and effect have changed." People were no longer "psychologically bound up with certain assumptions, and a common set of understandings … just isn't there. Our people have widely diverse views of the world and experiences of the world."[342] As broadcaster Tumamao Harawira observed, "We don't have a real-world experience of what it means to live in a world that is tapu and noa."

Time passes and customs change. As academic Hirini Moko Mead wrote:

> Mātauranga Māori continues to evolve both in the way it is understood and in the range of ways it is applied in today's world. Within the basket of knowledge itself, some ideas are held to be crucial and critical, while other ideas are subject to amendment or better left alone, and there is a wide range of new ideas to select from and to embrace.[343]

Among these new ideas is the use of karakia in domains beyond the sacred; these are reflections of tikanga as "spontaneous and organic" growing from our "earthly reality".[344] Karakia, with their focus on creation, the gods and the forces that brought Māori to Aotearoa New Zealand, are not just calls to higher powers, but stories of who we are and how we think, making them powerful statements of identity.

For example, contemporary Māori musicians combine the power of music and the eloquence of old karakia in their work or compose new ones. Many tribal reports, while written largely in English, open with a karakia, as do books and academic theses written by Māori. Recordings of karakia are on the internet so people can learn them.

As academic Amster Reedy said, the issue is authenticity: "The point about karakia and kawa is not how far back you can go but how far forward you can take it. We should not put ourselves in the position of living in the past, but should see that our culture is very relevant to the world that our children and grandchildren will live in."[345]

Karakia in music, film and literature are part of the "evolving and dynamic nature of tikanga".[346] People may no longer live strictly by tapu and noa, but to hear the distinctive cadence and words of a karakia in a news setting or in music ensures the link to the past is not forgotten; karakia have the power to focus our minds on the primacy of whakapapa, the spiritual realm and the mana of te reo Māori.

However, the way in which tikanga is reworked brings caveats. In adapting Māori practices for new contexts, wrote Meihana Durie, a "theoretical and philosophical base that is derived from mātauranga Māori" must be maintained, and this required "a type of leadership that can mediate between yesterday and tomorrow".[347] Those leaders needed to be thoroughly versed in reo and tikanga, but aware that tikanga had to adapt to survive.

The public nature of the journalist's work means that there is great incentive for the best possible exponents of te reo and tikanga to be chosen for on-air work. To use something inauthentically risks an immediate and embarrassing correction by your own community. However, journalists took different approaches with karakia according to their backgrounds and understandings. *Te Karere* presenter Scotty Morrison performs ancient karakia for a wide variety of purposes, just as the ancestors did, to help heal illness or remove psychological harm wrought by others. This work brings responsibilities, he said, among them delivering word-perfect chants, having the right manawataki (cadence) to gain the gods' attention, the ability to be the kauwaka (vessel) for atua, dealing with heightened levels of tapu and also handling the dynamics of the situation for which karakia are needed. In his media work, Scotty does not use ancient incantations "to protect the integrity and sanctity of those karakia".

Scotty Morrison.
JAE FREW

In contrast, *Manako* host Tumamao Harawira recites ancient karakia on radio, but only when he has time to recite them in full; this is to maintain "the integrity of the karakia". Below is one he often used to open *Manako*:

> Whakatau hā, whakatau hā
> Whakatau hā te rangi e tū iho nei
> Whakatau hā te papa e takoto nei
> Whakatau hā te mātuku mai i Rarotonga
> Ko ia i rukuhia manawa pou roto
> Ko ia i rukuhia manawa pou waho
> Whakatina kia tina, te more i Hawaiki
> Haumi ē, hui ē, taiki ē

This chant and its variants are believed to date from the era of migration; its age and obscure language makes an accurate translation difficult.[348] However, the chant's wairua, or its essence, evokes the Māori migration from Hawaiki. It contains several metaphors relating to firmness and stability, such as the sky above and the earth below, and the strength of the more, the tap root, and Hawaiki as a source of ritual power, strength and identity. Harawira saw the chant as a good way "to set the stage" for his show; it was also short, taking up twenty seconds of a one-minute intro.

Fellow *Manako* host Eruera Lee-Morgan said it was important for broadcasters to be creative in their use of language, and he did not believe that imaginative reworking diminished "the stuff of our ancient past". In one opening, he used a core element of the chant above – the phrase "whakatau hā" – to unify the elements that needed to be present: acknowledgement of the primal parents; acknowledgements to the dead; greetings to the living; and an invitation to listeners to enter the figurative marae of *Manako*. He interpreted "whakatau hā" in this context as "welcome".

This was the mihi to Ranginui and Papatūānuku:

> Whakatau hā, whakatau hā, whakatau hā te rangi e tū iho nei, whakatau hā te papa e takoto nei.
>
> [Welcome, welcome, welcome the sky father, welcome the earth mother.]

The next part paid homage to the dead, describing them in terms of Hinenuitepō, the guardian of the dead:

> Whakatau hā ō tātou tini aituā ki a Hine-nui-te-pō.
>
> [Welcome our numerous deceased dwelling in the realm of Hine-nui-te-pō.]

Lee-Morgan then turned to the living, using the metaphor of Tāne, who created the world of light after pushing his parents apart:

> Whakatau hā tātou ko te hunga ora ki a Tāne-te-waiora.
>
> [Welcome us, the living, in the realm of Tāne-te-waiora.]

Listeners were greeted:

> Whakatau hā koutou e ngā iwi o te motu ki te marae areare o *Manako* e whakatau nei i a koutou.
>
> [Welcome the tribes of the country to the marae of *Manako* hereby greeting you.]

This appealing reworking weaves links between the past and present, and between all those linked at that moment by their shared listenership. It's also pithy: The words above took eighteen seconds to deliver in an introduction of just over a minute. Lee-Morgan summed up his approach with the phrase, "He iti te kupu kia nui te kōrero", or "a short address expresses a great deal". Brevity and clarity, he said, are at the heart of the "art of oratory ... no matter what the platform is, on marae or on the airwaves".

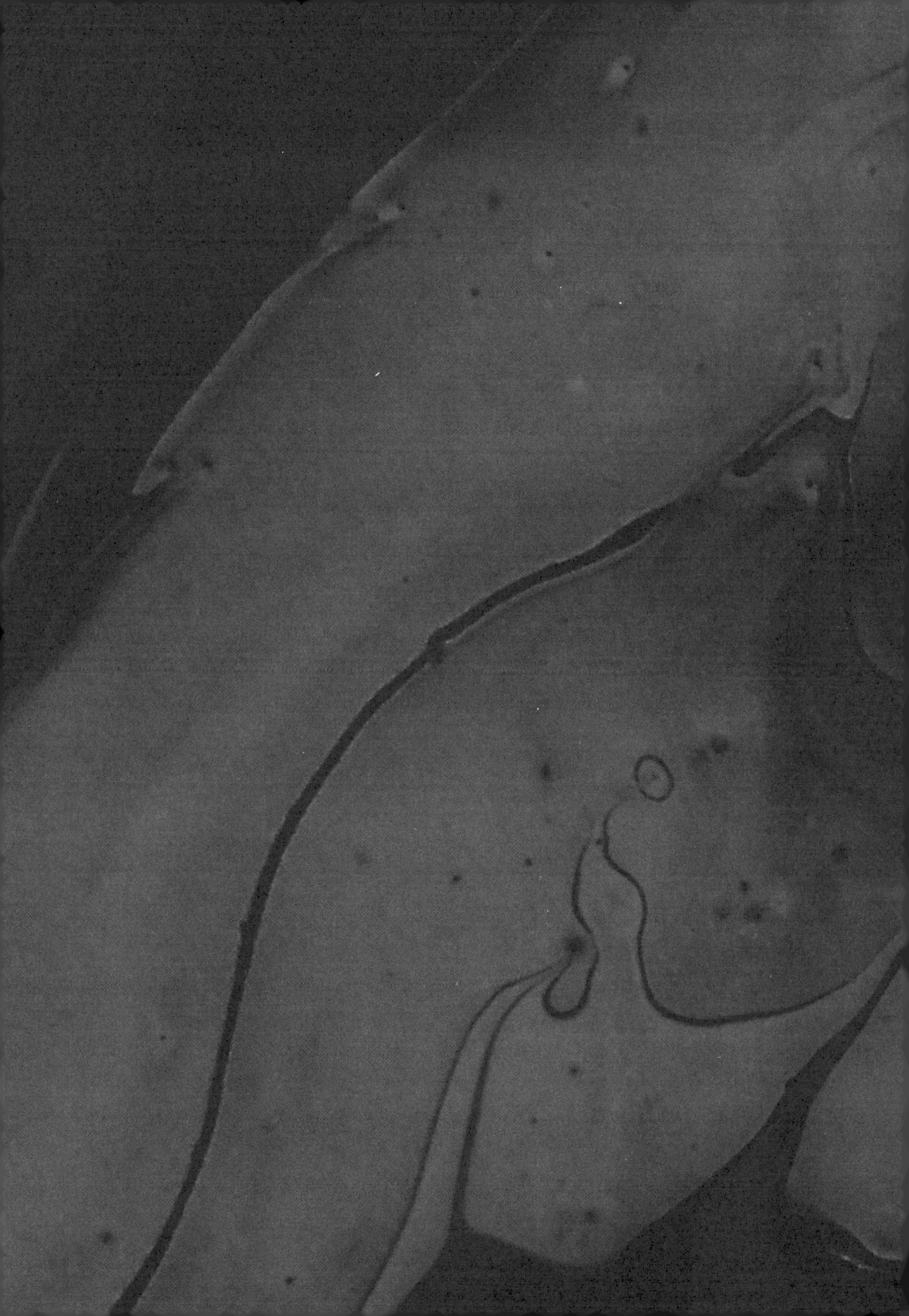

# KO TE WERO

## TIKANGA, RELATIONSHIPS AND THE MĀORI REPORTER

Journalists describe tikanga as a set of values, a way of seeing themselves and the world, and a guide to decision-making based on the teachings of their iwi.[349] To Gloria Taumaunu, tikanga is "a code of good practice". To Annabelle Lee-Mather, tikanga is "the way you connect to other people, to your environment. It encapsulates your philosophies, it guides your behaviour". For Arana Taumata, tikanga encapsulates "a unique set of values that I live by". For Raiha Paki, a life shaped by tikanga means that:

> We speak Māori at home, my child speaks only Māori. We do karakia and we sing a lot of waiata; it's just the language that we operate in. We do the basic tikanga stuff ... when we have manuhiri we look after them, we operate by aroha and manaakitanga ... and the same when I am at mahi. Tikanga is something you can't turn off.

For those who had grown up in tikanga and te reo – the majority of this book's participants – cultural lenses strongly shaped the way they engaged with the world and its spiritual dimension. Those who had learned about te reo and tikanga later in life, a minority, had incorporated various practices and perspectives into their lives to varying degrees.

However, what united every single reporter was their attention to cues about expected behaviour. Following tikanga on marae or in private homes was not just about showing respect and aligning with their own values; it was also about ensuring that others were not made to feel uncomfortable. Discussing this, several reporters quoted the proverb "When in Rome, do as the Romans do". Radio reporter Ana Tapiata quoted part of a well-known whakataukī: "He aha te mea nui o te ao? He tangata, he tangata, he tangata" (What is the most important thing in the world? It is people, people, people). As a reporter, she said, "everything comes down to that relationship, even if it's a short relationship. It's about trying to create an environment that's comfortable for the person that you're interviewing".

Cultural practices that differed from those with which reporters were familiar were not remarked upon in the interests of manaaki. Annabelle Lee-Mather gave an example:

> No offence to Te Arawa, but I go into their marae, and I see all the old kuia [women] sitting on the ground while the young men sit on chairs and I think, 'What the …?' But I'll never question it. It's not my marae; it's not my place to challenge what they do on their marae. So you just go with the flow. But that doesn't mean that I don't think in my head, 'None of my tāua [elders] would sit on the ground for any of my young male cousins.' They'd tell them to nick off.

Reporters unsure of what they could do somewhere usually sought advice and, on marae, they usually approached an elder. However, they might not get the same advice from two different people and, at times, inadvertently caused offence. All reporters could do was apologise, said RNZ reporter Shannon Haunui-Thompson:

> So one group of people who are at the marae, say 'Yes, please come, please interview,' but then you get the odd kuia or kaumātua saying 'Hey, what are you doing there? Get off, get back in the carpark!' kind of thing. You've just got to say, 'Look, sorry, we were told we were allowed here, we were told we were allowed to record here, but if you don't want me here, that's fine' – I'll just move on. It's not worth getting into an argument over those kinds of things. There's always another way.

### TIKA, PONO AND AROHA: A FUNDAMENTAL APPROACH

Tika, pono and aroha are a fundamental approach to life and professional activities in te ao Māori. We can translate the tripartite as "doing the right thing with integrity and with love";[350] Catholic leader Pā Henare Tate described tika, pono and aroha as "principles of action and encounter".[351] The concepts are so pervasive in Māori thought that they were the motto of a nineteenth-century newspaper, appear in various twentieth-century songs and even offer a lens for academic research into Māori literature.[352] They also shape the value statements of organisations. One is Whakaata Māori; its value statement translates tika, pono and aroha in a way that emphasises how they should be expressed in a Māori business context, not just a journalistic one:

- **Kia tika:** Kia ngaio, kia mau ki ngā taumata tiketike. Be professional and maintain high standards.

- **Kia pono:** Kia pono, kia tika, kia ngākau tapatahi. Be truthful, honest and act with integrity.

- **Kia aroha:** Kia mataara, kia whakaaro nui ki tētahi atu. Be respectful and demonstrate empathy.

Māori Television adds a fourth value:

- **Kia Māori:** Kia mau kia ū ki te hōhonutanga o ngā tikanga Māori. Maintain and uphold core Māori values.

For reporter Kereama Wright, tika, pono and aroha were the cornerstones of his childhood and the values he aims to transmit to his own children. To him, tika, pono and aroha encompass.

> He mihi ki te tangata, he kawe i ngā mahi katoa i runga i te tika, i te pono [acknowledging people, doing things with fairness and maintaining integrity], acknowledging each person's mana, try not to trample on each person's mana in amongst all the ... daily activities of a normal home.

> And then, in the workplace, it's obviously trying to transfer all those into everything that we do ... out in the field, with different talent, it's not always easy ... because different situations or circumstances provide different challenges.

Asked his guiding principles in journalism, Julian Wilcox, a former head of news at Whakaata Māori, said that his interviewees should expect that he would act "in accordance with tika, pono and aroha". He gave several examples, among them explaining in full to people why he wanted to talk to them, keeping the camera off until subjects were ready and ensuring they were comfortable with proceedings:

> I think there's the expectation that even though you may have done all the groundwork on the telephone, when you get into their house, get onto their marae, when you sit down in front of them, they need to know and feel and touch and growl or whatever with you first, so you go through it all again. They say, 'Yep, OK, ready to go.' Bang, you do the interview, you finish, then you put it [the camera] away and ask, 'How do you feel about that?'
>
> And you never, ever, go empty-handed. Always take something, even if it's a packet of biscuits. Many an interview has eventuated

Julian Wilcox.
WHAKAATA MĀORI

because of the relish I provided to the obligatory cup of tea from the host.

Tika, pono and aroha acquire different nuances in the context of newswork. **Tika** can translate as being correct and, in a Māori paradigm, that means things are done according to accepted standards of output or behaviour. Academic Hirini Moko Mead defined the word as "appropriate behaviour; good grace"[353] and the Williams dictionary defined it as "just, fair, right and correct"[354]. Pā Henare Tate wrote that as a principle of action, "tika includes the elements of <u>what</u> should be done, <u>how</u> it should be done, and <u>why</u> it should be done."[355]

The reporters in this research said that in a work context, tika also meant being accurate. "Tika to me is getting it right, getting your facts right," said executive producer Arana Taumata. "That's a fundamental of journalism." To Maramena Roderick, a story that was tika displayed "accuracy, fairness and balance". In the context of Māori journalism, she added, tika also meant having the courage to ask the questions that needed to be asked, even if doing so made both parties uncomfortable: "Ask the questions. Search for knowledge and don't be afraid to." She said:

> I remember a story where I asked a kaumātua whether his iwi deserved to have their land returned. Another Māori journalist commented: 'I'm glad you asked that because I've been brought up differently, not to question my kaumātua.' If I hadn't asked, someone else would have, and it could have been spun very differently. But the answer was so honest and dignified it effectively closed down any negative follow-up.

Likewise, Arana Taumata saw tika in journalism as working without fear or favour and adhering to journalistic principles. He understood why some Māori were suspicious of the media and felt that Māori journalists should focus on the positive. However, he said, Māori culture had always valued transparent and robust public discussion: "Our people used to debate issues hard on the marae," he said. "Back in the day, if leadership was found to be

Maramena Roderick.
SUPPLIED

wanting, people would ask questions. They would demand answers from their rangatira."

For Maramena Roderick, the word tika also encapsulated good judgment. "I expect that when crews are on the marae, proper protocols are met, that they have spoken to the right people, that they have permission to film on that marae." She was also clear what was not tika: "When we go to tangihanga, when we're at these sad events, I don't want to see any of my reporters taking selfies. You see that a lot now. I find that self-promotion appalling."

**Pono** translates as true, valid, honest and genuine. Manuel Beazley, Catholic vicar for Māori in Tāmaki Makaurau, wrote, "When there is pono, there is a sense of truth and integrity about the occasion or the interaction."[356] In journalism, pono was generally interpreted as being open and honest about what one sought and why. Ana Tapiata saw pono as acting with integrity: "People will … make a call in relation to your actions." However, Arana Taumata said the desire to be entirely transparent could be tested when dealing with contentious issues or evasive people: "Sometimes it can be really challenging … but I've always found that being honest and upfront with people and not being deceitful [will] … work very well for you."

**Aroha** translates as love, compassion and charitableness towards others. Wrote Beazley: "When acting in a spirit of aroha, our words and actions express not only love but also a myriad of other elements such as compassion, respect and empathy for others and for the environment around us."³⁵⁷ Within the interlocking nature of tikanga, aroha is an expected dimension of whanaungatanga and an essential part of manaakitanga.³⁵⁸

Tumamao Harawira said that aroha is not only about emotions: "it's the thought pattern that you have. The word aroha, you break it into two words: It's aro [to pay attention to] and hā [breath, essence] and that means to acknowledge someone's life force, acknowledge someone's mauri." This understanding, he said, reminded him to be temperate, not tabloid, in the way he wrote news.

For Shannon Haunui-Thompson, aroha in journalism encompasses the recognition that engaging with a reporter can be stressful: "You have to have empathy, you have to have love for the people in your story ... it's their story and they're letting you into their lives, telling some very vulnerable moments sometimes."

Aroha also means practical help. After an earthquake in Kaikōura in 2016 displaced hundreds of people, MTS reporters who flew in by helicopter took food and water to distribute. Said Maramena Roderick, "You do so because it's the right thing to do. I didn't have to ask them." Showing aroha did not compromise newsgathering: "I don't think you lose objectivity by doing what you can to help."

Aroha is also a critical part of reporter relationships with colleagues. *Marae* producer Tini Molyneux described her colleagues as whānau, in this context meaning that people united in a purpose supported each other: "When I've gone out, I've always – me and the cameraman and whoever our crew is – gone out as a whānau. We've got each other's backs and always explain to each other what it is you're doing and what it is you want from the stories. So if you go in as a team, you're more likely to achieve that."

Manuel Beazley wrote that tika, pono and aroha were necessarily intertwined because "aroha is at once the source of tika and pono and it is also the fruit of tika and pono."³⁵⁹ Someone approaching their activities with thoughtfulness, care and concern for others will be motivated to do them well. If the activities in one's private and public life are carried out to the accepted and expected standards, everyone

Tini Molyneux.
LAWRENCE SMITH, STUFF

benefits and a virtuous circle is built by the interlocking strands of tika, pono and aroha.

## JOURNALISM, MANA AND MANAAKITANGA

Behaving for the wellbeing of the collective is a critical concept in Māori life. Personal and group relationships are mediated by the high value placed upon mana. Mana is a quality bestowed by the gods from whom we descend (mana atua), but mana is also inherited from an illustrious lineage (mana whakapapa) or bestowed by the iwi for important contributions (mana tuku iho).[360] The mana of others must be respected, and their humanity and dignity recognised. This is effected by demonstrating manaakitanga, a closely linked concept that involves treating people with care and concern for their wellbeing, and this was a prime concern for the journalists in this study. For radio journalist Justine Murray, manaakitanga was her "utmost whakaaro" [thought] in interviews: "It's important to enter and leave a space with your mana and the other person's mana intact … kaua rā e whakaiti i te tangata, ahakoa ko wai" (don't diminish or denigrate the person, no matter who).

Tumamao Harawira believed manaakitanga relaxed people and that led to a good interview:

> Manaakitanga ... is one of the key things that I use, to get people to open up. If they can understand that the way that you're talking and the questions that you're asking are coming from a place of warmth, a place of love and a place of understanding, then they are going to be more open.
>
> It's almost like the exact opposite of how mainstream media would interview, they would interview with a certain aggressiveness in the nature, in the way that they ask questions. And it gets the exact opposite of what they want. The aggressiveness actually breeds aggressiveness.

Julian Wilcox had a strategy to remind himself about the maintenance of others' mana and his own: "You've got to treat everyone, whoever you talk to, like their mother is sitting beside them. There are very few instances in the world where mothers don't think their sons and daughters are the greatest alive, and if you keep that in mind, that keeps not just their mana intact, but your own mana intact."

Irena Smith said to be "pushy and forceful" in pursuit of a story risked trampling someone's mana: "I'm not prepared to stand on anyone's mana to get what I need. But I feel like I can still get what I need by taking the approach that I take, which is to establish that I'm there to do a job, and I'm gonna try my hardest to get that job done without stepping on your personal mana."

The interwoven nature of Māori life and the imperative to uphold mana meant that reporters tried to avoid discourtesy, even if they disliked someone. Wepiha Te Kanawa said, "Who am I to step on that mana? Because that's all a person has – their mana." Maintaining people's mana was particularly important when reporters interviewed people who were not fluent speakers and who might be dealing with language anxiety. Journalists often employed aroha and manaakitanga in understanding interviewees' anxiety and avoiding judgment while trying to get the best possible grabs from them.

Manaakitanga also encompassed caring for those unused to the media. For example, *The Hui* producer Annabelle Lee-Mather paid attention to interviewees' appearance: "If they're looking a bit roughed up, you just say, 'Have a look in the mirror, I'll straighten your tie' ... he mana tō ia tangata, and he kawenga tō te hunga pāpāho ki te āta tiaki i a rātou" (everyone has mana, and journalists are obliged to take great care with them).

At Whakaata Māori, manaaki was part of the "office dynamics," said Gloria Taumaunu, and that usually took the form of tuakana/teina. This means older sibling, younger sibling and captures the cultural norm that older, more experienced people looked after their juniors. She explained:

> A lot of the staff are inexperienced when they walk through that door, including myself. There's a whole lot of learning that goes on, and hapa [mistakes] and hē [difficulties], and you have to manaaki those kaimahi [staff] as they are coming up and learning more ... to me, if you have a good sense of manaaki tangata, that person will come out with the mātauranga needed, but also a sense of dignity; their dignity is still intact.

### NEWSROOM DILEMMAS

However, the principle of manaakitanga could conflict with the desire to get a good story. Julian Wilcox recounted two instances at MTS when a decision to prioritise manaakitanga led to stories being delayed. The first concerned the death on 20 July 2011 of notable former politician Whetū Tirikātene-Sullivan. She was seventy-nine and had been a high achiever: social worker, dancer, designer, sportswoman, academic and Parliamentarian for nearly thirty years. However, in accordance with her wishes, media were not informed of her death and, despite her stature, there was no tangi.

From a Māori perspective, both decisions were unusual. Whakaata Māori's newsroom found out about the death the day after it happened, but was told by the Minister of Māori Affairs not to break the news until the family was ready. The newsroom was in a dilemma, Wilcox said: the death was news, as was the lack of a tangi, and the newsroom had the facts. Although the minister had no power to control what reporters chose to do, he was genuinely respected and his words carried weight. The risk, said Wilcox, was that if the newsroom went against the family's wishes, reporters might be refused access when the whānau was ready to talk. The story was held.

Two days after her death, Tirikātene-Sullivan was farewelled by her immediate family in a private service; *Te Kāea* was then given permission to break the news. Her younger brother, Kukupa, appeared live to explain that his sister had asked that her death be kept quiet to protect her family. The next day, Wilcox interviewed Kukupa at his home. At the end of their discussion, he asked Kukupa to deliver a poroporoaki, or farewell address to his sister, to the camera. He did so as if addressing her at a tangi, then segued into a family waiata. It was touching and authentic television that might not have come about had the newsroom put timeliness before manaakitanga.

The other instance when manaakitanga trumped news imperatives involved rugby league coach Stephen Kearney – but here, said Wilcox, there was no journalistic payoff, and MTS was scooped in the process. The coach's grandmother, who was well-known in her community, died suddenly in the week he was to take the Kiwis rugby league team into its first test against Australia; at the time, squad and coach were in Australia preparing. MTS had a reporter on site who got an interview with one of the players about the kuia's death and how this might affect her grandson's test preparation.[361] The story was an hour from going to air when the team's media manager rang and asked that the story not be aired, as it would upset the family. Wilcox argued against this, as mainstream media also had the story. But, at the last minute, he removed it from the line-up: "I thought about what Stephen's whānau would think about Māori TV doing this story about his grandmother passing away and how it's affecting their brother or son ... and he's got his Anzac test."

The next morning, a mainstream breakfast show broke the story. Recalled Wilcox: "Everyone was going, 'We got scooped! We had the story!' and I said, 'Yeah, some things are worth doing sometimes.' Even if it doesn't directly pay you back." Manaaki didn't lead to any favours from the rugby establishment later on, he said. Reflecting, however, he wondered if the story was more gossip than news. "Wearing my

Māori hat, I can understand if someone doesn't want that to be put on the Māori news." He added, "His grandmother died, yes; he didn't go back, yes; yes, it probably was having an effect on the Kiwis team. But when you think about it, that's his whānau. And whānau is the most important thing to everyone, eh."

## WHANAUNGATANGA: RELATIONSHIPS

The above stories illustrate that Māori journalists pay close attention to the impact of their decisions on others, a consideration driven by the realities of a small, inter-related society. Whanaungatanga is an important dimension of tikanga, and the close ties across Māori society bring advantages and disadvantages for reporters. "Aotearoa is a small world, and te ao Māori is even smaller," said Julian Wilcox. "The chances of you needing to speak to people again is pretty high – and relationships in this game are crucial." Oriini Kaipara said that relationships had entwined professional, personal and cultural planes, and building relationships was important not just for your story, "but for your own credibility and reputation as a Māori first and foremost, then as a Māori journalist".

In te ao Māori, the word whanaungatanga means a kinship network that provides "a cultural framework for Māori identity".[362] Add the prefix whaka (to cause something to happen) to the word whanaungatanga, and you have whakawhanaungatanga, which describes the process by which relationships are formed. Julian Wilcox described this in terms of meeting an interviewee:

> If they know me, then I don't have to reintroduce myself. If they don't know me, then I can say, 'This is who I am, and by the way I'm your cousin or nephew, or so and so's cousin, or so and so's relation,' because you have to establish those relationships … you should expect that to occur and prepare accordingly.

These exchanges could take some time. Said Radio Waatea manager Bernie O'Donnell, "Drives me crazy! But that's exactly how it happens, and long may it reign."

Oriini Kaipara on the *Newshub* set.
SUPPLIED

Several reporters who started their careers in the early days of Māori news, when Māori were often suspicious of any media, said that whakawhanaungatanga was critical to overcoming resistance. "There were barriers that you had to break down," said Arana Taumata. "Hononga [connection] was a very important tool."

Many of the journalists reported that while younger generations often took an informal approach to whakawhanaungatanga, not necessarily seeking much detail about the journalist before them, elders often preferred to sit down with a cup of tea to talk. Said Kereama Wright, "That's their tikanga of manaakitanga. And as a journalist with a 4 p.m. deadline, that's always hard, to accept that cup of tea, because of the time constraints. The only way in is to have that initial conversation, is to have that cup of tea and a biscuit, and I get that."

The intergenerational, interlinked nature of whanaungatanga was vividly illustrated for Ana Tapiata when she was stockpiling election preview stories in 2014. The political candidate she was interviewing didn't speak te reo, so directed Tapiata to her grandfather's house so he could speak for her. At the house, the candidate's grandmother appeared at the door and called the reporter and her camera operator in with a karanga or call, much to their surprise. However, once they got inside, Tapiata found that the grandfather and his wife had enjoyed a long working relationship with her late father, and that made Tapiata significant to them. "I didn't even have a relationship with them," she said, "but they had it with my father and therefore it was with me."

After the grandfather had spoken, Tapiata talked about her parents. Then everyone ate together, doing the interview afterwards. Tapiata and the camera operator didn't have a strict deadline, but was conscious of time. Still, she said, tikanga dictated they followed the wishes of their hosts, and that was useful from a reporter's perspective: "I think what that does is slow down the process, to allow you to focus on what you're supposed to be doing later."

Although whanaungatanga could give journalists an advantage, Oriini Kaipara warned that tribal ties could never be taken for granted:

> You still have to work hard and make your own mark. Getting through doors off the back of someone you know, I feel, can be a burden because you're riding on their good work or reputation. You have to live up to that. There's no two ways about it. If not, it's on you and it also falls on them.

## THE DRAWBACKS OF REPORTING ON YOUR OWN COMMUNITY

In a small and inter-related world with an age-related pecking order, journalists find that negative feedback can be swift and painful. Whakaata Māori current affairs producer Carmen Parahi said:

> Our community is smaller; we know more people personally, or my cousin knows that person, or my cousin's cousin knows that aunty who's married on that side, who knows that person … if you do something wrong, it comes back to you faster than if you were in mainstream. And it comes through personal channels rather than official ones, and I think it's a real battle for a lot of Māori journalists.

Another battle for journalists was the poor image of journalists among some Māori. Oriini Kaipara said, "We're all tarnished with the same brush: 'We're all media. We're all the same. We're vultures'. Those are just some of the constant remarks I've seen and heard about media.

Carmen Parahi.
SUPPLIED

I know it stems from a lot of poor media coverage of Māori in the past to this present day. It sucks, because we're not all like that."

Negative feedback often accused reporters of harming their own people, said Maramena Roderick: "The criticism gets personal. It's not aimed at the organisation, it's to that person, how they have sullied the name of their whānau or iwi, when in fact they did their job honestly. So that can be hurtful for reporters. They need to get a very hard skin, actually."

On the other hand, an organisation's failings might be heaped on an individual reporter. Oriini Kaipara was at a tribal hui as a private individual when a speaker singled her out for a perceived failing by her employer: "I got called out in front of my iwi, my peers, and iwi leaders. I laughed it off but took it seriously. I went back to my office and called a hui with my seniors, told them it wasn't a good look for our company, and then pushed for a special broadcast around the issue."

Kereama Wright said that to be a Māori journalist means living with tension between kinship and work roles: "We're all conflicted … we're all whānau, so it's hard to do a story on someone without it upsetting someone from your whānau, because we're all so tight-knit." Carmen Parahi added, "Non-Māori journalists can pop into a situation and get out unscathed – or scathed, but don't care about it – whereas a Māori journalist will go into a situation and feel the weight of responsibility, even if they don't know these people; someone they know might know them."

A fear of negative feedback from one's own people could inhibit reporting. News editors reported that young journalists, in particular, could struggle to ask necessary but confronting questions out of discomfort and a fear of negative consequences. A number of senior journalists were concerned that new reporters were not getting enough training and support in this area. Among them was Mihingarangi Forbes, who said that that skill-building required training and good mentors: "What you see and hear around you matters. Do our Māori newsrooms have the key mentors working alongside our budding reporters? Is the balance in a Māori newsroom right? Are there enough experienced journalists? Have they spent decades challenging those in power on behalf of the vulnerable?" In her experience, she said, this wasn't the case.

Newsroom leaders also identified an aversion among some of their staff to doing stories that showed Māori in a negative light. Some reporters felt pressure to focus on positive, good-news stories about Māori as a counterbalance to many years of negative and racist representations in mainstream media. Carmen Parahi said she felt that this was one reason Māori journalism was perceived to be less adversarial than the mainstream: "It's because it's very difficult for us to be, especially when there's this overriding feeling that Māori as a group of people have got to fight for everything anyway … so who are we as journalists to add to that?"

While it was easy for Māori to relate to other Māori, she often had to remind journalists about the need to remain fair, accurate and balanced: "Because it's Māori Television, they feel there is a perception that Māori Television is always on the side of Māori … we're on the side of te reo and tikanga Māori, but as Māori journalists … it's important that they [stories] are neutral but delivered respectfully, and I think that's what makes us different."

For Julian Wilcox, journalism in the Māori world has to mean "holding our people to account as well". He understood why some found that problematic:

> For years, mainstream media has hammered us, hasn't told our positive stories, and for once … we have a couple of platforms that enable us to be able to tell our stories … but you've got to be able to tell the black and the white, the good and the bad … I would rather that my people hold me to account than the Pākehā journalists I don't know and don't trust.

While Māori journalists had to stick to the "main tenets of broadcasting, fairness, balance and accuracy", Wilcox added, tikanga brought "that process of tika, pono, aroha, whanaungatanga – all those Māori values that underpin the way that we interact with each other".

Numerous reporters said that Māori politicians, in particular, expected an easier ride from their own. On that theme, Maramena Roderick said, "Occasionally you hear the odd 'You're there for us,' and of course, we're there for our stories, but don't mistake that with, 'You're there for me and you're going to do it the way I want you to do it.' That then … breaks the normal protocols of fairness, or opens us up to editorial interference."

The challenge for Māori broadcasting was upholding editorial independence in a small world, she said: "We are all constantly pressured. There is a perception that because we are there for our people, we can be influenced to a point of interference. That's unacceptable. We are there for all our people, not just those in positions of power."

Numerous journalists said that they gave controversial or negative stories on their immediate iwi to journalists from other tribes in order to avoid perceptions of a lack of objectivity. "People don't want to do bad stories on their own iwi," said Gloria Taumaunu. "We can do these stories, but they need to be given to the right people to do."

Whanaungatanga could be a double-edged sword. On uncomplicated stories, inside knowledge and existing relationships might be a bonus. But editors might also expect staff to use those same attributes to pursue negative stories within their own tribe. This could put reporters in a difficult position, said one who preferred not to be named: "I'd say to them, 'I don't feel comfortable going to do this story' … and they'd use excuses like 'You're the most senior journalist that can tackle this that's rostered on at the moment.'" There were, the reporter said, arguments over the issue. After she reported a drawn-out court case involving extended family, several personal relationships suffered. That was the point at which she started moving out of hard news to avoid jeopardising long-standing relationships: "I started to shrink back ... when you stand out, your bosses are going to make you do the big stories, so I started to find entertainment and arts stories that were safe journalistically. I was sent less to do the hard-hitting stories. And I was quite happy with that, personally."

## ASKING THE HARD QUESTIONS

In te ao Māori, we are raised to revere elders and leaders. However, in a tribal society with an age-related hierarchy, reporters who push for answers or display scepticism at what they are told can be accused of a lack of manaakitanga. This isn't unique to Māori reporters, of course: "Most people don't like to be rude or confrontational, particularly to those in leadership," said Annabelle Lee-Mather. "Learning to ask hard questions while maintaining relationships comes with experience."

Kereama Wright said that when he was a junior journalist, he had to consciously give himself permission to ask what needed to be asked. He was raised with the words "Kaua e whakahōhā, kaua e whakahōhā i ngā pakeke!" (Don't be annoying, don't annoy your elders), and when he started at *Te Karere*, learning on the job, those words echoed:

> It's kind of what I had in the back of the mind, 'kaua e whakahōhā' [don't be a nuisance]. But then, early in, I realised 'no, you need to be the hōhā [nuisance]'. In order to do this work, you need to be the hōhā. Ki te kore koe e whakahōhā, kāore koe e whai kaikōrero, kāore he kaupapa, nē? [If you don't make a nuisance of yourself, you won't get your interviewee, and you won't have the story, will you?]

He decided he would ask the necessary questions, but with humility: "A tikanga that I've kind of created for myself is be the hōhā ... but be the hōhā with respect and be the hōhā ā-ngākau Māori nei [a nuisance, but with kindness and respect]. So a lot of the time, I approach everyone respectfully and ko te reo Māori te reo kōrero [and speak in Māori]."

Gloria Taumaunu took the same approach: "It's in how you handle things. You're not entitled to their whakautu [a response], or their whakaaro [thoughts], but you can ask respectfully." In addition, it was only fair to give notice of potentially confronting questions, which aligned with manaakitanga. Taumaunu said: "I think you have to make

Annabelle Lee-Mather (left) and Mihingarangi Forbes.
SUPPLIED

them aware that you are going to ask the questions. You can't lull them into 'Okay, it's just a kōrero, a chat,' and then hit them while they're sitting there in front of you, because you get them on the back foot."

Mihingarangi Forbes and Annabelle Lee-Mather have earned reputations for being unafraid to push for answers; to expect accountability, they believe, is no contravention of tikanga. Mihingarangi said, "Asking questions doesn't impinge on anyone's mana; it's their answer that does that." However, manaakitanga was key: "Making sure the person is treated with dignity is key." Annabelle took a similar stance: "Their answers will either enhance their mana or diminish it." She was upfront with interviewees about her intentions and reminded them of the possible outcomes:

> I say to them, 'I'm going to be asking you some tough questions that might make you feel uncomfortable, but this gives you the chance to front-foot this take [issue] in your own words. If I don't ask you, then people will think I've given you a patsy interview and that makes both of us look bad.' Most accept this. And if they don't, they don't – you just have to suck it up and do your job.

To avoid asking difficult but necessary questions, she said, was "An insult to both the talent and our audience … it's important to remind ourselves that our responsibility is to the ordinary Māori who pay our salary through the tax dollars that funds our programmes. Our job is to seek the truth for them."

### *NATIVE AFFAIRS* AND TE KŌHANGA REO NATIONAL TRUST

Forbes and Lee-Mather were among the *Native Affairs* team that investigated the financial dealings of Te Kōhanga Reo National Trust, asking questions on behalf of members of the kōhanga reo movement who felt their concerns were being dismissed. The collective, which represented sixty language nests, alleged that their schools were starved of cash and their buildings falling apart while the trust and its wholly owned commercial arm, Te Pātaka Ōhanga (TPO), made questionable purchases, stockpiled cash and refused to answer questions. The collective felt it had no option but to turn to *Native Affairs*.

The ensuing story, *A Question of Trust*,[363] outlined the collective's allegations and used publicly available information to show the trust had $13 million in reserves. However, the board refused to engage with journalists, despite repeated requests and written questions. The board also unsuccessfully tried to injunct transmission of *A Question of Trust*. However, it was forced to provide financial information in making its bid to block that broadcast, and *Native Affairs* successfully applied to use this information in a second programme, *Feathering the Nest*. This was based on records of credit-card transactions made by a board member and her daughter-in-law, the general manager of TPO, and showed lavish personal spending.

A Serious Fraud Office investigation concluded that, while there were issues with credit-card use and general governance at Te Kōhanga Reo National Trust, there was no criminal wrongdoing. However, a review of TPO, the commercial arm, under the Charities Act 2005 found serious wrongdoing and it was given a formal warning.[364] The trust board was required to make substantial changes to its staffing and procedures.[365]

This was investigative journalism that brought positive change. However, principal reporter Mihingarangi Forbes said that from the beginning of the investigation, she and colleagues were pressured from within Māoridom to drop it. "We all got emails and calls saying, 'just leave it alone' and 'why is a Māori organisation investigating another Māori organisation?' We should be able to put the microscope on our own."[366] The facts had to be established, she added, and a Māori organisation was best-placed to do so: "We understand what they are trying to do, and often have sympathy for their aims. But we won't let them hide behind tikanga if they're not tika [acting appropriately]."

After the allegations were first broadcast, the Kōhanga Reo National Trust Board complained to the MTS board in a bid to appeal to their peers. Jim Mather, then MTS chief executive and editor-in-chief, rejected the approach and directed the trust to the Broadcasting Standards Authority (BSA), one of several national watchdog agencies that hold the media to account. The trust board complained to the BSA that the broadcast was inaccurate, unbalanced and unfair. The BSA, whose members are experts in journalism, broadcasting and the law, rejected the assertion, saying that the story had high public interest and was a legitimate investigation into a publicly funded body.[367]

Still, some quarters of Māoridom said the approach *Native Affairs* took was "Pākehā-fied", bashing Māori and lacking respect. It was not, they said, tikanga Māori.[368] The reporters disagreed, saying that citing a breach of tikanga was a defensive smokescreen; they had tried to meet with the board. Forbes said:

> Tikanga Māori is kanohi ki te kanohi – face-to-face. So if that's the case, they should have met with us. They ignored us from the beginning and went to court. So this whole tikanga thing is easy to throw up in the air. Throw your arms in the air and talk about tikanga when it's not suiting you.[369]

One commentator wrote that sexism was part of the dynamic:

> The young, many of whom were female, journalists had the temerity to challenge the behaviour of the older, many of whom were male, members of the Māori establishment. The message from some disgruntled elders to the stroppy wāhine toa [warrior women] of Native Affairs seemed to be loud and clear: 'You be quiet, girlie!'[370]

Jim Mather left MTS in late 2013, and his successor, Paora Maxwell, was reported as having concerns about the tone of the approaches to the trust board. "When you challenge the establishment, you are going to get kickback," he said. "If there was any criticism from me, it is about the tone. Tone is difficult to balance and it is difficult whenever a younger person is inquiring about an older establishment person."[371]

MTS was subsequently blocked from covering kōhanga reo-related stories, and this remained the case five years later, when Keith Ikin started as MTS chief executive in early 2018. In an attempt to clear the impasse, he met with those who were on Te Kōhanga Reo National Trust Board at the time the scandal erupted:

> We sat down and I saw the hurt that they beared [sic] through the telling of that story and the way that story was told and the impact that it had on them. And so the issue around us ensuring that we have balance is important ... as Māori, yes, we hold decision-makers and we hold people in positions of power and positions of authority ... to account. But we have a wider responsibility in terms of tikanga Māori, whakaaro ki te tangata [considering the people involved] and in that circumstance ... I believe we got it wrong. I believe ... we lacked balance.[372]

As noted earlier, the BSA found that the reporting was not inaccurate, unbalanced and unfair. Still, two out of three Whakaata Māori CEOs had concerns about tone and balance. There is no evidence, however, that either publicly questioned the approach of the trust board in refusing to answer legitimate concerns and then seeking an injunction. None of the CEOs up until that time had been professional journalists. However, they were Māori leaders in a small pool of Māori who might be related, and with whom they might have longstanding relationships.[373] We don't know how influence and relationships behind the scenes may have played out in public pronouncements.

We do know, however, that the political environment around Māori Television is affected by "the highly complex Māori politics surrounding the appointment of the Māori TV board, and the close and interwoven politics of whānau, tribal allegiances, and personal friendships".[374] There were allegations of editorial interference at MTS while Paora Maxwell was CEO.[375]

The above suggests a fundamental misunderstanding in some quarters of Māoridom about the role of journalism in a democracy. Māori journalists see their role as do their mainstream counterparts: to deliver truthful, fair and balanced information to their community of interest and monitor those in power.[376] Tikanga and the Māori worldview informs the subjects chosen, the way in which news work is carried out and how it is presented. However, as the late veteran reporter Tāwini Rangihau said, "the ethics of journalism are the ethics of journalism in whatever language you're reporting in".[377] Such a role conception is reinforced and supported by a regulatory regime that applies to all news media in the shape of the BSA and the New Zealand Media Council; the same role conception has been noted in Indigenous journalism elsewhere.[378]

Critics of the *Native Affairs* reporters also ignored the fact that Māori culture has long valued open and robust public debates. As Parliamentarian Metiria Turei wrote at the time, "There is nothing un-Māori about confronting a misuse of power or asking questions of public figures. The open airing of issues is supposed to be a hallmark of hui [meetings] and kōrero."[379] Indeed, Māori media speaking truth to the Māori powerful is not a new issue. In 1994, Ripeka Evans, then chief executive of Te Māngai Pāho, said critical reporting was necessary:

> To question the Minister for Maori Affairs and his policies is not to attack Maori. To look critically at the structures of Maori organisations – such as Maori trust boards and other trusts and incorporations, or at the performance of some Maori leaders – is not necessarily to be hostile to Maori interests. Sunlight can in fact be a very good disinfectant. This comment is particularly true of ministers, bureaucracies and political organisations. However earnestly they believe they are doing their best, they are not themselves the clients.[380]

Some in the Māori world felt it was not culturally acceptable for the trust's leaders, revered stalwarts of the language revitalisation movement, to be questioned, and made their feelings known. Reflecting the debate, veteran reporter Maramena Roderick, who was not at MTS at the time, firmly rejected this view:

> What's forgotten in the kōhanga reo story is that it was a number of kōhanga reo themselves who raised the concerns. They protested. They had a right to be heard also. So what is a Māori way? Not to question? Not to do any story that may bring Māori into disrepute? That's not journalism. I don't even think it's Māori.

Lee-Mather said it was hard for her to challenge the trust board, as she regarded two of its members, Tīmoti Kāretu and Te Wharehuia Milroy, as mentors; they had been her teachers in elite language school Te Panekiretanga o te Reo. For months, *Native Affairs* encouraged the board to talk, she said: "I sent through the entire question line … we weren't trying to ambush them or catch them out … we just wanted to get them to the table and have this discussion and, of course, they wouldn't do it."

As she worked on the story, a proverb she had learned from the men stuck in her mind: "Takahia te tikanga kia ora ai te tikanga" (trample tikanga for the greater good):[381]

> I had to keep that in my head all the time because we were questioning the governance practices of the Kōhanga Reo National Trust and that included two men who I adore and hero-worship, and who have mentored me, who have been very generous kaiako [teachers] to me, and it was seen as a direct challenge to them. It wasn't – it was a challenge of the governance of that organisation and that case was a quintessential example of 'takahi te tikanga kia ora ai te tikanga'.

There were, she said, big issues at stake around the health of the kōhanga reo movement, and they had to be examined: "We did it because we wanted to draw attention to the fact that it's a bit broken and needs some people to come in and take a look at it and figure out how to make it better again."

Despite the "massive blowback" from those who felt that questioning elders was an attack on mana, Lee-Mather "felt good that those people who really needed a voice and a platform … got it". Viewers noticed, and in following months, *Native Affairs* was "inundated" with tip-offs: "Message after message about dodgy kōhanga, dodgy marae, dodgy kaumātua, dodgy sports clubs, dodgy this, dodgy that. Our people are crying out for an outlet to have their nawe [complaints] heard, and they don't want to take it to mainstream."

The *Native Affairs* team, while the most high-profile journalists to date to be accused of trampling tikanga, are not alone. Several journalists reported that when investigating stories, people had cited tikanga to try to prevent them asking questions or taking footage. Maramena Roderick described this as using tikanga as a weapon, and said, "Too often, Māori media are pressured from Māori who say, 'You can't do this story because of tikanga.' What they're really saying is 'Know your place.'" This was generally a signal, she said, that they didn't know the answer or were trying to hide something, "which immediately raises a big, fat, red flag". She added, "Those who have nothing to hide will be very upfront; they will ask for time to investigate. That's fair. But those who threaten are usually trying to hide, and that's a reason for media to dig even harder."

### INTERVIEWING KAUMĀTUA: GENTLY, GENTLY

As culture-related stories are often news, and as kaumātua are cultural guardians, they are often news subjects. A number of the journalists said they handled elders with more care, patience and solicitude than their own or younger generations, aware that their elders might be unfamiliar with interviews and/or might need time to formulate their thoughts. The key to interviewing kaumātua, said Shannon Haunui-Thompson, is talking face to face and having patience: "If you are wanting a quick-turnaround news story with a quick grab, don't even go there."

Several of the journalists in this book were clear that interrupting elders was disrespectful. This put Peata Melbourne in a difficult position when she was interviewing an elder who had a formal demeanour. Halfway through one of his sentences, the non-Māori camera operator suddenly stopped filming because there was an empty chair in the background that he wanted to frame out. "I kind of held my breath, because I was thinking 'don't do that!'" recalled Peata. "I don't think I would have cared if it was not a kaumātua, but I just don't like interrupting kaumātua for anything. It's a bloody chair, who cares?" She frowned but said nothing to the cameraman.

### WHEN TIKANGA AND JOURNALISM CLASH: HOW DO JOURNALISTS RESOLVE DILEMMAS?

It was clear to me, while filming reporters at work, that journalists did their best to align their tikanga with their journalistic work, particularly at places and events run on cultural protocol. Often, this was straightforward; journalists took cues about what overt expressions of tikanga might be required from the environment, letting their interviewee or host lead. This might mean a formal welcome, discussing whakapapa and sharing refreshments.

When finely balanced decisions had to be made about how to handle a story, a critical factor was the likely impact on ongoing relationships, as any breakdown had personal as well as professional consequences. In several areas, alignment between tikanga and journalistic work was harder to find, and there were several pinch points. What reporters appeared to experience at these times was cognitive dissonance.[382] None of them used the phrase, but analysis of their discussions around the issues fits neatly with the definition of American cognitive psychologist Leon Festinger. Cognition, he explained, is "any knowledge, opinion, or belief about the environment, about oneself, about one's behaviour".[383] The theory of cognitive dissonance says that people need their thoughts and behaviour to be consistent; our opinions and attitudes tend to exist in clusters that are internally consistent. "Two elements are dissonant if, for one reason or another, they do not fit together. They may be inconsistent or contradictory, culture and group standards may dictate that they do not fit, and so on."[384]

A number of journalists, like Julian Wilcox earlier in this chapter, conceptualised this discomfort through the metaphor of wearing a Māori hat and a journalist hat. The Māori hat, or Māori identity, sat first, and permanently, on one's head; the journalist hat sitting on top could be removed. Oriini Kaipara said it could be difficult for journalists to observe the values embodied by each hat at once: "The whole tikanga versus journalism – I feel that sometimes it's hard to wear the two at the same time, it really is. And when, in situations that I'm challenged to wear one or the other, that's when the internal conflict starts within me. It's terrible!"

Every journalist had stories about the times their role as Māori and their role as journalist caused cognitive dissonance. This discomfort sometimes arose because they didn't have time to focus on relationships as they normally would and felt bad about this, or because a situation brought variance between one's normal spiritual practice and the behaviours that news required. Such situations included going somewhere tapu or being waewae tapu at an unfamiliar marae but too short of time to carry out the necessary ritual. On the issue of entering a marae, hosts would not necessarily know whether or not a visiting reporter was waewae tapu. In fieldwork, I never saw reporters asked, and they were always greeted courteously. However, reporters themselves were certainly aware of their status.

When thoughts and behaviours are dissonant, people are driven to reduce the psychological discomfort it causes. Depending on the situation, these journalists had a range of responses, from apologising to hosts to make it clear the situation was less than optimal from a tikanga point of view to reciting a karakia or sprinkling water. Discomfort was often most pronounced when journalists had to impose their timetable on others during formal hui, pōwhiri or tangi on marae; they not only had to assess what they were expected to observe as guests, but they also had to manage the fact that key contacts might be unavailable for some time. Journalists reported that they had learned ways to interrupt people or move things along.

Festinger's experiments in cognitive dissonance led him to write that while some people had a low tolerance for dissonance and found it hard to deal with – he suggested they saw life in more black-and-white terms – some people could tolerate a large amount, and he couched this as an ability to deal with the 'greys' in cognition. He speculated that these people were able to compartmentalise "different cognitive clusters so they had nothing to do with one another".[385] We can perhaps apply this thinking to two situations I saw on the road with journalists, where twice journalists who were waewae tapu removed that issue from their thinking entirely. They both entered from the side of the marae without ceremony, and later told me they saw themselves as present to do a job as a journalist – in effect, temporarily foregrounding their journalistic identity above their Māori one.

Oriini Kaipara was one of several journalists who believed that Māori reporters were still feeling their way through the tikanga/

journalism conundrum, with every story bringing different considerations. Overall, said reporter Shannon Haunui-Thompson, being thoughtful was critical to managing the tensions:

> There's a whole lot of tikanga in te ao Māori, but there's a whole lot of tikanga around being a journalist, full stop, and it's always just a balance really. You have to be thoughtful in whatever situation you are in … for me, it's always tika, pono, manaakitanga … if I follow those … then … the mana for both parties is upheld.

# 10

## KO TE TAPU ME TE KAIRĪPOATA MĀORI

## THE INFLUENCE OF TAPU ON NEWS WORK

## THE CONCEPT OF TAPU AND NOA

Tapu and noa are potent forces in the Māori world and are often important considerations for Māori reporters for both personal and professional reasons. Tapu is a multi-layered concept often translated as sacred, prohibited, restricted, set apart, forbidden, or under the protection of a departmental god; academic Poia Rewi describes tapu as "an intimate connection with the divine" and also as "unparalleled respect for something because of its significance".[386] Activities that take place "under the patronage of the gods", as Māori Marsden wrote, are tapu, such as pōwhiri, house openings and tangi, all important sites for newsgathering.[387]

To break the conventions of formal ritual is to invite misfortune.[388] For example, at marae-based events, the space between hosts and guests is tapu while orators are speaking; it is the domain of Tūmatauenga, the god of war, and strong words are permitted.[389] A journalist walking across the area at that time would be breaching tikanga and, to a Māori way of thinking, would be placing themselves in spiritual and/or bodily danger.[390]

Extensions of tapu exist in order to keep oneself safe, physically and spiritually. For example, to sit on a table where food is prepared or eaten is tapu, because your rear is unclean.[391] Places can be made tapu by rāhui, or bans on access; for example, rāhui are placed on waterways where someone has died, due to the extreme tapu that accompanies death. Conservation rāhui are also placed in areas where depleted natural resources, such as shellfish beds, need time to replenish.[392]

Closely related to tapu is noa. When a situation moves from the realm of the sacred to the realm of the everyday, it has become noa. For example, a formal pōwhiri moves from tapu to noa when the visitors move from outsiders to insiders with the hongi, the pressed noses and the exchange of breath, and shared, cooked food.[393]

Although the word tapu is often translated as sacred, this doesn't quite capture its essence. Something tapu has a value that must be respected: "It places a sanction on a person, an object or a place. Tapu is largely a matter for the individual because it requires protective and disciplinary responses. It is more than mere native superstition, it acts as a means of social control."[394]

Radio reporter Justine Murray says that during her childhood, the tapu areas of the marae were "really drummed into us kids." She added: "We didn't realise as young kids that it was tikanga; it was just a way of doing things. Getting older you start to ask the 'why' questions and learn about te ao wairua [the spiritual world]."

Reporter Irena Smith said her mother raised her to have a strong sense of tapu and noa:

> You don't cut your nails at night-time, don't cut your hair at night-time ... your head is extremely sacred, you don't let people just touch your head and play with your hair. Some people might see those as ... things that aren't really needed in this day and age, but I guess that's how she was taught, so she passed those down to me.

Among our ancestors, there was a belief that if you cut your nails or hair at night, you might not see where the pieces went and they might be taken by a malevolent person to use against you.[395] The head is sacred because it contains the vulnerable brain, and tapu serves as a warning to take care.[396] In adulthood, Smith has been careful to keep tapu and noa separate in life and work, but doesn't observe other tikanga to the extent that her mother did, "because I think it's up to me".

## TAPU AND NOA IN THE NEWSROOM AND IN THE FIELD

The separation of tapu and noa remain important values in many kaupapa Māori organisations. At Whakaata Māori, all staff, whether Māori or not, are expected to observe tapu and noa, said Gloria Taumaunu. "Things like sitting on tables, and hairbrushes on tables, keeping those boundaries between tapu and noa – that's very important

Raiha Paki at her marae, Pākira in Waitahanui (Ngāti Tūwharetoa).

ERICA SINCLAIR PHOTOGRAPHY

here." She occasionally comes across people who don't observe these tikanga or are unaware of them, and takes a gentle approach to raising awareness: "My attitude is one of educating them rather than growling them. That's tikanga Māori as well – me manaaki te tangata, me manaaki hoki te hunga kūare [we must be kind to people and support those who are ignorant]."

In the field, journalists can find themselves in situations where they have to weigh up conflicts between tapu and news work. As an example, carved meeting houses under construction are tapu and women, being a source of noa in this context, are usually barred from going in until completion. *The Hui* reporter Raiha Paki, sent to cover an incomplete whare whakairo, needed shots of the carvers at work inside but would not enter the building herself: "Ko ngā tapu o te wāhine me te tapu o ngā tāne, kia kaua e miki rapu, kei takahi i te taha wairua o te whare, o ngā whakairo o ngā tūpuna" (You must not mix the tapu of men and women, lest you trample the spiritual essence of the house and the carvings of the ancestors).

Paki sent in her male camera operator while she waited in the carpark.

On another occasion, Paki wouldn't enter a burial cave that still contained bones: "That to me is tapu, so I didn't go in." Her cameraman was Samoan and "had no qualms" about entering. In contrast,

Wepiha Te Kanawa entered a burial cave for a story, but only after reciting a karakia to protect himself and his camera operator. Although both reporters perceived these places to be tapu and that they needed to protect themselves, they had different ways of balancing their spiritual beliefs with the need to get the reporting done.

Certain cultural practices are tapu and journalists may not be permitted to record them, particularly karakia recited in formal settings such as tā i te kawa, the ceremony held at dawn to lift tapu from a new building. Kereama Wright explained why:

> The tohunga [experts] don't like being recorded because they have concerns or fears that some people will try and learn their karakia through that recording … along with those karakia come tikanga, and some of them are incantations and there could be a spiritual and physical threat to someone who does not learn them properly. So it's about protecting themselves and protecting others.

When a new museum at the Waitangi Treaty Grounds was opened in a dawn ceremony in 2016, organisers asked journalists not to record a specific karakia. For RNZ reporter Shannon Haunui-Thompson, compliance was automatic: "If someone doesn't want something recorded or taken pictures of, it's not an issue." However, Arana Taumata said that it could be frustrating being unable to film such events, as they often promised beautiful images. He has sometimes been able to negotiate filming snippets of sacred karakia as background audio only. If he can't, he won't record them at all, and not just to conform to host wishes, but to protect himself: "I don't want to muck around with that sort of stuff [tapu]."

In her radio career, Ana Tapiata was sometimes asked not to record karakia, iwi stories and the recitation of genealogies. Such information is generally collectively held within a tribe, she said, and an individual may not have the right to make it public. "I think that from a Māori point of view, not all information is everybody's information," she said. "In mainstream, the idea is that 'I'm entitled to everything', whereas in Māoridom that's not true". Tribal entities are oriented and responsible to their own people and cultural practices, rather than the wider Māori or public sphere.

## REPORTING ON PŌWHIRI

In the past, people arriving at a marae might have peaceful or hostile intent; pōwhiri processes discerned that intent and provided a space for controlled discussion. Pōwhiri encapsulate a highly tapu set of processes that have persisted, unchanged, for hundreds of years; they "mediate the coming together of two sets of tapu and mana, the tapu and mana of the tangata whenua and the tapu and mana of the manuhiri".[397]

As a ritual, a pōwhiri passes from tapu to noa. The karanga, or female call that summons visitors, brings forth the dead and the state of tapu, and that tapu rests on all throughout the oratory and waiata that follow. At the conclusion of speeches, noa is reached with the hongi, the nose-press and exchange of breath that symbolically unites hosts and guests. At this point, participants can interact normally and visitors are able to move around the marae.[398]

Pōwhiri often preface a newsworthy activity for which reporters are present; sometimes, the pōwhiri itself is the event, particularly when dignitaries or celebrities are welcomed on their first visit to Aotearoa. Reporters said they had a cultural duty to follow marae protocol to the best of their ability while on the job. To formally enter a marae under the gaze of the locals was colloquially called 'going on'; reporters would usually enter a pōwhiri with the main group for whom the pōwhiri was being held.

Going on is particularly important when a journalist is visiting a marae for the first time. Newcomers are waewae tapu, or feet set apart; this places tapu on them that must be neutralised through ritual.[399] Radio reporter Justine Murray says that those who are waewae tapu "need to make that transformation tapu–noa" and she stresses that in engaging in ritual, a reporter is not merely an individual doing a job: "It's not just me going into a marae. It's my whakapapa, my genealogy, my tūpuna … I am not only bringing my physical ā-tinana [body] to the marae, but I'm bringing in my wairua as well as my ancestors."

For Kereama Wright, the very nature of pōwhiri – to clear the way between peoples – is a good way for a journalist to remove any "negativity" or "spiritual obstacles" that might exist between the parties and "ensure that our first contact is on positive terms". There is value in hosts seeing reporters adhering to protocol, he says: "I think they respect the fact that we're going through those practices … sometimes it has been the key to getting in there for a story. In other cases, not so much."

### TAPU AND TIME

However, journalists said they often attended pōwhiri with concerns about having enough time to balance formalities and interviews. Journalist Renee Kahukura Iosefa recalled that as a junior reporter, she entered a marae as waewae tapu and, following her beliefs, participated in the entire pōwhiri. However, by the time it ended, she had missed her deadline. Back in the office, a superior told her that when attending an event on a marae as a reporter, she didn't have time to sit through formalities. His advice was to perform a short karakia to spiritually clear the way before entering the marae, a strategy she adopted and has seen others use.

Conversely, turning up at an unfamiliar marae one day to find that there was no process made journalist Justine Murray uncomfortable. Although she was waewae tapu, her hosts dispensed with tikanga and took her straight on to the marae. Murray felt the situation, which she characterised as "not a good space to be in", affected the quality of her work: "At the start of that interview, I didn't feel good, and in fact, when I listen back, I can tell in the way I'm interviewing. Maybe it's nerves, because I knew that I had been on their marae … without being accorded the tikanga."

Once back in her car, she opened a bottle of water and sprinkled some drops over herself as she recited a karakia. She was trying to stem the conflict she felt between her identity as Māori and her role as journalist: "That is an example of me having to walk a tightrope as both producer and Justine, because I needed to leave that place with my story, but in order to get that story I had to go against my beliefs

Justine Murray.
SUPPLIED

and my own way of how I practise tōku Tauranga Moanatanga [my tribal practices]."

However, she wasn't passing judgment on the marae: "Kāore ahau i te whakawā, i te whakaiti i te tangata [I'm not judging or disparaging others] but some people ... practise differently than what I'm used to ... I sometimes have a little internal battle with myself." Justine said she has done karakia in similar work-related circumstances "about five times maybe".

Like Justine Murray, Mere McLean, a Whakaata Māori reporter at the time of interview, believes newsworkers faced with conflict between tikanga and news work have to take responsibility for themselves. Although McLean has been to nearly every marae in the Tūhoe region and is rarely waewae tapu, her camera operators are sometimes strangers at marae where no formalities are planned. She advises them to recite a protective karakia as they enter: "I always tell them, 'Karakia! Karakia within yourself because within your karakia, you're protecting your mauri and within your mauri you're asking their ancestors if you could come on to their marae.'" In her view, any breach of tikanga around entry to a marae has to be addressed: "If you don't take responsibility for yourself, don't blame the marae if something bad happened to you down the track."

However, three journalists who were interviewed for this book rationalised that it was not necessary for them to be welcomed onto unfamiliar marae under spiritual protocol as they were a third party present to do a job. Peata Melbourne filmed a story about a group of Auckland kaumātua who met at Hoani Waititi Marae in west Auckland, a place where she saw herself as waewae tapu. She greeted the visitors waiting at the marae gate with a cheerful "Mōrena!" then entered the marae around the side before proceedings began. This was not an issue for the hosts, who greeted her warmly. In explanation, Melbourne said, "they're not welcoming me on … at the end of the day I have been asked to come and be here, so that's my invitation … to be there without having to go through the formalities." Another Whakaata Māori reporter said that being given permission to attend tangi as waewae tapu covered her: "For me, the first contact initially makes you noa, whether you've gone to the marae or not … once you have the approval of the whānau pani, you have the covering … you're there to do this part of the job."

However, journalists I accompanied who skipped pōwhiri still followed the tikanga they could control, such as taking their shoes off in a whare nui and remaining seated while a speech was in train. This approach can be seen, perhaps, as a tikanga of convenience – avoiding the activities that hold journalists up, but acknowledging tikanga where performance rested with the individual.

## PULLING PEOPLE OUT OF CEREMONIAL OCCASIONS

Although pōwhiri-related time pressures can be mitigated with careful pre-planning, that isn't always possible, and reporters sometimes have to ask someone to leave a pōwhiri or hui for interview. Veteran reporter Hinerangi Goodman had no compunction:

> I do it in the most feared iwi, Tūhoe, but they know who I am, and they know I know our tikanga, and they know I have a job, too, they know I have deadlines. I always say, 'Aroha mai, mōhio ana koe ā te whā karaka te kaupapa nei' [I'm sorry, but you know the show's at 4 p.m.] … and they never question me or tell me to go away.

However, not all reporters have her social capital or confidence, and approaching someone during a formal event risked causing offence. Oriini Kaipara reflected that as a junior reporter, "it took a lot of courage for me to ... just pull them out and say, 'I need you to talk to me now'." Interrupting made her uncomfortable, as her upbringing had taught her to be patient.

Reporters said time pressures meant they cut corners on tikanga all the time, but it was important to mitigate this by acknowledging it to other parties. "Short-cuts are being made every day, every hour," said Gloria Taumaunu, "but the thing is ... you're up front with whatever your transgression was. You ask them for their forgiveness." She cited cutting whakawhanaungatanga short as an example:

> Like when you're ringing a whaea [older woman] to be a talent on a story, and she'll want to know are you married, where you're from, how many kids you've got ... and you have to go, 'Aroha mai Nan, hoi anō he poto te wā ki a tāua' [sorry, Nan, but we have very little time]. I always felt so rude on the phone because the reality is, five minutes max is the amount of time I can give to each phone call.

It's the nature of the news business, she said, that "tika and pono gets pushed out the door when ... your atua becomes time and story and news." However, journalists noted that Māori were becoming more accommodating as they became familiar with journalists' work: "They're a lot more lenient with us now than they used to be," said Peata Melbourne. So much so, said Mere McLean, that marae in Tūhoe were so used to her being unable to stay for post-pōwhiri meals that they bagged food for her to take away.

## COVERING TANGIHANGA

Tangihanga are among the most tapu and unchanged of rituals. They generally last three days, with the tūpāpaku welcomed on the first day with a pōwhiri, then lying in state until the third day, when farewells are made. In between there are songs, haka, tears, meals, whaikōrero and pōwhiri for arriving groups. Visually, tangihanga are arresting and are staples of Māori news, but they can present challenges for reporters:

tangihanga are times of increased tapu, heightened emotion and many guests, some of whom might not appreciate the presence of journalists.

Although some reporters would bypass general pōwhiri formalities if they were short of time, as discussed earlier, the consensus was that with tangihanga reporters should go on not just for their own tikanga but as a sign of respect for the deceased, who was providing their story. Hinerangi Goodman was among those who went on, even if she knew the host marae well. Otherwise, she said, "he haere pēnei i te whānako … it's like a thief in the night; you're going to get the story and didn't even pay your respects." Journalist Semiramis Holland spoke similarly:

> You cannot be labelled a kiore [mouse] in Māoridom. You need to be seen to be paying your respects first, to the tūpāpaku, before you can do anything else on that marae. It's just how it is. And you don't want that label when you're out and about in the community, especially the Māori community, or they won't let you back on. Your face will get remembered. They're watching. Māori are watching you very closely, and so you need to be seen to be adhering to tikanga.

*The Hui* reporter Raiha Paki also went on if she was covering a tangi, aware she was representing not just her employer, but her family:

> Outside of my mahi [work], I have whakapapa and I have my own mana and so do my parents and my grandparents, and so if I'm seen to be disrespectful, or mēnā kei te hē taku kawe i a au i roto i ērā ao, ka hoki ērā kōrero ka whakamā i tō whānau, kāore e kore [or if I don't behave appropriately in these places, it will come back and doubtless embarrass my family].

However, there were occasions when reporters just didn't have time and, once again, karakia were important. Arana Taumata would do a personal karakia to acknowledge the tūpāpaku "for my own protection … as we know, the tangihanga is probably the most tapu event and so I was always acutely aware of that, and that's not something that can be trifled with." He would also apologise to the hosts, saying that while their story was important, to show it to the world he had to meet a deadline. Asked how hosts responded, he said, "That's the beautiful thing about our people. Gosh, I couldn't think of one person that was offended by it."

Marae haven't always been so open to tangi being filmed. MTS producer Hone Edwards was at *Te Karere* in the 1980s when it started filming tangi: "People just freaked … it wasn't so much seeing us and the camera crews at tangis, it was seeing it on air that night … everything just slammed shut, because Māoridom were trying to … ascertain to what extent they would allow that kind of exposure on issues that were kind of sacrosanct."

## THE ARRIVAL OF THE 'TELE-TANGI'

However, as tikanga, technology and broadcasting have found an accommodation with each other, Māori have become more willing to have reporters document funerals and broadcast them live. Any conceptual barriers to broadcasting tangi appeared to fall in 2006, when the final day of the tangihanga for Dame Te Atairangikaahu, the sixth Māori monarch, was broadcast live on Television New Zealand and Whakaata Māori. The 'tele-tangi' was visually compelling and attracted more than 430,000 viewers.[400]

Since then, the tangihanga of many other notables have been livestreamed, and one driver has been to allow participation by those

The tangihanga for Dame Te Atairangikaahu, the sixth Māori monarch, was broadcast live on Television New Zealand and Māori Television.

NZME

unable to attend or living overseas. For example, the livestream of the 2013 tangihanga of popular Parliamentarian Parekura Horomia drew 29,000 log-ins from 103 different countries.[401] An important point about livestreaming tangihanga is that they capture the very best speakers and performers, so play an important role in presenting exemplars of reo and tikanga.

Another contentious issue in Māori journalism is whether reporters should speak to direct relatives of the deceased at tangi. Close relatives of the deceased, called kirimate, are under the tapu of death and are left to grieve. A common tikanga is that three generations around the deceased do not speak publicly,[402] and for many years those people would not speak to reporters either. However, in the past decade, that had changed, says producer Hone Edwards, with some families accepting requests to speak. After politician Parekura Horomia died in office in 2013, Kereama Wright asked if a member of the family might be interviewed for television. One of his brothers agreed, given the interest in the politician's life. "I was surprised," Wright recalled, "but I took the opportunity."[403]

However, such interviews remain rare enough that reporters may explain to viewers why they have come to pass. For example, when then Whakaata Māori reporter Maiki Sherman covered the tangi of Ngāti Hine leader Erima Henare, his son Peeni, a Parliamentarian, was interviewed.[404] Maiki explained why in her story:

> Reporter voice-over: "Ehara i te tikanga e kitea whānuitia ana, arā, kia whakapuaki kōrero te kirimate. Heoi ko tā Ngāti Hine he poipoi i ana uri kia tū pakari ai rātou ki ngā take katoa. He tauira o te kāwai whakapapa i ahu mai ai a Erima Henare."

> *Subtitles: It's unusual for the immediate bereaved family to speak. However, Ngāti Hine believes it's important to raise their descendants to stand strong on all matters. It's an example of the prestigious lineage of which Erima Henare is a descendant.*

> Grab, Hirini Henare, an elder: "Kāhore mātou āwangawanga ki tērā mō Ngāti Hine tīmata mātou ō mātou tamariki kia tū pakari rātou heoi anō i a mātou i konei koia tō mātou hiahia tū mai."

*Subtitles: We are not concerned by that, as we of Ngāti Hine teach our children to stand strong. So on this occasion we want them to do the same.*

It appears that this tribe doesn't adhere to the tikanga of kirimate as do others, for the reason cited above. However, the reporter was aware that as the tikanga of silence was widely known, a departure needed to be explained.

Mere McLean was torn over interviewing kirimate. As a journalist, she wanted to talk to someone as close as possible to the deceased: "That is the scoop." But as Māori, "I don't want to do that, lest I trample the mana of that family. But with my reporter's hat on, I have to ask the question … in my opinion, that's breaking tikanga." In the past, she had often sought an interview from a designated spokesperson, but now went straight to a family member to ask. She felt that most of the people who agreed to be interviewed were aware of the tikanga of kirimate but put it aside for what they perceived as a greater need: "Maybe they feel this death can teach other people something. Usually the families that have experienced suicide are the ones that would kōrero to me, because … they don't want … another family to go through it."

## SEEKING GUIDANCE ON TIKANGA-RELATED ISSUES

Among the journalists and news managers I spoke to, there was agreement that reporters on the ground were best placed to manage any tikanga-related dilemmas that arose. Said Maramena Roderick of Whakaata Māori: "Our journos come from their own tikanga base, as did I. They bring that with them. Nothing I say is going to be of more value to them than what their own have already taught them."

Kereama Wright trusted his instincts, saying he was brought up "being conscious of te taha wairua and te whakarongo ki te ngākau [of my spiritual side and listening to my feelings]." However, if he needed to talk something over, he went to his father, Rawiri Wright, a former print reporter:

> I just ring him about different encounters that I have, that's when it's fresh in the mind. So after I've finished and I feel like maybe I might have stepped over the line with somebody, I'll give ... my father a call, just to get a gauge on his thoughts on it.
> He's been a pou [pillar of support] of mine.

Wright recalled how his father's advice helped him when one of his stories attracted criticism. After more than forty whales died on a rural beach, the local iwi decided to decapitate them in order to extract a special oil encapsulated in their heads, thereby reviving an ancient custom that had long been dormant. They invited Kereama to document it. To him, the crux of the story was the revival of an ancient practice: "I was fascinated. And I thought, 'Man, this is something that our kids need to see.' I felt it was important for us to show that tikanga is still alive, as a Māori news outfit. That's news, that's Māori news."

In the intro to the story, the presenter warned viewers that some of the images might be distressing. The visuals showed men slicing through a whale's head and then rolling it away, as well as heads lined up on the grass. Experts overseeing the work gave informative interviews. Kereama believed showing viewers what was happening to the corpses was "Important to give them an idea of what happens – it's reality. After those whales are dead, the next part of the tikanga comes into play and I felt it was important to show that. But a lot of Māori disagreed with that."

The story, when posted on Facebook with two photographs of the heads, generated a great deal of discussion. Many posters objected to severed heads being shown: "Some traditions are best left unseen," wrote one. Some were happy to see an ancient practice being revived, and talked of the whales being a gift from Tangaroa, god of the sea. But there was concern that putting the story online left tikanga Māori open to criticism, as one poster wrote: "… But in all reality fb is not the place for advertising this. as like some said on here people who view this from all over the world that don't have any clue on what is actually going on here could turn this into a world wide hate frenzie against our culture …"

Wright wasn't surprised about the polarised reaction: "I was expecting it, because you don't see whale heads on TV every day." But as criticism mounted, misgivings set in: "You do start doubting yourself and second-guessing yourself." He called his father, "just to ask him if I did step over the line." Dad didn't think so: "He's all about telling Māori stories from a Māori worldview," says Wright. "If you were to look at the story from the Māori worldview, you'd understand, and no offence would set in."

Mere McLean used to talk to her late grandmother about work-related tikanga issues. She now discusses any dilemmas with her whanaunga Hinerangi Goodman, who spent more than twenty years working on *Te Karere*. Like many Tūhoe, Mere is of the Ringatū faith, and she takes tikanga issues to church elders if she has a problem.

## THE KAUNIHERA KAUMATUA AT WHAKAATA MĀORI

The human body is tapu, and a corpse highly so; the tapu of death would generally preclude filming. However, as tikanga evolves with the times, so tikanga within journalism can flex if overriding issues of political or social importance exist. This arose for the staff of *Native Affairs* in 2011 after the fatal police shooting of a man named Anthony Ratahi. His family believed that the police had overreacted in shooting to kill – the fatal shot was through his left eye – and asked Whakaata Māori reporter Semiramis Holland to film his body in the morgue in Wellington. Holland felt uncertain about this, so called her producers for advice. One of them, Annabelle Lee-Mather, advised her to film: "You've got to get it when it's there; you can't go back and re-enact that stuff," she recalled. "So we thought we'd get it and figure out our plan afterwards."

*Native Affairs* head Julian Wilcox approached kaunihera member Huirangi Waikerepuru for advice, as both he and the victim were both from Taranaki. Waikerepuru advised the journalists to follow the family's wishes. Lee-Mather called another member of the pan-tribal council, Canon Hone Kaa, who was an experienced broadcaster (see Chapter 4). His advice, she says, was "if the whānau are okay with it, the taha wairua will be okay, because you are secure in what this whānau wants."

Aware that there would be criticism of the decision to show a body, especially one with such graphic injuries, producers moved carefully, said Lee-Mather:

> We knew we wanted to put it on air, but we knew that we had to cross off some tikanga boxes to make sure that we were safe, that Māori TV was safe, that Semi's mana was safe, that the whānau weren't acting willy-nilly.
>
> We needed to show that we weren't just running around filming dead people and we needed to show that there was consideration and that there had been a process. So we needed to talk to people who we considered had high tikanga values and mātauranga Māori value and who were respected within the Māori community and get their guidance … we felt like with all of their powers combined, that we had their blessing, and their whakaaro and guidance, that we would be okay.

Holland said she trusted the elders' guidance: "After the discussions, I didn't have a problem with it, especially when Huirangi and Hone Kaa were involved. I was going to go with what they said … because they are tikanga experts."

Other Māori journalists aired their reservations about filming a body. In response, Parliamentarian Metiria Turei said she didn't feel that tikanga had been breached. The fact the family had suggested filming showed "the high level of trust Māori whānau have in the Māori media to treat our issues and our people with sensitivity and openness. Mainstream media would never have gotten so close."[405]

However, the Kaunihera Kaumātua appeared to have fallen into abeyance by 2016. That year, RNZ reported that its members had not been consulted for several years and were unhappy about the situation. Members Kīngi Īhaka and Huata Holmes said there had been no formal notification that the group had disbanded.[406] Whakaata Māori head Shane Taurima, who assumed his role in 2019, told me that he wasn't sure why the kaunihera had faded away, but was exploring what sort of advisory group would best support Whakaata Māori staff on issues where tikanga intersected with the business of broadcasting. In general, he said, it was best that reporters dealt directly with whānau and iwi on any issues that arose, adding that staff were able to draw on a range of expertise among colleagues and also within their own networks. In addition, Whakaata Māori has a team dedicated to supporting kaimahi on reo and tikanga matters that is headed by Dr Hinurewa Poutu, the kaikōkiri reo, or director of te reo Māori. Whakaata Māori also has a kāhui of local Waikato-Tainui pakeke who meet regularly with management and staff and support the company with pōwhiri, whakatau, karakia and internal and external events.

## WHEN TIKANGA ITSELF IS THE STORY

Tikanga is such a strong influence on Māori life that tikanga itself – or a breach of it – can become news. In 2016, Peata Melbourne, then at *Te Karere*, reported how an American company, fineartsamerica.com, printed the heads of rangatira (chiefs) on NZD$100 shower curtains and sold them online.[407] The images were real people painted by Gottfried Lindauer in the nineteenth century, but one image appeared to be a mokomokai, or preserved head. Mixing the head, which is tapu, with things related to washing of the body is offensive – "those are things you keep really, really separate," said Melbourne – and using images of real ancestors to make money caused great dismay. "There were just so many things wrong with it," she said. "There was the intellectual property scenario; there was the tikanga Māori scenario; they were non-New Zealanders." In compiling the story, "I tried to keep my calm. I actually got quite angry, because we contacted the people whose website it was and when they spoke to us, we basically just got shoved off."

The importance of the story was highlighted by the length of the first package: An unusual five minutes thirty-nine seconds, compared to usual *Te Karere* story lengths of about two minutes. Although that first package had various experts outlining why the company's move was offensive, the disapproval of both reporter and anchor was clear, if tempered. At the end of one live cross, host Scotty Morrison asked Melbourne if she would be following up the story. Melbourne replied:

*Āe, ka tika ka whai au engari kei tēnā kei tēnā o ngā kaitaurima te mana ki te whai i tēnei take arā ki te tono atu ki te kamupene me te tango i ngā whakaahua.*

*Subtitles: Oh yes, I will be. But all patrons can also submit complaints to the company to have the images removed.*

As Morrison linked to the next clip, he said, "Te whakarihariha, nē hā", or "Isn't it disgusting". Here, within a Māori paradigm, the assumption was made that viewers would be similarly affronted and that license could be taken to embody that in the language of the presenters and reporters, and even suggest a remedy – that viewers should make their displeasure known. Here, in defence of tikanga, the show took an activist stance. This story, along with others, prompted a concerted social media campaign that saw the offending images taken down within twenty-four hours. However, the following day, a Rotorua man found his own face on the same site, available for printing on carry bags, duvets and cushions; he hadn't been approached to give consent.[408] Melbourne interviewed a lawyer who said that copyright laws did not protect Māori culture. In a live cross to the anchor, she opined that this situation was "āhua koretake" (pretty hopeless).

Cultural appropriation is a perennial topic in Māori language news; as Māori culture has become more visible and appreciated in Aotearoa New Zealand and overseas, so outsiders have tried to commodify it. There have been protests against overseas fashion labels using moko on models, Israeli cigarettes called Maori Mix and beer brands named after ancestors Hinemoa and Tūtānekai.[409] Linking beer and cigarettes with Māori culture causes particular offence; neither existed in Aotearoa New Zealand before colonisation, yet Māori have been disproportionately and negatively affected by both.[410]

## CASE STUDY: DEALING WITH DEATH ON *KAWE KŌRERO – REPORTERS*

In the Māori world, we are very conscious of the tapu of death. So how is mention of death handled in the studio – and what resources

In the minutes before *Kawe Kōrero* goes to air, Kawe practises his opening line while the floor manager attends to a technical issue. Centre is Peata Melbourne and right is Gloria Taumaunu.

ATAKOHU MIDDLETON

do reporters draw on to take care of their own spiritual health? I saw some good examples at Whakaata Māori during a live broadcast of *Kawe Kōrero – Reporters*, a light and fast-paced bilingual news talk show that ran on Māori Television from 2016 to 2018. On this particular night, there were three people in the studio: Host Kawe Roes and two colleagues, Peata Melbourne and news editor Gloria Taumaunu. Their job was to discuss the news circulating on social media, with interviewees brought into the studio using video chat applications.

This show turned out to be unusually sombre. The first story was about high-profile netballer Tania Dalton, who had died suddenly that morning from a brain aneurysm, aged forty-five. She was Pākehā, but very well known in the Māori world. The second story was about the funeral, in Tonga, for the nation's Queen Mother, ninety-year-old Halaevalu Mata'aho, who had died in Auckland. As the latter story ended, Roes turned to the camera and delivered a scripted outro:

> E ngā mate, haere atu rā. Ki te ao mārama, e hoa mā. Ā muri ake i te pūreirei whakamatua, ka hoki mai anō mātou ki te matapaki marau.
>
> [Translation: You the dead, go to your rest. Now to the world of the light, my friends. After the ad break, we'll be back to discuss more topics.]

Kawe Roes.
WHAKAATA MĀORI

The phrase "You the dead go to your rest" is a mihi mate, a greeting to the dead widely used in reo Māori oratory that has been imported into Māori news (see Chapter 8). It is followed by a mihi ora, a greeting to the living, here "To the world of light my friends."

One sentence to the dead and one to the living is a minimum and reflects the Māori view that the physical world and the spiritual realm are integrated. According to *Kawe Kōrero – Reporters* producer Hone Edwards, inserting the mihi after stories involving deaths simply follows tikanga: "It's a clean delineation between dealing with the dead and dealing with the living". The mihi are "cultural stops" that keep staff safe, "because they have … strong spiritual beliefs, and I'm always aware of respecting those boundaries".

Edwards doesn't script individual mihi mate/mihi ora for non-Māori; to do so, he said, isn't culturally appropriate. In this case, the deaths involved a Pākehā and a Tongan. But to reflect tikanga for the benefit of both viewers and staff, both women were acknowledged as well as the many dead who had gone before, and the focus returned to the living.

As the outro ended and the trio was off-camera, Roes, his expression one of discomfort, raised his hands and turned them inwards, then outwards three times, palms outward, as if flicking something unwanted off them. Such symbolic gestures speak as eloquently as our voices do[411] – and here, the gesture spoke of unease. Body-language analysts call this sort of movement an 'away gesture' as it symbolically says 'get away from me – stay away from my body', with a connotation of negation or refusal.[412]

For Roes, the gesture was an attempt to mentally distance himself. He felt uneasy that there had been two consecutive stories about death:

> I was like, 'Jeekers, hell, this is some pretty hard-core death stuff. This is some pretty tapu, toimaha [weighty]-type business', so I could feel my goose bumps and the hair around my head and my neck all standing to attention when I was doing 'haere ngā mate, rātou ki a rātou' [Go you dead, the dead to the dead]. And I think at that moment it sort of hit in that, 'Jeekers, you know, you're talking about dead people.'

He then said, to his two companions, "Been like having a tangihanga angle." Melbourne smiled briefly at him and remarked "Was a bit, eh?" Roes replied, "Was heavy for part one," grimacing momentarily. At the same time, Melbourne, her words overlapping with those of Roes, said "just death, death, death". She later said that she also found the two stories "quite heavy" fare for a "quite light" show.

Gloria Taumaunu had been silent to this point. As Melbourne said "death" the first time, Taumaunu, expressionless and with her eyes downcast, raised her right hand, palm towards her and hand cupped, and mimed flicking something over her head. She was doing a metaphorical whakanoa, or a removal of the tapu surrounding death.[413]

Taumaunu said later that at the time she made the gesture, she was also conveying a wordless karakia to the wāhi ngaro, to those who have gone before, who are a source of strength for her. She was feeling "a bit of tingle, a bit of taumaha [spiritual heaviness]" and some discomfort with "āhuatanga tapu" – subjects imbued with tapu – being treated in a necessarily superficial way given the show's short-bites format:

> You do have to acknowledge your feelings about it, because it's not sitting right with you ... I decided that what was required at that moment, was an imaginary ruirui wai [sprinkling of water] ... that was a physical way of addressing the taumahatanga [heaviness] ... ask for that clearance ... because I always want to conduct myself in an appropriate manner.

Her whakanoa was "for my own self":

> You've got to move your mind from something taumaha [heavy or serious] to being able to talk about something light; you know, you've got to give permission to yourself to move on ... and if anything, it was that, so you're not just so blasé about moving from one person's mate [death] on to another kaupapa. If anything, it's a sign of respect to the kaupapa you've just spoken about.

Karakia is, for Taumaunu, a natural response to anything that makes her feel ill-at-ease: "It comes in the heavy times, at times of stress, and if you are someone who's spiritual, you karakia whenever you've had a bad day." She adds that karakia "puts you in that space where you're centred, you centre yourself ... having said that, you need to be able to understand the power of karakia to enjoy its benefits."

As she was finishing her whakanoa, Roes glanced at her and said, "Ashes to ashes, dust to dust, that is us, let's get to kapa haka [the next item]." On the first "ashes", he flicked his right arm and hand out in front of him as if he were brushing something away, then on the first "dust" did the same with his other hand. Here he was enacting scattering ashes into a grave, a phrase and gesture associated with Judaeo-Christian culture. The phrase "ashes to ashes" is a ritualistic, fixed phrase that is rooted in the Bible, became part of the set text of the Anglican burial service and is now a widely used proverb – and often a parody – about the impermanence of human life.[414] Roes later said that he was feeling the need to lighten his mood before the next story. His words and gestures were a case of "just moving on, that was part one, it's over and dusted, now let's get into part two, let's get into that head space". Live television, he said, didn't allow much time to adjust between segments: "When you do a tangihanga at a marae ... you have literally a day to process those emotions and that feeling. When you have a TV show, you have 30 seconds."

## CASE STUDY: REPORTING IN A WĀHI TAPU

Iwi may place conservation rāhui over areas where natural resources need time to replenish or people's interaction with a natural feature needs to change. While on the road with journalists, I saw something of a tussle between a television reporter, whom we'll call Rēhia, and an iwi leader, whom we'll name Tai, over what could and couldn't be filmed in a wāhi tapu where a conservation rāhui had been imposed.

The wāhi tapu was a spring of great significance to the three iwi that co-managed it. After suffering decades of people swimming and diving in the spring, the iwi had imposed a rāhui that banned any human contact with the water, such as swimming, diving, wading, taking water and drinking. Signs made the conditions clear: "Thank you for respecting this wāhi tapu by avoiding contact with the water."

Rēhia wanted to do a story about the extensive work the three iwi had done to conserve the site. Standing at the water's edge with Tai, she asked if he would stroke the water with his hands for the camera in order to show the link between iwi and water. As a visual journalist, Rēhia needed to show as well as tell, and that required strong images. Tai refused, as this breached the rāhui and he didn't want to do anything to undermine it. If people saw him touching the water on national television, he said, they'd think the rāhui was meaningless: "They'll be saying, 'here he is, well we'll go and have a swim.'"

Rēhia tried to persuade Tai, saying she needed pictures that expressed his connection with the spring. Tai, trying to appease her, said he could put the tip of his walking stick in the water instead, but Rēhia was not receptive. She later told me she thought the iwi were being unnecessarily strict about the rāhui, especially as she had been told the springs were used by ancestors for childbirth rituals. Her perception of what was acceptable in a wāhi tapu diverged from that of the iwi. To her, such a place was "sacred, and respect goes with it … they just don't want people swimming and diving and desecrating it. But touching it, it's not that bad. I've just gotta see how I can get around that."

The next day, Rēhia decided she wanted her camera operator to put a waterproof camera in the spring to capture what she knew would be spectacular sub-surface pictures. Unable to get hold of Tai, she called the tribe's public affairs officer and tried to get permission from her alone, promising to gift the footage as a taonga for the iwi as a sweetener. Permission wasn't forthcoming, with the officer saying that assent could come only from the leaders of the three relevant iwi. Knowing the assent of three people would be harder to secure and take longer than that of one, and under time pressure, Rēhia suggested the permission of one of the leaders would be enough. The officer promised to see what she could do.

After the phone call, I asked Rēhia what she thought would happen. She said she expected a refusal, and appeared unhappy. She briefly entertained the idea of bypassing the public relations officer entirely and going to one of the other two iwi for permission, but quickly discarded this, knowing the risk this posed to the maintenance of relationships.

A few hours later, there had been no response and the time was drawing near for Rēhia and her camera operator to leave to catch a plane. Rēhia instructed the camera operator to put the camera in the water and gather footage, reasoning she should get some images as journalistic insurance while awaiting a decision. At this point, Rēhia's identity as a reporter was to the fore, and the pictures came above all other considerations. What was less clear is whether, as Māori, she saw herself responsible for upholding the mana whenua of the iwi, even though they were not present. Later that day, Rēhia explained:

> I wasn't prepared to sit there and wait for four hours. Sometimes you make a choice, and a decision, just you've gotta do it ... what if they phoned me tomorrow and said, 'Yeah, absolutely, Rēhia, absolutely you can do that' and then I didn't have it because I didn't do it? So sometimes you just go with what you need to do at that time.

As the pair were on the way to the airport, a text arrived from the public relations officer with a polite refusal.

Back at the office, Rēhia told her producer she had taken underwater footage but without permission. The producer said, "If your water was tapu and some reporter turned up and chucked their camera in it, would you like that?" Still, Rēhia had the footage edited into the story; the producer admitted that the images were beautiful, and left Rēhia to see if she could secure retrospective permission.

When Rēhia told Tai she had footage and again sought permission, he again politely refused. As a compromise, he said that he would try and locate some pre-rāhui underwater footage owned by the iwi for her to use. However, this search was unsuccessful. Over succeeding days, Rēhia continued negotiating with Tai, stressing that her story would emphasise the importance of the rāhui. Tai asked his peers what they thought; the answer was no. Under pressure, Tai said that if Rēhia used the footage, it would be without his permission, and he was not to be linked to it in any way.

To use the footage without being able to identify its provenance would leave Rēhia and her employer open to criticism, and she couldn't take that risk. Without explicit permission, she stripped the footage from the edit. Instead, she located some attractive aerial footage of the springs and inserted it into her report. Discussing the situation later, Rēhia said she knew she couldn't alienate the iwi – she needed to display respect and an understanding of the iwi's position. A practical reason was that she had heard of another story in the area she wanted to pursue, so would have to talk to the same leaders again; she couldn't afford to irritate them. As she was a member of one of the three iwi that co-managed the springs, any offence caused may become known, affecting her professional and personal reputation. She said:

> At the end of the day it's about relationships, and for us as Māori journos, you've got to keep your relationships really tight. To me that's worth more than anything … I've got whakapapa connections down here so I'd love to come back and see these whānau again and say 'Kia ora, kia ora, kei te pēhea koe?' [Hi! How are you?] and not be 'Oh no (they're not being welcoming) …'

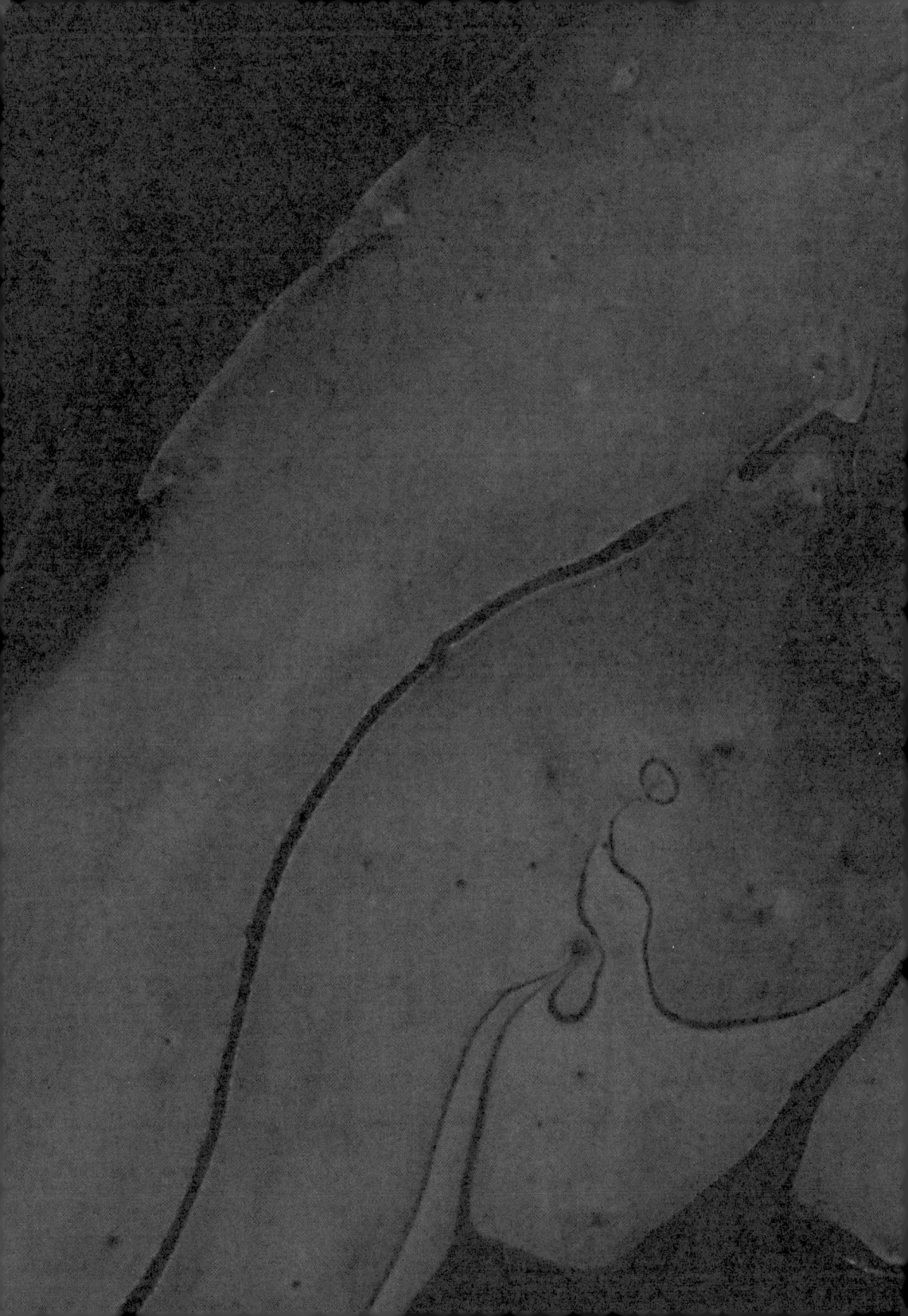

# KEI MUA

# 11

## WHAT LIES AHEAD?

In October 2018, as this book was taking shape, the then Minister for Māori Development, Nanaia Mahuta, a Labour Parliamentarian, announced a review of the entire Māori broadcasting sector to ensure it was "fit for purpose" in the digital age, calling the process the Māori Media Sector Shift.[415] Situation analysis identified a range of issues, among them a number of silos with little cooperation, minimal investment in talent development, low production budgets compared to mainstream media and queries over whether the sector's governing sector policy and legislation remained relevant.[416]

Following consultation, Mahuta released her proposals for change in June 2020. In general, they envisioned a more connected and collaborative industry. Among the proposals was a Centre for Media Excellence, based at Whakaata Māori, to provide skills training in journalism and technical areas through partnerships with academic institutions. This was greeted positively, as a lack of journalism and technical training has been an ongoing issue.[417] The proposal of a 100 percent reo Māori national Māori radio service met a mixed response, with concerns that such a station would have a negative impact on iwi radio.

However, the proposal of a single Māori daily news outlet at Māori Television, with iwi media funded to contribute content, met stiff and immediate opposition from journalists. It is important to clarify here that such centralisation would have affected *Te Karere* and the iwi radio news contract held by Radio Waatea, but not current affairs programmes such as *Marae* and *The Hui*. Resistance centred on the ways on which a single outlet would limit the diversity of Māori voices, opinions and stories.[418]

In late 2020, the Labour Party won a second consecutive term in government, with oversight of Māori media passing to former broadcaster Willie Jackson, who has a long history in Māori media. He was no fan of the suggestions that had been made and appointed his own advisory board to revisit the review. Its members were Auckland University of Technology academic and broadcaster Ella Henry, the chair; iwi radio leader and Whakaata Māori board chair Peter-Lucas Jones;

*Te Karere* presenter and language revitalisation expert Scotty Morrison; *The Hui* producer Annabelle Lee-Mather; film producer Nicole Hoey; iwi communications manager Jason Ake, a former radio, television and print journalist; and producer Bailey Mackey, a former *Te Karere* reporter.[419]

On Māori media, Jackson's goals are no secret. He has publicly stated that he wants to see better alignment between Māori media and other state-funded media, such as Radio New Zealand and Television New Zealand. Māori media, he says, needs to be more fairly funded compared to its state-owned Anglophone counterparts: he wants to "make sure we get a fairer slice of the pie".[420] Review group chairperson Ella Henry has made similar comments and has also reiterated the need for structured training for the sector, saying that "Māori media has not had an equitable share of sector funding and the workforce lacks capacity. It is clear that polytechnic and university courses have been under-delivering for Māori."[421]

Jackson's advisory group reported a suite of proposals to the Minister in mid-2021, and Te Puni Kōkiri, which handles Māori media policy, started working on a detailed business case and strategic plan. At the time of writing, the day-to-day businesses of responding to successive COVID-19 outbreaks has slowed much government policy work, and no details on the future shape of the Māori media sector have been announced. In the meantime, Te Māngai Pāho, which is now platform-agnostic given the realities of the digital age, continues funding Māori journalism as it has for so many years. In 2021, TMP decided it would no longer pay for programming that was less than 30 percent in te reo and thus aimed at language learners; such programming now rests with New Zealand On Air. TMP now funds in two bands: 30–70 percent reo content, which targets receptive language learners, and 70 percent+, which targets fluent speakers. These categories encompass the news and current affairs long-stayers, so for *Te Karere*, *Marae*, *The Hui* and the news services on Te Reo Irirangi o Waatea, it's business as usual with the hope that positive change is to come. Tē tōia, tē haumatia – a secure future for Māori journalism requires a plan, a well-resourced workforce and a clear path forward.

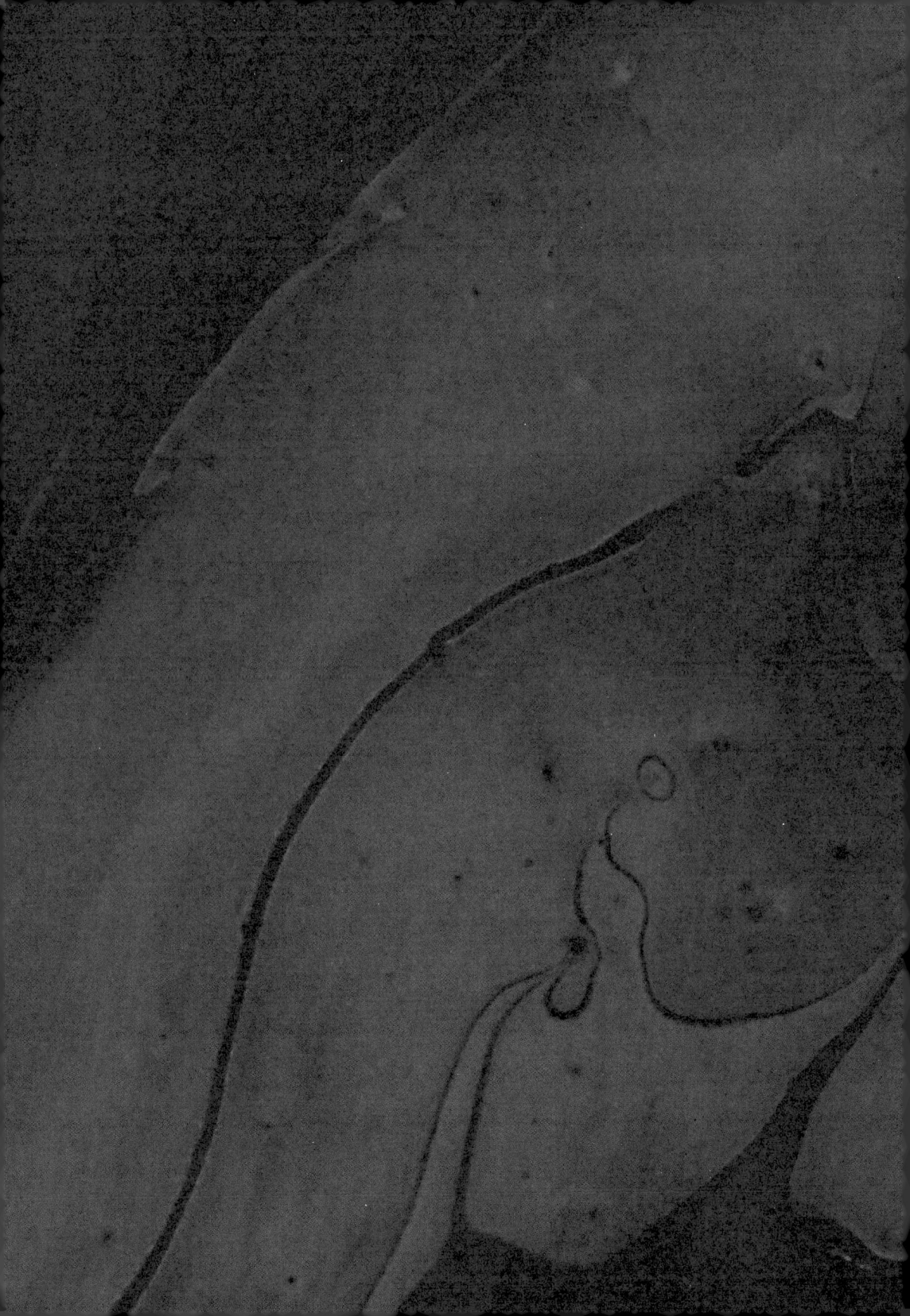

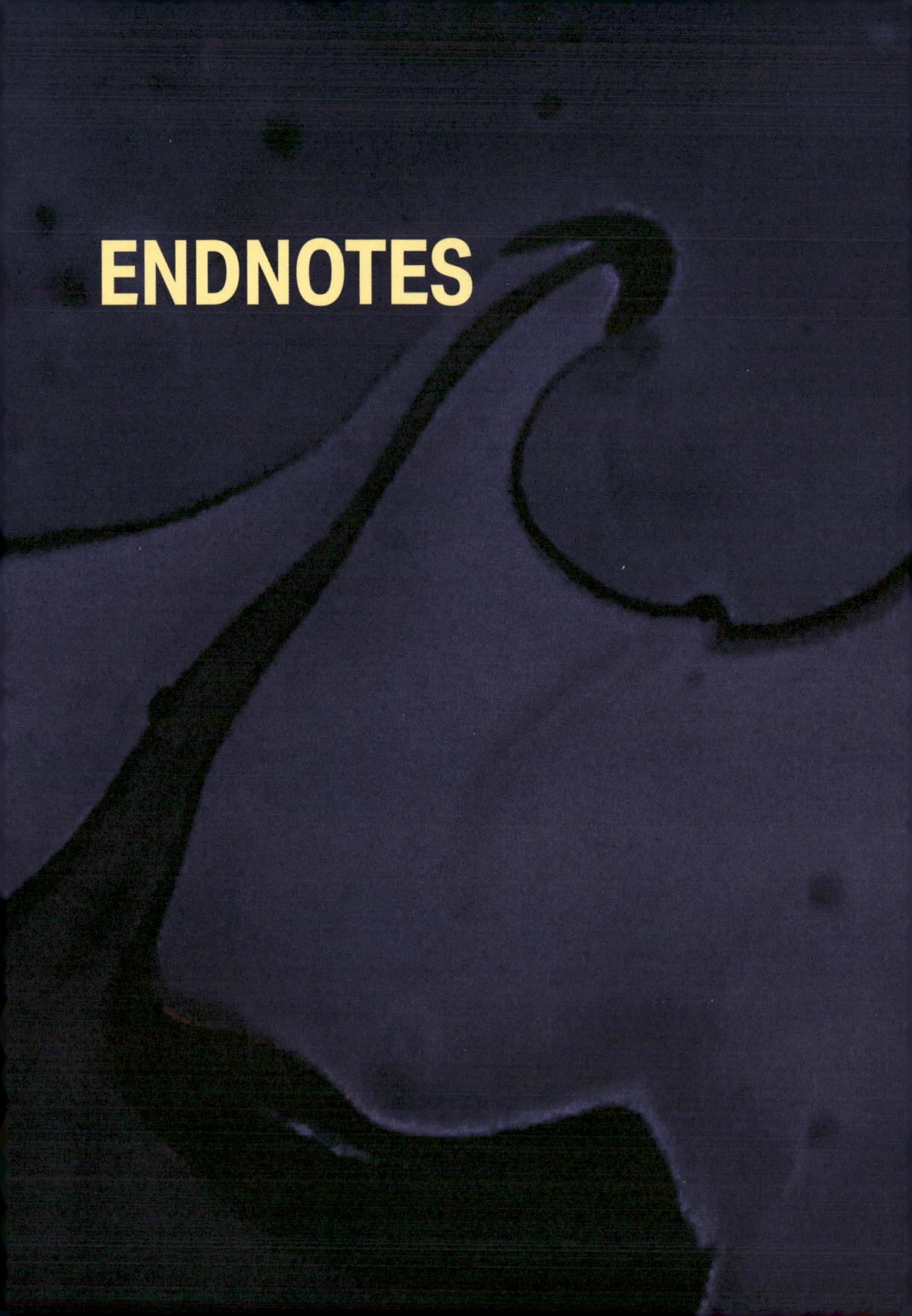

# ENDNOTES

1. Statistics New Zealand. (2014). *Measuring te reo Māori speakers: A guide to different data sources.*
2. New Zealand on Air. (2022). *About/Mō.*
3. Williams, K. (2020, November 29). Our truth, tā mātou pono: Stuff introduces new Treaty of Waitangi based charter following historic apology. *Stuff.*
4. Donnell, H. (2020, July 3). Forcing the issue of race at the Herald. Mediawatch, Radio New Zealand.
5. Turei, L. (2021, June 20). Kāhu, nzherald's home of Māori content, takes flight. *New Zealand Herald.*
6. Deguara, B. (2021, March 12). Complaint about Stuff's use of 'Kia ora, Aotearoa' thrown out by media council. *Stuff.*
7. Johnsen, M. (2021, March 10). BSA to stop hearing complaints about te reo Māori on air. RNZ.
8. O'Connor, M. (2021, September 17). HRC to stop hearing individual complaints on use of te reo Māori. RNZ.
9. Hollings, J., Hanusch, F., Balasubramanian, R., & Lealand, G. (2016). Causes for concern. *Pacific Journalism Review, 22*(2), pp. 122–138.
10. Middleton, A. (2020). 'Kia hiwa rā! The influence of tikanga and the language revitalisation agenda on the practices and perspectives of Māori journalists working in reo-Māori news.' PhD, Auckland University of Technology.
11. Smith, C. (2000). Straying beyond the boundaries of belief: Māori epistemologies inside the curriculum. *Educational Philosophy & Theory, 32*(1), p. 45.
12. Walker, R. (1978). The relevance of Māori myth and tradition. In *Tihe mauri ora: Aspects of Māoritanga.* Methuen, p. 19.
13. Rewi, P. (2010). *Whaikōrero: The world of Māori oratory.* Auckland University Press, p. 9.
14. Stephens, T. (2004). Māori television. In R. Horrocks & N. Perry (Eds.), *Television in New Zealand: Programming the Nation.* Oxford University Press, p. 107.
15. Wiri, R. (2001). 'The prophecies of the great canyon of Toi: A history of Te Whāiti-nui-a-Toi in the western Urewera mountains of New Zealand. PhD thesis, University of Auckland, p. 25.
16. Mead, H. M. (2003). *Tikanga Māori: Living by Māori values.* Huia, p. 12.
17. Durie, M. K. (2012). *Tikanga in changing worlds.* In A. Mikaere & J. Hutchings (Eds), *Kei tua o te pae: Changing worlds, changing tikanga – educating history and the future.* New Zealand Council for Educational Research and Te Wānanga o Raukawa, pp. 77–78.
18. Parr, C. (1963). Māori Literacy 1843–1867. *Journal of the Polynesian Society, 72*(3), pp. 211–234.
19. Biggs, B. (1968). The Maori language past and present. In E. Schwimmer (Ed.), *The Maori people in the nineteen-sixties: A symposium.* Longman Paul.
20. The first English-language newspaper had come out two years earlier. The *New Zealand Gazette*, published from 21 August 1839 to 25 September 1844, was the mouthpiece of the New Zealand Company, a private enterprise that, wrote Michael King in the *Penguin History of New Zealand* (2003), "sought to establish a 'Better Britain' or 'Britain of the South', in which English class distinctions were preserved" (p. 172).
21. McRae, J. (2014). Māori newspapers and magazines – ngā niupepa me ngā moheni. *Te Ara The Encyclopedia of New Zealand.* Manatū Taonga Ministry for Culture and Heritage.

22  Curnow, J. (2002). A brief history of Māori-language newspapers. In J. Curnow, N. Hopa, & J. McRae (Eds.), *Rere atu taku manu: Discovering history, language and politics in the Māori-language newspapers*. Auckland University Press, p. 20.

23  Hocken, T. M. (1909). *A bibliography of the literature relating to New Zealand*. J. Mackay, p. 545.

24  Paterson, L. (2004). 'Nga reo o nga niupepa: Māori language newspapers 1855–1863'. Thesis, University of Otago, p. 20. https://ourarchive.otago.ac.nz/handle/10523/146

25  Paterson, L. (2013). Te Hōkioi and the legitimization of the Māori nation. In B. Hokowhitu & V. Devadas (Eds.), *The fourth eye: Māori media in Aotearoa New Zealand* (pp. 124–142). University of Minnesota Press.

26  McKay, R. A. (1940). *A history of printing in New Zealand, 1830–1940*. R. A. McKay.

27  Ibid., p. 42.

28  Paterson (2013), p. 130.

29  Paterson (2013), p. 134.

30  *The Jubilee Te Tiupiri*. (1898). *1*(1), p. 4. http://www.nzdl.org/cgi-bin/library.cgi?gg=full&e=d-00000-00---off-0niupepa--00-0----0-10-0---0---0direct-10---4-------0-1lpa--11-en-50---20-home-Te+Tiupiri--00-0-1-00-0-0-11-1-0utfZz-8-00&a=d&cl=CL1.29&d=37_1_1.6

31  Translation by Curnow, J., Hopa., N., & McRae, J. (Eds.) (2006). *He pitopito kōrero nō te perehi Māori: Readings from the Māori-language press*. Auckland University Press, p. 19.

32  Paterson, L. (2006). *Colonial discourses: Niupepa Māori, 1855–1863*. University of Otago Press, p. 32.

33  Ibid., p. 35.

34  Ibid., p. 13.

35  Ballara, A. (1993). Story: Niniwa-i-te-rangi. In *Te Ara the Encyclopedia of New Zealand*. Manatū Taonga Ministry for Culture and Heritage.

36  McRae, J. (2002). E manu, tēnā koe! 'O bird, greetings to you': The oral tradition in newspaper writing. In J. Curnow, N. Hopa, & J. McRae (Eds.), *Rere Atu Taku Manu: Discovering History, Language and Politics in the Māori-Language Newspapers* (pp. 42–59). Auckland University Press.

37  Ibid., p. 45.

38  *Te Korimako* 1, Maehe 1882, p. 2. http://www.nzdl.org/cgi-bin/library.cgi?gg=full&e=d-00000-00---off-0niupepa--00-0----0-10-0---0---0direct-10---4-------0-1l--11-mi-50---20-about---00-0-1-00-0-0-11-1-0utfZz-8-00&a=d&cl=CL1.19&d=25_0_1.2

39  Note that the spelling of the name Uetahi is probably an error, as was common in the 1800s when papers were typeset by hand. Reliable sources record "He mahi nā Uetaha, e hokia", or "Uetaha's work will be finished". According to Mead & Grove (2003), Uetaha was a descendant of Porourangi, the eponymous ancestor of Ngāti Porou, and became "the proverbial figure for someone whose work was always completed on time" (p. 93). Mead, H. M., & Grove, N. (2003). *Ngā pēpeha a nga tipuna*. Victoria University Press.

40  This translation is from Curnow et al. (2006), pp. 54–55.

41  Orbell, M. (1985). *The natural world of the Maori*. Collins: David Bateman, pp. 180–181.

42  McRae (2002), p. 49.

43  This translation is from Curnow et al. (2006), p. 193.

44  In Scanlan, C. (2000). Birth of the inverted pyramid: A child of technology, commerce and history. In *Reporting and writing: Basics for the 21st century* (pp. 195–198). Oxford University Press.

45  Ibid.

46  Hastings, D. (2013). *Extra! Extra: How the people made the news*. Auckland University Press, p. 172.

47  McRae (2002), p. 55.

48  Ibid.

49. Ibid., p. 52.
50. In Pool, I. (2015). *Colonization and Development in New Zealand Between 1769 and 1900: The Seeds of Rangiatea*. Springer.
51. Marsden, M. (2003). *The woven universe: Selected writings of Rev. Māori Marsden* (T. A. C. Royal, Ed.). Estate of Rev. Māori Marsden, p. 30.
52. Dale, W. (1931). The Maori language: Its place in native life. In P. M. Jackson (Ed.), *Maori and education: Or the education of natives in New Zealand and its dependencies* (pp. 249–260). Ferguson & Osborn Ltd.
53. Parsonage, W. (1952). Maori language teaching in New Zealand Schools. In M. Black (Ed.), *Report of the seventh science congress, Christchurch, May 15–21, 1951* (pp. 191–197). Royal Society of New Zealand.
54. Waitangi Tribunal. (1986). *Report of the Waitangi Tribunal on the te reo Maori claim (Wai 11)*. Department of Justice.
55. Ibid., p. 10.
56. Derby, M. (2014). Newspapers – first newspapers, 1839–1860. *Te Ara The Encyclopedia of New Zealand*. Manatū Taonga Ministry for Culture and Heritage.
57. Keegan, J. (2000). *The first world war*. Vintage; Lascelles, P. (2014). 'Remembering seafarers: The (missing) history of New Zealanders employed in the mercantile marine during World War I'. Masters thesis, Massey University.
58. Beyond Russia. (2019, August 13). *Debunked: There was no 'wolf truce' between Russia & Germany during WWI*. https://www.rbth.com/history/330804-there-was-no-wolf-truce-russia-germany; Linnell, J., et al. (2002). *The fear of wolves: A review of wolf attacks on humans*. NINA Oppdragsmelding, 731, pp. 1–65.
59. McCallum, J. (2013). Maihi, Rehutai. *Te Ara The Encyclopedia of New Zealand*. Manatū Taonga Ministry for Culture and Heritage.
60. Allen, C. (2002). *Blood narrative: Indigenous identity in American Indian and Māori literary and activist texts*. Duke University Press, p. 40.
61. Sturm, J. (1993, April). Three men and their mags. *Landfall*, *185*, pp. 6–7.
62. Schwimmer, E. (2004). The local and the universal: Reflections on contemporary Maori literature in response to 'Blood Narrative' by Chadwick Allen. *Journal of the Polynesian Society*, *113*(1), p. 14.
63. Ibid., p. 11.
64. Allen (2002).
65. *Te Kaea* 1, December 1979, p. 3.
66. Ibid.
67. *Tu Tangata* 1, August 1981, p. 2. https://paperspast.natlib.govt.nz/periodicals/TUTANG19810801.2.6
68. *Tu Tangata* 9, December 1982, p. 30.
69. *Tu Tangata* 33, December 1986, p. 40.
70. *Tu Tangata* 36, June 1986, p. 2.
71. Stuart, I. (2002). Māori and mainstream: Towards bicultural reporting. *Pacific Journalism Review*, *11*(1), p. 52.
72. Mannion, R. (1993, July 8). Māori newspaper bucks the trend. *The Dominion*, p. 9.
73. Ibid.
74. *Tu Mai magazine goes online*. (2010). [Press release], para. 4.
75. Duncan, S. (2013). Consume or be consumed: Targeting Māori consumers in print media. In B. Hokowhitu & V. Devadas (Eds.), *The fourth eye: Maori media in Aotearoa New Zealand*. University of Minnesota Press, p. 92.
76. Fox, D. (2011, July). The Mana story. *Mana* 100, p. 12.
77. Ibid.
78. *Mana* 1, January/February 1993, p. 1.
79. Heiss, A. (2003). Part five: Maori literature. In *Dhuuluu Yala to talk straight*. Aboriginal Studies Press, p. 207.
80. *More people reading Mana magazine*. (2008, May 28) [Press release], para. 6.
81. *Mana* 13, Winter 1996, p. 1.
82. Fox (2011), p. 13.

83  Melbourne, P. (2014, April 2). Mana magazine takes time out. *Te Karere*. TVNZ.

84  Kōwhai Media relaunches Mana magazine, aims to capture digital eyes (2014, June 17). *StopPress*. http://stoppress.co.nz/news/same-waka-new-crew-mana-magazine-be-re-launched

85  McDonald, D. (2017, July 8). Mana magazine editor lashes out at its publishers after production line stops. *Stuff*.

86  Huria, G. (1995, Autumn). Editorial. *Te Karaka*, 1, p. 4.

87  Kaa, J. (2012). The tribal empire writes back: A review of three iwi periodicals. *Te Pouhere Korero*, p. 107.

88  Tafuna'i, F. (2011). Celebrating 50 issues of *Te Karaka*. *Te Karaka*, winter 2011, p. 11.

89  Smith, J., & Ruckstuhl, K. (2011). The case of *Te Karaka*: Ngāi Tahu print media before and after settlement. *AlterNative*, 6(1), pp. 25–37.

90  In *Te Hookioi magazine* (n.d.). [Video]. Waikato-Tainui. https://vimeo.com/287560291

91  Wong, R. (2020, August 31). Tihei Kahungunu celebrates five years in print and online. *Hawke's Bay Today*, paras. 2–3.

92  Hayden, L. (2017, October 2). Introducing The Spinoff Ātea, an online community for Māori perspectives and insight. *The Spinoff*, para 6.

93  Sullivan, J. (1987). *A history of broadcasting news 1921–1962*. Radio New Zealand Sound Archives, p. 11.

94  Ibid., p. 13.

95  Ibid.

96  Ibid.

97  Ibid., p. 16.

98  Lemke, C. (1995). 'Maori involvement in sound recording and broadcasting 1919 to 1958'. Master's thesis, University of Auckland.

99  Perkins, J. (2000, June 11). Te reo o te tangata whenua: The story of Māori radio (No. 8). In *The story of Radio in New Zealand 1921–1996*. Radio New Zealand.

100  Ibid.

101  Walker, P. (2014). Māori radio reo irirangi. *Te Ara The Encyclopedia of New Zealand*. Manatū Taonga Ministry for Culture and Heritage.

102  Day, P. (1994). *The radio years: A history of broadcasting in New Zealand* (Vol. 1). Auckland University Press in association with the Broadcasting History Trust, p. 124.

103  Hall, J. H. (1980). *The history of broadcasting in New Zealand: 1920–1954*. Broadcasting Corporation of New Zealand, p. 25.

104  Matamua, R. (2014). Te reo pāpāho me te reo Māori – Māori broadcasting and te reo Māori. In R. Higgins, P. Rewi, & V. Olsen-Reader (Eds.), *The value of the Māori language Te hua o te reo Māori* (Vol. 2, pp. 331–348). Huia.

105  See Lemke (1995); Perkins (2000).

106  te Ua, H. (2005). *Hēnare te Ua: In the air*. Reed Books, p. 174.

107  Matamua, R. (2009). Māori radio broadcasting: A brief history. *He Pukenga Kōrero*, 9(1), p. 47.

108  Lemke (1995), p. 127.

109  Lineham, P. (2013). Oriwa Tahupōtiki Haddon. *Te Ara The Encyclopedia of New Zealand*. Manatū Taonga Ministry for Culture and Heritage.

110  In Sullivan (1987).

111  Fowler, L. (1974, September). Lack of war reports gives birth to 'Maori news'. *Marae*, 1(3–4), p. 46.

112  Soutar, M. (2015). Ngā pakanga ki tāwāhi Māori and overseas wars – The 28th (Māori) Battalion. *Te Ara The Encyclopedia of New Zealand*. Manatū Taonga Ministry for Culture and Heritage.

113  te Ua (2005), p. 174.

114  Lemke (1995); Sullivan (1987).

115  Beatson, D. (1996). A genealogy of Māori broadcasting: The development of Māori radio. *Continuum: Journal of Media & Cultural Studies*, 10(1), p. 77.

116  S. Johnston, personal communication, 26 February 2021.

117  Fowler (1974), p. 46.

118  te Ua, quoted in Perkins (2000).
119  Waka for vessel, ruku for dive and moana for sea. It was one of the interpretations Parker was "rather fond of." In Nixon, J. (1986, October 18). Spirit voice. *New Zealand Listener*, p. 44.
120  Fowler (1974), p. 76.
121  In Perkins (2000).
122  Ibid.
123  For an excellent biography of Parker that draws on oral history tapes made just before his death in 1986, see Lemke (1995).
124  Fowler (1974).
125  Lemke (1995).
126  te Ua, H. (2013). Fowler, Percy Leo. *Te Ara The Encyclopedia of New Zealand*. Manatū Taonga Ministry for Culture and Heritage; 'The Māori on Radio' (1965, February 12). *New Zealand Listener*, p. 8.
127  te Ua (2013).
128  Matamua, R. (2006). 'Te reo pāho: Māori radio and language revitalisation'. PhD thesis, Massey University.
129  Day, P. (2000). *Voice and vision: A history of broadcasting in New Zealand* (Vol. 2). Auckland University Press in association with the Broadcasting History Trust.
130  McGill, D. (1964, October 2). Kua ngaro te kōrero. *New Zealand Listener*, p. 11.
131  Matamua (2009).
132  See Beatson (1996); Day (1994); Fox, D. (2002). Honouring the treaty: Indigenous television in Aotearoa. In J. Farnsworth & I. Hutchison (Eds.), *New Zealand television: A reader* (pp. 260–269). Dunmore Press; Mill, A. (2005). The Māori radio industry. In K. Neill & M. Shanahan (Eds.), *The great New Zealand radio experiment*. Thomson Learning and Dunmore Press.
133  Maori radio begins in Auckland. (1988, August). *Te Iwi o Aotearoa*, pp. 14–15.
134  Tamihana, S., & Kipping, P. (1990, October). Breaking sound barriers: Irirangi women. *Broadsheet*, 182, p. 14.

135  Whaanga, P. (1990). Radio: Capable of carrying a bicultural message? In P. Spoonley & W. Hirsh (Eds.), *Between the lines: Racism and the New Zealand media*. Heinemann Reed, p. 67.
136  Waitangi Tribunal. (1999). *The radio spectrum management and development final report* (Wai 776).
137  It has since been replaced by Te Ture mō te Reo Māori 2016 (The Māori Language Act 2016).
138  Benton, R. (2015). Perfecting the partnership: Revitalising the Māori language in New Zealand education and society 1987–2014. *Language, Culture and Curriculum*, 28(2), pp. 99–112.
139  Matamua (2014).
140  Walker, P. (1986, December). Rūnanga radio lures the listeners. *Tu Tangata*, 33, p. 16; Whaanga, P. (1987, June). Real Maori radio takes to the air. *Tu Tangata*, 36, p. 6.
141  Whaanga (1987).
142  Bourke, C. (1990, May 28). The marae of the airwaves. *New Zealand Listener*, 127, p. 88.
143  Radio Ngāti Porou. (2008). *Te reo irirangi o Ngāti Porou: Te reo whakakotahi i te Iwi, 1987–2008: 21 years*. Radio Ngāti Porou.
144  Whaanga, P. (1994). Ngā piki me ngā heke The ups and downs of Maori radio. In P. Ballard (Ed.), *Power and responsibility: Broadcasters striking a balance* (pp. 137–145). Broadcasting Standards Authority.
145  Some iwi have set up commercial stations. There are seven Māori radio stations that receive a free frequency for broadcast as enshrined in legislation, but have commercial aims so are ineligible for TMP funding. They are Sun FM (Whakatāne); Reo FM (Ngāti Raukawa, Ōtaki); Ake Ngāti Whātua 1179AM (Auckland); Sunshine and Tai FM (both in Kaitaia and part of Te Hiku Media, owned by the Far North iwi Ngāti Kuri, Te Aupouri, Ngai Takoto, Te Rārawa and Ngāti Kahu); Heat 99.1FM (Te Arawa, Rotorua); and Ngāti Whakatōhea (Ōpōtiki).

146  Horrocks, R. (2004). The history of New Zealand television: 'An expensive medium for a small country'. In N. Perry & R. Horrocks (Eds.), *Television in New Zealand: Programming the nation* (pp. 20–43). Oxford University Press.

147  Matamua (2009); Pihama, L., & Mika, C. (2013). The Treaty of Waitangi and policy in Māori broadcasting. In V. Tawhai & K. Gray-Sharp (Eds.), *Always speaking: The Treaty of Waitangi and Public Policy*. Huia; Vercoe, M., & Williams, J. (1994, February). Showdown at Downing Street. *Mana*, pp. 50–53.

148  Horrocks (2004); Mill (2005); Waitangi Tribunal (1999).

149  Dunleavy, T. (2008). New Zealand television and the struggle for public service. *Media, Culture & Society*, 30(6), pp. 795–811; Mill (2005).

150  T. Hood, manager, corporate services, Te Māngai Pāho, personal communication, 18 January 2021.

151  National Maori radio service hits the airwaves. (1996, May). *Te Māori*, p. 7; Searancke, R. (1996, February). Shambolic process undermines National Māori Radio Service. *Te Māori News*, p. 5.

152  McGarvey, R. K. (1997, June). Ruia Mai: Te ratonga irirangi o te motu. *Pu Kāea*, p. 5.

153  Sarney, E. (1996, October 16). Static crackles between the Māori broadcasters. *New Zealand Herald*, p. 13.

154  Knight, R. (1997, May 21). Māori language radio news service survives. *New Zealand Herald*, p. 9; Norris, P., & Comrie, M. (2005). Changes in radio news 1994–2004. In K. Neill & M. W. Shanahan (Eds.), *The great New Zealand radio experiment* (pp. 175–194). Thomson Learning and Dunmore Press; Te Māngai Pāho. (1998). Annual report.

155  Campbell, L. (2004, June). Funding cut silences Ruia Mai. *Te Waha Nui*, p. 13.

156  Norris and Comrie (2005).

157  The package included a two-minute, satirical audio cartoon in te reo about current events called Reta ki a Māmā (Letter to Mum) by Waihoroi Shortland and Rereata Mākiha.

158  Wilson, H. (Ed.). (1994). Whakarongo mai e ngā iwi. In *The radio book 1994* (pp. 99–114). New Zealand Broadcasting School.

159  Cited in Watkin, T. (2000, June 3). Mana Maori News – the voice of Maori. *New Zealand Herald*, p. 14.

160  Fox, D. (2011, July). The Mana story. *Mana* 100, p. 12.

161  Knight, R. (1999, July 8). Mud flies over loss of Maori news. *New Zealand Herald*.

162  Drinnan, J. (2011, May 12). 'Pākehā radio' – broadcaster savages RNZ's Māori news cut. *New Zealand Herald*, p. 1.

163  The charter is at https://www.rnz.co.nz/about/charter

164  Rose, J. (2016, February 28). RNZ challenged on level of Māori content. In *Mediawatch*, Radio New Zealand.

165  Boyd-Bell, R. (1985). *New Zealand television: The first 25 years*. R. Methuen, p. 195; Stephens (2004), pp. 107–115.

166  See Fox (2002), pp. 260–269; Reweti, D. (2006). Māori and broadcasting. In M. Mulholland (Ed.), *State of the Māori nation: Twenty-first century issues in Aotearoa*. Reed; Stephens, 2004.

167  Stephens, T. (2014). He kura takitahi he kura takimano. In R. Higgins, P. Rewi, & V. Olsen-Reeder (Eds.), *The value of the Māori language Te hua o te reo Māori*. Huia, p. 372.

168  Barclay, B. (2015). *Our own image: A story of a Māori filmmaker*. University of Minnesota Press, p. 76.

169  Young, D. (1978, July 1). Māori TV: A presence for a people. *New Zealand Listener*, pp. 22–23.

170  Boyd-Bell (1985); Fox (2002).

171  Stephens (2004).

172  Fox (2002), p. 62.

173  Reweti (2006), p. 180.

174  Stephens (2014), pp. 372–375.

175 Fox, D. (1990). *Te Karere* and the struggle for Māori news. In P. Spoonley & W. Hirsh (Eds.), *Between the lines: Racism and the New Zealand media* (pp. 103–107). Heinemann Reed.

176 Charlton, C. (1984, September). *Te Karere* is flying solo. *Tu Tangata*, 19, p. 3.

177 Fox (2002).

178 Whiteside, A. (Director) (2010). Whai Ngata – Māori broadcasting pioneer. NZ On Screen.

179 Boyd-Bell (1985); Fox (1990, 2002); Stephens (2004).

180 Abel, S. (2002). Carol Archie: Reporting as an alternative discourse. In J. Farnsworth & I. Hutchison (Eds.), *New Zealand television: A reader* (pp. 111–118). Dunmore Press; Archie, C. (2007). *Pou kōrero: A journalists' guide to Māori and current affairs*. New Zealand Journalists Training Organisation; Harawira, W. (2008, April 16). *Challenges facing indigenous broadcasters* [speech]. Pacific Media Summit, Apia, Samoa, 16–18 April 2008; Reweti, 2006.

181 Walker, R. (1984, June). Too little, too early. *Metro*, p. 150.

182 Stephens (2014), p. 373.

183 Whiteside (2010).

184 Charlton (1984).

185 Fox (2002); Tahana, Y. (2009). Double jubilee celebrations for Te Karere. *New Zealand Herald*, p. 4. Tahana, Y. (2011, August 2). English subtitles go live on Maori news. *New Zealand Herald*, p. 6.

186 Fox (2002), p. 266.

187 Harawira (2008), p. 2.

188 Hubbard, A. (1996, April 27). Watching your language. *New Zealand Listener*, 153, pp. 32–35; Burns, D. (1997). *Public money, private lives. Aotearoa Television – the inside story*. Reed; Horrocks (2004), pp. 20–43.

189 Stephens (2014), p. 373.

190 More Maori. (1986, November 15). *New Zealand Listener*, pp. 28–29.

191 Curry, J. (Director). (1986, November 10). *Nga take Maori* (No. 1). TVNZ.

192 Cave, S. (1987, November 21). Face to face. *New Zealand Listener*, p. 34. Coddington, D. (2012, February 25). Deborah Coddington: Forthright opinion seems to unsettle the blinkered. *Herald on Sunday*.

193 *More Maori* (1986).

194 Cave (1987).

195 Ibid, para. 5.

196 Braunias, S. (1987, March 28). Titiro, whakarongo, korero. *New Zealand Listener*, 115, pp. 30–31.

197 Pullar-Strecker, T. (2014, December 12). TVNZ details outsourcing of Māori, Pacific shows. *Stuff*.

198 Logan, C. (1990, April 23). Marae mornings. *New Zealand Listener*, 126, p. 62.

199 Drinnan, J. (2014, October 23). TVNZ to outsource most of Maori unit. *New Zealand Herald*.

200 McCurdy, D. (2004, April 4). Now the story really begins for Maori TV. *New Zealand Herald*, para. 12.

201 Wickliffe, T. (2014, October). What's going on in Māori media? *Pīpīwharauroa*, 13, para. 2.

202 Nicol-Reed, M. (2004, May 2). Same country, new perspective. *Sunday Star-Times*, E29, para. 14.

203 Macdonald, J. S. (2008). 'Who talks, what they talk about, and how much they say: A study of bulletin structure and source use in New Zealand free-to-air television news programmes'. Master's thesis, Massey University.

204 *Bringing issues to Te Tepu*. (2010, February 8). [Press release]. Māori Television; *Chris Winitana to host Te Tepu*. (2012, June 12). [Press release]. Māori Television.

205 Kinita, D. (2015, March 31). Whanau to the fore as father and son front new TV show. *New Zealand Herald*.

206 Radio New Zealand. (2018, November 22). Māori TV cuts news and current affairs programmes, paras 5–6.

207  Dansey, H., & Dansey, T. R. D. (2000). Dansey, Harry Delamere Barter. *Te Ara The Encyclopedia of New Zealand*. Manatū Taonga Ministry for Culture and Heritage.

208  The Taranakian, (1987, vol. 76). New Plymouth Boys' High School.

209  Whai Ngata. (n.d.). NZ On Screen.

210  Thomas, R. (2008). 'The making of a journalist: The New Zealand way'. PhD thesis, Auckland University of Technology.

211  Hannis, G. (2017). Journalism education in New Zealand: Its history, current challenges and possible futures. *Asia Pacific Media Educator*, 27(2), pp. 233–248.

212  Hollings, Hanusch, Balasubramanian, & Lealand (2016).

213  Ministry of Education and Ministry of Business, Innovation and Employment. (2014). *Tertiary education strategy 2014–2019*.

214  Hannis (2017).

215  Whelan, B. (2021). 'He whakangungu kairīpoata nō Aotearoa: Journalism education of this place'. PhD thesis, Auckland University of Technology.

216  Boynton, J. (2018, September 11). Is iwi dialect under threat? Radio New Zealand. https://www.radionz.co.nz/news/m%C4%81ori-language-week/366227/is-iwi-dialect-under-threat

217  Statistics New Zealand. (2013). Iwi Individual profile: Tūhoe.

218  Keegan, P. (2017). *Understanding Te Kupenga 2013 data*. http://peterjkeegan.github.io/mstats01.html

219  Whaanga, P. (1987, July). Newspaper surveys show lack of Māori journos. *Tū Tangata*, 35, p. 3.

220  Wilson, G. (2005). Breaking the circuit: A discussion paper about Maori and Pacific Island coverage in the New Zealand news media. Unpublished report for the Journalists Training Board, p. 22.

221  Transfield, S. (1982). Polynesian youth get a taste of the media. *Tu Tangata*, 8, p. 23.

222  Wilson (2005), p. 21.

223  G. Wilson, personal communication, 22 March 2016.

224  P. Whaanga, personal communication, 6 March 2016.

225  Ibid.

226  Rawiri Wright resigns from Waiariki Polytechnic. (1994, December). *Te Maori News*, p. 27.

227  A. Schuler, personal communication, 24 September 2018.

228  Schuler, A. (2003). *The empowering effect of ethics*. Journalism Education Association of New Zealand conference. Western Institute of Technology at Taranaki, 4–5 December 2003, p. 1. http://img1.wsimg.com/blobby/go/82228004-cb16-4269-a778-c4f1ceeb757a/downloads/1cs5513v1_684510.pdf?ver=1635912968544

229  Ibid., p. 3.

230  D. Scadden, personal communication, 26 September 2018.

231  Taylor, J. (2011, July 7). Maori journalism progress hindered by skills shortage. *Daily Post*.

232  Two other polytechnic-based journalism schools also closed at this time, victims of falling enrolments and the vulnerability occasioned by their small size: the Western Institute of Technology in New Plymouth in 2014 and Southland Institute of Technology in 2015 (Hannis, 2017).

233  Ikin, K. (2018, December 7). Address to national Māori journalism hui, Massey University, Auckland.

234  A. Schuler, personal communciation, 24 September 2018.

235  Johns, R. (2013, March 11). Waiariki Māori journalism course lacking numbers. *Te Karere*.

236  Mead, A. (1994). Maori leadership. *Te Pua*, 3(11), pp. 11–20.

237  Ibid., p. 12.

238  Tait, M. (24 July 2014). Sibling rivalry in news. *New Zealand Herald*. https://www.nzherald.co.nz/nz/news/article.cfm?c_id=1&objectid=11298722

## ENDNOTES

239 Ibid., paras 8–9.

240 Winder-Murray, H. (2018, December 4). *Iwi radio to television*. Te Hiku Media.

241 McGarvey, R. K. (1997, June). Ruia Mai: Te Ratonga Irirangi o te Motu. *Pu Kāea*, p. 5.

242 Rakuraku, M. (2009, February 22). Te Ahi Kaa. Radio New Zealand; Taumata, A. (2018, November 11). Māori media: Work hard, but fight hard too. *E-Tangata*.

243 Myllylahti, M., & Hope, W. (Eds). (2020). *New Zealand media ownership 2020*. Journalism Media and Democracy research centre, AUT.

244 New Zealand On Air. (2021, April 22). *NZ On Air appoints head of journalism*. [Press release].

245 New Zealand On Air. (2021, July 14). *Significant funding injection to boost Māori journalism*. [Press release].

246 Day, P. (1990). *The making of the New Zealand press: A study of the organizational and political concerns of New Zealand newspaper controllers, 1840–1880*. Victoria University Press; Hollings, Hanusch, Balasubramanian, & Lealand (2016).

247 Fox, D. (1992). The Māori perspective of the news. In M. Comrie & J. McGregor (Eds.), *Whose News?* (pp. 170–180) Dunmore Press.

248 Deverson, T., & Kennedy, G. (Eds.). (2005). *New Zealand Oxford Dictionary*. Oxford University Press, p. 45.

249 Holmes, J. (2003). Narrative structure: Some contrasts. In C. B. Paulston & G. R. Tucker (Eds.), *Sociolinguistics: The essential readings* (1st ed.). Blackwell, p. 133.

250 Adds, P., Bennett, M., Hall, M., Kernot, B., Russell, M., & Walker, T. (2005). *The portrayal of Māori and te ao Māori in broadcasting: The foreshore and seabed issue*. Broadcasting Standards Authority, p. 21.

251 Bell, A. (1991). *The language of news media*. Blackwell; Hall, S. (1981). The determination of news photographs. In J. Tunstall (Ed.), *The manufacture of news: Social problems, deviance and the mass media* (Revised fourth edition, pp. 226–243). Constable; Hall, S., Critcher, C., Jefferson, T., Clarke, J., & Roberts, B. (1978). *Policing the crisis: Mugging, the state, and law and order*. Macmillan; Schudson, M. (2011). *The sociology of news* (2nd ed.). WW Norton & Co.

252 Tremewan, P. (1986, December). Objectivity or Pakeha bias? *Tu Tangata*, 33, p. 42.

253 Gravengaard, G., & Rimestad, L. (2012). Elimination of ideas and professional socialisation. *Journalism Practice*, 6(4), pp. 465–481; Gravengaard, G., & Rimestad, L. (2014). Socializing journalist trainees in the newsroom: On how to capture the intangible parts of the process. *Nordicom Review*, 35, pp. 81–95; McGregor, J. (1991). *News values and the reporting of Māori news* [Working paper]. Department of Human Resource Management, Faculty of Business Studies, Massey University; McGregor, J. (2002, July 10). Restating news values: Contemporary criteria for selecting the news. Australian & New Zealand Communication Association Conference, Gold Coast, Queensland; Thomas (2008).

254 Galtung, J., & Ruge, M. H. (1965). The Structure of foreign news. *Journal of Peace Research*, 2(1), pp. 64–91; Harcup, T., & O'Neill, D. (2016). What is news? News values revisited (again). *Journalism Studies*, 18(12), pp. 1470–1488; McGregor (2002).

255 Bell (1991).

256 The story is at https://www.youtube.com/watch?v=uDfYVpa5xFY&t=3s

257 Scott, J. (2014). Radio journalism. In G. Hannis (Ed.), *Intro: A beginner's guide to journalism in 21st-century Aotearoa/New Zealand* (1st ed, pp. 253–267). New Zealand Journalists Training Organisation.

258 Broadcasting Standards Authority. (2006). *Significant viewpoints: Broadcasters discuss balance*; Comrie, M. (2012). Double vision: Election news coverage on mainstream and indigenous television in New Zealand. *The International Journal of Press/Politics*, 17(3), pp. 275–293; Macdonald (2008).

259 Archie (2007).

260 The story is at https://www.rnz.co.nz/news/te-manu-korihi/318982/govt-sorry-for-taking-iwi%27s-land

261 The first settlement under the Waitangi Tribunal process was made in 1989 in respect of Waitomo Caves. As of January 2021, a total of ninety-one deeds of settlement have been signed between the Crown and claimant groups, to a total value of approximately $2.2 billion.

262 Bellett, D. (1995). Hakas, hangis, and kiwis: Māori lexical influence on New Zealand English. *Te Reo*, 38, pp. 73–103; Macalister, J. (2006). The Maori presence in the New Zealand English lexicon, 1850–2000: Evidence from a corpus-based study. *English World-Wide*, 27(1), pp. 1–24.

263 Benton (2015); Crewsden, P. (2017, September 1). Why Stuff is introducing macrons for te reo Māori words. stuff.co.nz

264 de Bres, J. (2009). The behaviours of non-Maori New Zealanders towards the Maori language. *Te Reo*, 52, pp. 17–45; Kennedy, G., & Yamazaki, S. (2000). The influence of Māori on the New Zealand English lexicon. In *Corpora galore: Analyses and techniques in describing English: Papers from the nineteenth international conference on English language research on computerised corpora* (ICAME 1998). Rodopi, pp. 33–44.

265 Macalister (2006); Macalister, J. (2008). Tracking changes in familiarity with borrowings from te reo Maori. *Te Reo*, 51, p. 75.

266 Middleton, A. (2022). Tūtira mai! Reporting a Tiriti o Waitangi settlement ceremony for public radio through a Māori lens. *Te Kaharoa*, 15(1), p. 35. https://doi.org/10.24135/tekaharoa.v15i1.395

267 Ibid.

268 Taaonga Tuku Iho. (2018). *Te Hookioi*, 67, pp. 31–32.

269 Middleton (2022), p. 35.

270 Middleton (2020), p. 232.

271 Higgins, R., & Rewi, P. (2014). ZePA: Right-shifting: Reorientation towards normalisation. In R. Higgins, P. Rewi, & V. Olsen-Reeder (Eds.), *The value of the Māori language Te hua o te reo Māori* (vol. 2, pp. 7–32). Huia.

272 Rewi, T., & Rewi, P. (2015). The ZePA model of Māori language revitalization: Key considerations for empowering indigenous language educators, students, and communities. In J. Reyhner, L. Martin, L. Lockard, & W. Gilbert (Eds.), *Honoring our elders* (pp. 136–153). Northern Arizona University; Te Māngai Pāho. (2018). *Annual report 2017/2018*.

273 Smith, L., & Piripi, H. (2012). *Ngā whetū kapokapo Māori language evaluation framework*. Te Māngai Pāho, p. 16.

274 Middleton (2020), p. 232.

275 Statistics New Zealand. (2014). *Measuring te reo Māori speakers: A guide to different data sources*, p. 8.

276 T. Hood, TMP corporate services manager, personal communication, 19 June 2019.

277 Higgins & Rewi (2014), p. 26.

278 Middleton (2020), p. 234.

279 Ibid.

280 Ibid., p. 235.

281 Ibid.

282 Ibid.

283 Ibid.

284 Ibid., p. 236.

285 Ibid., p. 241.

286 Ibid., p. 242.

287 Ibid.

288 Ibid.

289 Ibid.

290 Te Huia, A. (2013). 'Whāia te iti kahurangi, ki te tuohu koe me he maunga teitei: Establishing psychological foundations for higher levels of Māori language proficiency'. PhD thesis, Victoria University of Wellington. 2015.

291 See Hura, N. A. (2015, September 19). Ending the shame of not speaking the reo. *E-Tangata*; Hura, N. A. (2017, April 23). How one approach to learning Māori

conquers the shame factor. *The Spinoff*; Walker, F. (2017, September 14). Learning te reo: My pathway out of shame. *Stuff*.

292  Chrisp, S. (2005). Māori intergenerational language transmission. *International Journal of the Sociology of Language*, 172, pp. 149–181. Cowell, J. T. H. (2017). Tūwhitia te hopo, Mairangatia te angitū. *Te Kaharoa*, 10(1); Metge, J. (1986). *In and out of touch: Whakamaa in cross-cultural context*. Victoria University Press.

293  Middleton (2020), p. 243.

294  Ibid.

295  Ibid., p. 244.

296  Ibid.

297  Ibid.

298  Ibid.

299  Ibid., p. 245.

300  Ibid.

301  Ibid., p. 246.

302  Ibid., p. 234.

303  Ibid., p. 246.

304  Fishman, J. (1991). *Reversing language shift: Theoretical and empirical foundations of assistance to threatened languages*. Multilingual Matters.

305  Te Māngai Pāho. (n.d.). Why we are here. tmp.govt.nz

306  McAnulty, B., Francis, B., & Price, S. (2014). *TVNZ report into alleged misconduct within Māori and Pacific programmes department*. Television New Zealand, p. 9.

307  Fong, S. H. (2014, May 1). Q+A with Te Haumihiata Mason of Te Taura Whiri i te Reo Māori. *Te Kāea*. www.maoritelevision.com

308  Ihaka, J. (2014, May 1). Call for simpler te reo on TV. *New Zealand Herald*. www.nzherald.co.nz; Winitana, C. (2011). *My language, my Inspiration*. Huia Publishers and Te Taura Whiri i te Reo Māori.

309  Temara, P. (2016, March 9). Growing leaders in Te Panekiretanga. [Speech]. Mana Tāne Ora conference, Blenheim, 9–11 March 2016.

310  Matamua, R., & Temara, P. (2010). Te reo Māori in 2020. In P. Papa & L. Blake (Eds.), *He pī ka rere: Te tauira 1* (pp. 39–45). Te Wānanga o Aotearoa, p. 41.

311  Stephens, T., Edwards, H., & Hūria, J. (2009). Te Kāhui o Māhutonga: Review of the Māori Television Service Act 2003. Te Puni Kōkiri, pp. 13–14.

312  The standards are defined in Smith & Piripi (2012).

313  Middleton (2020), p. 270.

314  Ibid., p. 271.

315  Dragonfly Data Science: Kōkako for language monitoring. (2015, September 4). www.dragonfly.co.nz; Harawira, W. (2016, September 13). *Māori computations. Native Affairs*. Māori Television Service.

316  Middleton (2020), pp. 268–9.

317  Ibid., p. 241.

318  Unless cited, sources in this chapter come from the broadcasts under discussion and from personal communications.

319  Barlow, C. (1991). *Tikanga whakaaro: Key concepts in Māori culture*. Oxford University Press; Mahuta, R. T. (1974). 'Whaikoorero: A study of formal Māori speech'. Master's thesis, University of Auckland; Rewi (2010).

320  Williams, H. W. (1971). *A dictionary of the Māori language* (7th ed.). Legislation Direct.

321  Hīroa, T. R. (1949). *The coming of the Maori*. Māori Purposes Fund Board, p. 389.

322  Rewi (2010), p. 152.

323  Middleton (2020), p. 113.

324  According to Deverson & Kennedy (2005).

325  Shirres, M. P. (1997). *Te tangata: The human person*. Accent Publications, p. 66.

326  Rewi (2010), p. 144.

327  Metge, J., and Jones, S. (1995). He taonga tuku ihō no ngā tūpuna: Māori proverbial sayings – a literary treasure. *The Journal of New Zealand Studies*, 5(2).

328  Statistics New Zealand. (2014).

329 Brooke-White, V. (Ed.). (1981). *Whaikoorero: Ceremonial farewells to the dead*. Continuing Education Unit, Radio New Zealand, pp. 21–22.

330 Metge & Jones (1995), p. 3.

331 McRae, J. (2017). *Māori oral tradition: He kōrero nō te ao tawhito*. Auckland University Press, p. 66.

332 Metge & Jones (1995), p. 5.

333 Ibid.

334 In Mead & Grove (2003), p. 292.

335 Parker, B. (1966, March). Nga whakatauki: Maori proverbs and sayings. *Te Ao Hou*, 54.

336 Metge & Jones (1995), p. 6.

337 In Mead & Grove (2003), p. 169.

338 Durie (2012), p. 78.

339 Shirres (1997), p. 90.

340 Durie, M. K. (2011). 'He kawa oranga: Māori achievement in the 21st century'. PhD thesis, Massey University, p. 78.

341 Quoted in Durie (2011), pp. 110–111.

342 Quoted in Durie (2011), p. 111.

343 Mead, H. (2012). Understanding mātauranga Māori. In *Conversations on Mātauranga Māori*. New Zealand Qualifications Authority, p. 12.

344 Durie (2011), pp. 114–115.

345 Quoted in Durie (2011), p. 129.

346 Durie (2012), p. 80.

347 Durie (2012), p. 85.

348 For insight into how this karakia has been understood by various iwi, see Orbell, M., and McLean, M. (2002). *Songs of a kaumatua*. Auckland University Press, pp. 49–51.

349 Unless cited, sources in this chapter come from personal communications.

350 Peters, R. J. (2000). 'Tika, pono and aroha in three novels by Patricia Grace'. Masters thesis, Massey University, p. 1.

351 Tate, H. (2010). 'Towards some foundations of a systematic Māori theology'. PhD thesis, Melbourne College of Divinity, p. 113.

352 For example, newspaper *Te Waka Maori O Ahuriri* (1863–71) bore the motto "Ko te Tika, ko te Pono, ko te Aroha". The well-known song written by Henare Te Owai of Ngāti Porou in 1933 contains this verse: Mā wai rā e taurima te marae i waho nei?/Who will attend to the marae outside?/Mā te tika, mā te pono me te aroha e/ Tika, pono and aroha will be the attendants. Also see Peters (2000).

353 Mead (2003), p. 368.

354 Williams, H. W. (1971). *A Dictionary of the Māori Language* (7th ed.). Legislation Direct.

355 Tate (2010), p. 127.

356 Beazley, M. (2017, June 1). A role for everyone. *Tui Motu InterIslands Magazine*, pp. 6–7.

357 Ibid.

358 Mead (2003).

359 Beazley (2017).

360 Duncan, S., & Rewi, P. (2018a). Ritual today: Pōwhiri. In M. P. J. Reilly, G. Leoni, L. Carter, S. Duncan, L. Paterson, M. T. Ratima, & P. Rewi (Eds.), *Te Kōparapara: An introduction to the Māori world* (pp. 121–136). Auckland University Press; Mead (2003); Tauroa, H., & Tauroa, P. (2009). *Te marae: A guide to customs & protoco*. Raupo.

361 The story is at https://www.teaomaori.news/kiwis-coach-mourns-grandmothers-passing

362 Ka'ai, T., & Higgins, R. (2004). Te ao Māori: Māori world-view. In T. Ka'ai, J. Moorfield, M. Reilly, & S. Mosley (Eds.), *Ki te whaiao*. Pearson Education New Zealand, p. 18.

363 *A question of trust*, part 1. https://www.maoritelevision.com/news/national/native-affairs-question-trust-part-1; *A question of trust*, part 2. https://www.maoritelevision.com/news/education/native-affairs-question-trust-part-2; *Feathering the nest*, part 1. https://www.maoritelevision.com/news/national/native-affairs-feathering-nest-part-1; *Feathering the nest*, part 2. https://www.maoritelevision.com/news/national/native-affairs-feathering-nest-part-2

364 Potaka, B. (2014). Te Pataka Ohanga Limited: Charities Services investigation report. Department of Internal Affairs.

365 Forbes, M. (2015, August 31). Minister sidelines Kohanga Reo board. Checkpoint, Radio New Zealand; Small, V., Kirk, S., & Watkins, T. (2013, October 15). Parata calls meeting over accusations. *Stuff.*

366 Steward, I. (2013, October 13). Fur flies when Māori TV takes on Te Kohanga Reo. *Sunday Star-Times*, p. 6.

367 Broadcasting Standards Authority. (2014). BSA declines to uphold Kōhanga Reo Trust's complaint (adjudication No. 2013–071).

368 Drinnan, J. (2013, October 25). Māori TV probe labelled too pushy. *New Zealand Herald*, C6.

369 Wichtel, D. (2014, March 8). Standing her ground. *New Zealand Listener*, p. 32.

370 Armstrong, D. (2015, June 29). It's not Māori TV's job to be respectful. stuff.co.nz, para. 5.

371 Drinnan, J. (2014, November 7). John Drinnan: Changes ahead for Maori TV. *New Zealand Herald*, C9. 5

372 Ikin, K. (2018, December 7). Speech. National Māori Journalism Hui, Massey University, Auckland.

373 Forbes, M. (2016). Navigating the waters of Māori broadcasting. In E. Johnson, G. Tiso, S. Illingworth, & B. Bennett (Eds.), *Don't dream it's over: Reimagining journalism in Aotearoa New Zealand* (pp. 91–104). Freerange Press.

374 Drinnan, J. (2015, June 26). Radio NZ seeks cure to ratings malaise. *New Zealand Herald*, para. 33.

375 Grant, N. (2015, June 4). Forbes quits Maori TV's Native Affairs. *National Business Review*; McAllen, J. (2015). Mihingarangi Forbes back in control. *Sunday Star Times.*

376 Archie (2007); Forbes (2016); Hanusch, F. (2014). Dimensions of Indigenous journalism culture: Exploring Māori news-making in Aotearoa New Zealand. *Journalism, 15*(8), pp. 951–967.

377 Broadcasting Standards Authority. (2006). *Significant viewpoints: Broadcasters discuss balance.* Broadcasting Standards Authority, p. 65.

378 Markelin, L. (2017). Indigenous voices in the global public sphere: Analysis of approaches to journalism within the WITBN network. *Journal of Applied Journalism & Media Studies, 6*(3), pp. 443–461. https://doi.org/10.1386/ajms.6.3.443_1

379 Turei, M. (2013, October 30). Metiria Turei: Our own will rightly hold us to account. *The Ruminator*, para. 7.

380 Evans, R. (1994). The negation of powerlessness: Maori feminism, a perspective. *Hecate, 20*(2), p. 6.

381 See the discussion in Kāretu, T., & Milroy, W. (2018). *He kupu tuku iho: Ko te reo Māori te tatau ki te ao.* Auckland University Press.

382 Festinger, L. (1957). *A theory of cognitive dissonance.* Tavistock.

383 Ibid., p. 3.

384 Ibid., p. 13.

385 Ibid., p. 271.

386 Rewi (2010), pp. 70, 105.

387 Marsden (2003), p. 6.

388 Manihera, T. U., & Pēwhairangi, N. (1992). Learning and tapu. In M. King (Ed.), *Te ao hurihuri: Aspects of Māoritanga* (pp. 9–14). Reed Books.

389 Duncan, S., & Rewi, P. (2018b). Tikanga: How not to get told off! In M. Reilly, S. Duncan, G. Leoni, L. Paterson, L. Carter, M. Rātima, & P. Rewi, Eds.), *Te kōparapara: An introduction to the Māori world* (pp. 30–47). Auckland University Press; Tauroa & Tauroa (2009).

390 Mead (2003).

391 Mead (2003); Tauroa & Tauroa (2009).

392 Marsden (2003); Maxwell, K. H., & Penetito, W. (2007). How the use of rāhui for protecting taonga has evolved over time. *MAI Review, 2007*(2), p. 15; Mead (2003).

393 Duncan & Rewi (2018a).

394 Tauroa & Tauroa (2009), p. 151.

395 August, W. T. (2004). 'The Māori female: Her body, spirituality, sacredness and mana. A space within spaces'. Masters thesis, Waikato University; Mead (2003).

396 Hooker, M. (2008). *Makawe: Gaining an understanding of the tikanga for hair.* M & J Hooker.

397 Duncan & Rewi (2018a), p. 124.

398 Tauroa & Tauroa (2009).

399 Mead (2003).

400 NZ On Screen. (n.d.). Tangi for Te Arikinui Dame Te Atairangikaahu. https://www.nzonscreen.com

401 Newshub. (2013, February 5). Army drafted in to feed mourners at Horomia's tangi. Radio New Zealand. (2013, May 13). Thousands tuned into webcast of Horomia's tangi.

402 Karetū, T. (2010). Te whaikōrero. In *Te Pīnakitanga ki te Reo Kairangi: Whaikōrero* (pp. 6–7). Te Wānanga o Aotearoa; Kelly, J. (2015). 'Ngā tikanga o te uhunga i Te Nehenehenui'. Masters thesis, Auckland University of Technology; Rewi, P. (2005). 'Te ao o te whaikorero'. PhD thesis, University of Otago.

403 *Te Karere*. (2013, May 2). Parekura Horomia's brother talks about upbringing. TVNZ. https://www.youtube.com/watch?v=I8e-leWDRfI

404 Māori Television. (2015, May 8). Ka mihi atu te whānau o Erima Henare ki te motu mō te āwhina i a rātou. https://www.teaomaori.news/mi/ka-mihi-atu-te-whanau-o-erima-henare-ki-te-motu-mo-te-awhina-i-ratou

405 Turei (2013, October 30), para. 4.

406 Forbes, M. (2016, July 7). Māori TV kaumatua feels left out in the cold. Radio New Zealand.

407 Melbourne, P. (2016, June 20). Outrage at shower curtains depicting Māori ancestors for sale. *Te Karere*.

408 Melbourne, P. (2016, June 21). Māori man reacts to his face on shower curtain for sale. *Te Karere*.

409 Arthur-Worsop, S., & Miller, C. (2016, July 21). Birkenhead beer brewery threatened over image use of Maori legend of Hinemoa and Tutanekai. *New Zealand Herald*; Kenny, K. (2014, September 26). Storm over fashion magazine moko. stuff.co.nz; Stokes, J. (2006, April 28). Tobacco giant apologises to Maori. *New Zealand Herald*; Young, M. (2018). Tā Moko and the cultural politics of appropriation. *Sites: A Journal of Social Anthropology and Cultural Studies, 15*(2).

410 Cook, M. (2013, September 5). Māori smoking, alcohol and drugs – tūpeka, waipiro me te tarukino. *Te Ara The Encyclopedia of New Zealand*. Manatū Taonga Ministry for Culture and Heritage.

411 McNeill, D. (2009). Gesture and communication. In K. Brown & J. Mey (Eds.), *Encyclopedia of Language & Linguistics* (2nd ed., pp. 299–320). Elsevier.

412 Müller, C., Bressem, J., & Ladewig, S. (2013). Towards a grammar of gestures: A form-based view. In C. Müller, A. Cienki, E. Fricke, S. Ladewig, D. McNeill, & S. Tessendorf (Eds.), *Body language communication: An international handbook on multimodality in human interaction* (Vol. 1, pp. 7607–7733). De Gruyter Mouton.

413 Mead (2003); Sullivan, C. L. T. (2012). 'Te okiokinga mutunga kore – The eternal rest: Investigating Māori attitudes towards death'. MA thesis, University of Otago.

414 Jeffrey, D. L. (1992). Ashes to ashes. In *A dictionary of biblical tradition in English literature* (1st ed.). Wm. B. Eerdmans Publishing, p. 60; Kitchin, G. (1967). *A survey of burlesque and parody in English*. Russell & Russell.

415 Mahuta, N. (2018). Future focussed review of Māori media sector. [Press release]. http://www.beehive.govt.nz/release/future-focussed-review-m%C4%81ori-media-sector

416 Mahuta, N. (2019). Te ao pāpāho ki tua Māori media sector shift – An overview of the current state of the sector as of March 29, 2019. [Report]. https://www.tpk.govt.nz/en/a-matou-kaupapa/maori-media

417 Middleton, A. (2019, February 17). Māori media revamp: Where's the focus on quality journalism? *E-Tangata*. https://e-tangata.co.nz/reo/maori-media-revamp-wheres-the-focus-on-quality-journalism/; Te Puni Kōkiri (2020). Te ao pāpāho Māori/Māori media sector: He ara hou/shift options. (2020). https://www.tpk.govt.nz/en/a-matou-kaupapa/maori-media

418 Forbes, M. (2020, June 18). Mihi Forbes: This will silence Māori media voices. *The Spinoff*. https://thespinoff.co.nz/atea/18-06-2020/mihi-forbes-this-will-silence-maori-media-voices/; McLachlan, L.-M. (2020, June 12). Fears the future of *Te Karere* Māori news is on the line. Radio New Zealand. https://www.rnz.co.nz/news/te-manu-korihi/418900/fears-the-future-of-te-karere-maori-news-is-on-the-line

419 Jackson, W. (2020, November 25). Expert independent advisory group appointed to strengthen the future of Māori broadcasting. The Beehive. http://www.beehive.govt.nz/release/expert-independent-advisory-group-appointed-strengthen-future-m%C4%81ori-broadcasting

420 Jennings, M. (2021, June 8). Māori media in for a big shake-up, para 31. Newsroom. https://www.newsroom.co.nz/page/mori-media-in-for-a-big-shake-up

421 Ibid., para 24.

# BIBLIOGRAPHY

## PUBLISHED BOOKS AND JOURNAL ARTICLES

ABEL, S. (2002). Carol Archie: Reporting as an alternative discourse. In J. Farnsworth & I. Hutchison (Eds.), *New Zealand television: A reader* (pp. 111–118). Dunmore Press.

ADDS, P., BENNETT, M., HALL, M., KERNOT, B., RUSSELL, M., & WALKER, T. (2005). *The portrayal of Māori and te ao Māori in broadcasting: The foreshore and seabed issue.* Broadcasting Standards Authority.

ALLEN, C. (2002). *Blood narrative: Indigenous identity in American Indian and Māori literary and activist texts.* Duke University Press.

ANDERSON, A., BINNEY, J., & HARRIS, A. (2014). *Tangata Whenua: An illustrated history.* Bridget Williams Books.

ARCHIE, C. (2007). *Pou kōrero: A journalists' guide to Māori and current affairs.* New Zealand Journalists Training Organisation.

BARCLAY, B. (2015). *Our own image. A story of a Māori filmmaker.* University of Minnesota Press, p. 76.

BARLOW, C. (1991). *Tikanga whakaaro: Key concepts in Māori culture.* Oxford University Press.

BEATSON, D. (1996). A genealogy of Māori broadcasting: The development of Māori radio. *Continuum: Journal of Media & Cultural Studies, 10*(1), p. 77.

BEAZLEY, M. (2017, June 1). A role for everyone. *Tui Motu InterIslands Magazine*, pp. 6–7.

BELL, A. (1991). *The language of news media.* Blackwell.

BELLETT, D. (1995). Hakas, hangis, and kiwis: Māori lexical influence on New Zealand English. *Te Reo,* 38, pp. 73–103.

BENTON, R. (2015). Perfecting the partnership: Revitalising the Māori language in New Zealand education and society 1987–2014. *Language, Culture and Curriculum, 28*(2), pp. 99–112.

BIGGS, B. (1968). The Maori language past and present. In E. Schwimmer (Ed.), *The Maori people in the nineteen-sixties: A symposium* (pp. 65–84). Longman Paul.

BOYD-BELL, R. (1985). *New Zealand television: The first 25 years.* R. Methuen.

BROADCASTING STANDARDS AUTHORITY. (2006). *Significant viewpoints: Broadcasters discuss balance*. bsa.govt.nz

BROOKE-WHITE, V. (Ed.). (1981). *Whaikoorero: Ceremonial farewells to the dead*. Continuing Education Unit, Radio New Zealand.

BURNS, D. (1997). *Public money, private lives. Aotearoa Television – the inside story*. Reed.

CHRISP, S. (2005). Māori intergenerational language transmission. *International Journal of the Sociology of Language*, 172, pp. 149–181.

COMRIE, M. (2012). Double vision: Election news coverage on mainstream and indigenous television in New Zealand. *The International Journal of Press/Politics*, 17(3), pp. 275–293.

COWELL, J. T. H. (2017). Tūwhitia te hopo, Mairangatia te angitū. *Te Kaharoa*, 10(1), pp. 17–41.

CURNOW, J. (2002). A brief history of Māori-language newspapers. In J. Curnow, N. Hopa, & J. McRae (Eds.), *Rere atu taku manu: Discovering history, language and politics in the Māori-language newspapers* (p. 20). Auckland University Press.

CURNOW, J., HOPA, N., & MCRAE, J. (Eds.) (2006). *He pitopito kōrero nō te perehi Māori: Readings from the Māori-language press*. Auckland University Press.

DALE, W. (1931). The Maori language: Its place in native life. In P. M. Jackson (Ed.), *Maori and education: Or the education of natives in New Zealand and its dependencies* (pp. 249–260). Ferguson & Osborn Ltd.

DAY, P. (1990). *The making of the New Zealand press: A study of the organizational and political concerns of New Zealand newspaper controllers, 1840–1880*. Victoria University Press.

DAY, P. (1994). *The radio years: A history of broadcasting in New Zealand* (Vol. 1). Auckland University Press in association with the Broadcasting History Trust.

DAY, P. (2000). *Voice and vision: A history of broadcasting in New Zealand* (Vol. 2). Auckland University Press in association with the Broadcasting History Trust.

DE BRES, J. (2009). The behaviours of non-Maori New Zealanders towards the Maori language. *Te Reo*, 52, pp. 17–45.

DEVERSON, T., & KENNEDY, G. (EDS.). (2005). *New Zealand Oxford Dictionary*. Oxford University Press.

DUNCAN, S. (2013). Consume or be consumed: Targeting Māori consumers in print media. In B. Hokowhitu & V. Devadas (Eds.), *The fourth eye: Maori media in Aotearoa New Zealand* (pp. 76–97). University of Minnesota Press.

DUNCAN, S., & REWI, P. (2018a). Ritual today: Pōwhiri. In M. P. J. Reilly, G. Leoni, L. Carter, S. Duncan, L. Paterson, M. T. Ratima, & P. Rewi (Eds.), *Te kōparapara: An introduction to the Māori world* (pp. 121–136). Auckland University Press.

DUNCAN, S., & REWI, P. (2018b). Tikanga: How not to get told off! In M. P. J. Reilly, G. Leoni, L. Carter, S. Duncan, L. Paterson, M. T. Ratima, & P. Rewi (Eds.), *Te kōparapara: An introduction to the Māori world* (pp. 30–47). Auckland University Press.

DUNLEAVY, T. (2008). New Zealand television and the struggle for public service. *Media, Culture & Society, 30*(6), pp. 795–811.

DURIE, M. K. (2012). Tikanga in changing worlds. In A. Mikaere & J. Hutchings (Eds.), *Kei tua o te pae: Changing worlds, changing tikanga – educating history and the future* (pp. 77–86). New Zealand Council for Educational Research and Te Wānanga o Raukawa.

EVANS, R. (1994). The negation of powerlessness: Maori feminism, a perspective. *Hecate, 20*(2), p. 6.

FESTINGER, L. (1957). *A theory of cognitive dissonance*. Tavistock.

FISHMAN, J. (1991). *Reversing language shift: Theoretical and empirical foundations of assistance to threatened languages*. Multilingual Matters.

FORBES, M. (2016). Navigating the waters of Māori broadcasting. In E. Johnson, G. Tiso, S. Illingworth, & B. Bennett (Eds.), *Don't dream it's over: Reimagining journalism in Aotearoa New Zealand* (pp. 91–104). Freerange Press.

FOX, D. (1990). Te Karere and the struggle for Māori news. In P. Spoonley & W. Hirsh (Eds.), *Between the lines: Racism and the New Zealand media* (pp. 103–107). Heinemann Reed.

FOX, D. (1992). The Māori perspective of the news. In M. Comrie and J. McGregor (Eds.), *Whose News?* (pp. 170–180). Dunmore Press.

FOX, D. (2002). Honouring the Treaty: Indigenous television in Aotearoa. In J. Farnsworth & I. Hutchison (Eds.), *New Zealand television: A reader* (pp. 260–269). Dunmore Press.

GALTUNG, J., & RUGE, M. H. (1965). The structure of foreign news. *Journal of Peace Research, 2*(1), pp. 64–91.

GRAVENGAARD, G., & RIMESTAD, L. (2012). Elimination of ideas and professional socialisation. *Journalism Practice, 6*(4), pp. 465–481.

GRAVENGAARD, G., & RIMESTAD, L. (2014). Socializing journalist trainees in the newsroom: On how to capture the intangible parts of the process. *Nordicom Review, 35*, pp. 81–95.

HALL, J. H. (1980). *The history of broadcasting in New Zealand: 1920–1954*. Broadcasting Corporation of New Zealand.

HALL, S. (1981). The determination of news photographs. In J. Tunstall (Ed.), *The manufacture of news: Social problems, deviance and the mass media* (Revised fourth edition, pp. 226–243). Constable.

HALL, S., CRITCHER, C., JEFFERSON, T., CLARKE, J., & ROBERTS, B. (1978). *Policing the crisis: Mugging, the state, and law and order*. Macmillan.

HANNIS, G. (2017). Journalism education in New Zealand: Its history, current challenges and possible futures. *Asia Pacific Media Educator, 27*(2), pp. 233–248.

HANUSCH, F. (2014). Dimensions of Indigenous journalism culture: Exploring Māori news-making in Aotearoa New Zealand. *Journalism, 15*(8), pp. 951–967.

HARCUP, T., & O'NEILL, D. (2016). What is news? News values revisited (again). *Journalism Studies, 18*(12), pp. 1470–1488.

HASTINGS, D. (2013). *Extra! Extra: How the people made the news*. Auckland University Press.

HEISS, A. (ED.) (2003). Part five: Maori literature. In *Dhuuluu Yala to talk straight* (pp. 189–219). Aboriginal Studies Press.

HIGGINS, R., & REWI, P. (2014). ZePA: Right-shifting: Reorientation towards normalisation. In R. Higgins, P. Rewi, & V. Olsen-Reeder (Eds.), *The value of the Māori language Te hua o te reo Māori* (vol. 2, pp. 7–32). Huia.

HĪROA, T. R. (1949). *The coming of the Maori*. Māori Purposes Fund Board.

HOCKEN, T. M. (1909). *A bibliography of the literature relating to New Zealand*. J. Mackay.

HOLLINGS, J., HANUSCH, F., BALASUBRAMANIAN, R., & LEALAND, G. (2016). Causes for concern. *Pacific Journalism Review, 22*(2), pp. 122–138.

HOLMES, J. (2003). Narrative structure: Some contrasts. In C. B. Paulston & G. R. Tucker (Eds.), *Sociolinguistics: The essential readings* (1st ed, pp. 114–138). Blackwell.

HOOKER, M. (2008). *Makawe: Gaining an understanding of the tikanga for hair*. M & J Hooker.

HORROCKS, R. (2004). The history of New Zealand television: 'An expensive medium for a small country'. In N. Perry & R. Horrocks (Eds.), *Television in New Zealand: Programming the nation* (pp. 20–43). Oxford University Press.

JEFFREY, D. L. (1992). Ashes to ashes. In *A dictionary of biblical tradition in English literature* (1st ed., p. 60). Wm. B. Eerdmans Publishing.

KAA, J. (2012). The tribal empire writes back: A review of three iwi periodicals. *Te Pouhere Korero*, pp. 103–107.

KA'AI, T., & HIGGINS, R. (2004). Te ao Māori: Māori world-view. In T. Ka'ai, J. Moorfield, M. Reilly, & S. Mosley (Eds.), *Ki te whaiao* (pp. 13–25). Pearson Education New Zealand.

KARETŪ, T. (2010). Te whaikōrero. In *Te Pīnakitanga ki te Reo Kairangi: Whaikōrero* (pp. 6–7). Te Wānanga o Aotearoa.

KĀRETU, T., & MILROY, W. (2018). *He kupu tuku iho: Ko te reo Māori te tatau ki te ao*. Auckland University Press.

KEEGAN, J. (2000). *The first world war*. Vintage.

KENNEDY, G., & YAMAZAKI, S. (2000). The influence of Māori on the New Zealand English lexicon. In *Corpora galore: Analyses and techniques in describing English: Papers from the nineteenth international conference on English language research on computerised corpora* (ICAME 1998, pp. 33–44). Rodopi.

KING, M. (2003). *Penguin History of New Zealand*. Penguin Books.

KITCHIN, G. (1967). *A survey of burlesque and parody in English*. Russell & Russell.

LINNELL, J., ANDERSEN, R., ANDERSONE, Z., BALCIAUSKAS, L., BLANCO, J., BOITANI, L., BRAINERD, S., BREITENMOSER, U., KOJOLA, I., LIBERG, O., LØE, J., OKARMA, H., PEDERSEN. H., PROMBERGER, C., SAND, H., SOLBERG, E., VALDMANN, H., & WABAKKEN, P. (2002). *The fear of wolves: A review of wolf attacks on humans*. NINA Oppdragsmelding, 731, pp. 1–65.

MACALISTER, J. (2006). The Maori presence in the New Zealand English lexicon, 1850–2000: Evidence from a corpus-based study. *English World-Wide*, 27(1), pp. 1–24.

MACALISTER, J. (2008). Tracking changes in familiarity with borrowings from te reo Maori. *Te Reo*, 51, p. 75.

MANIHERA, T. U., & PĒWHAIRANGI, N. (1992). Learning and tapu. In M. King (Ed.), *Te ao hurihuri: Aspects of Māoritanga* (pp. 9–14). Reed.

MARKELIN, L. (2017). Indigenous voices in the global public sphere: Analysis of approaches to journalism within the WITBN network. *Journal of Applied Journalism & Media Studies*, 6(3), pp. 443–461.

MARSDEN, M. (2003). *The woven universe: Selected writings of Rev. Māori Marsden* (T. A. C. Royal, Ed.). Estate of Rev. Māori Marsden.

MATAMUA, R. (2009). Māori radio broadcasting: A brief history. *He Pukenga Kōrero*, 9(1), pp. 46–51.

MATAMUA, R. (2014). Te reo pāpāho me te reo Māori – Māori broadcasting and te reo Māori. In R. Higgins, P. Rewi, & V. Olsen-Reader (Eds.), *The value of the Māori language Te hua o te reo Māori* (Vol. 2, pp. 331–348). Huia.

MATAMUA, R., & TEMARA, P. (2010). Te reo Māori in 2020. In P. Papa & L. Blake (Eds.), *He pī ka rere: Te tauira 1* (pp. 39–45). Te Wānanga o Aotearoa.

MAXWELL, K. H., & PENETITO, W. (2007). How the use of rāhui for protecting taonga has evolved over time. *MAI Review, 2007*(2), p. 15.

MCKAY, R. A. (1940). *A history of printing in New Zealand, 1830–1940*. R. A. McKay.

MCNEILL, D. (2009). Gesture and communication. In K. Brown & J. Mey (Eds.), *Encyclopedia of Language & Linguistics* (2nd ed., pp. 299–320). Elsevier.

MCRAE, J. (2002). E manu, tēnā koe! 'O bird, greetings to you': The oral tradition in newspaper writing. In J. Curnow, N. Hopa, & J. McRae (Eds.), *Rere Atu Taku Manu: Discovering History, Language and Politics in the Māori-Language Newspapers* (pp. 42–59). Auckland University Press.

MCRAE, J. (2017). *Māori oral tradition: He kōrero nō te ao tawhito*. Auckland University Press.

MEAD, A. (1994). Maori leadership. *Te Pua, 3*(11), pp. 11–20.

MEAD, H. M. (2003). *Tikanga Māori: Living by Māori values*. Huia.

MEAD, H. M. (2012). Understanding mātauranga Māori. In *Conversations on Mātauranga Māori* (pp. 9–12). New Zealand Qualifications Authority.

MEAD, H. M., AND GROVE, N. (2003). *Ngā pēpeha a ngā tīpuna*. Victoria University Press.

METGE, J. (1986). *In and out of touch: Whakamaa in cross-cultural context*. Victoria University Press.

METGE, J., AND JONES, S. (1995). He taonga tuku iho nō ngā tūpuna: Māori proverbial sayings – a literary treasure. *The Journal of New Zealand Studies, 5*(2), pp. 3–7.

MILL, A. (2005). The Māori radio industry. In K. Neill & M. Shanahan (Eds.), *The great New Zealand radio experiment* (pp. 195–213). Thomson Learning and Dunmore Press.

MÜLLER, C., BRESSEM, J., & LADEWIG, S. (2013). Towards a grammar of gestures: A form-based view. In C. Müller, A. Cienki, E. Fricke, S. Ladewig, D. McNeill, & S. Tessendorf (Eds.), *Body language communication: An international handbook on multimodality in human interaction* (Vol. 1, pp. 7607–7733). De Gruyter Mouton.

NORRIS, P., & COMRIE, M. (2005). Changes in radio news 1994-2004. In K. Neill & M. W. Shanahan (Eds.), *The great New Zealand radio experiment* (pp. 175–194). Thomson Learning and Dunmore Press.

ORBELL, M. (1985). *The natural world of the Maori*. Collins and David Bateman.

ORBELL, M., AND MCLEAN, M. (2002). *Songs of a kaumatua*. Auckland University Press.

PARKER, B. (1966, March). Nga whakatauki: Maori proverbs and sayings. *Te Ao Hou*, 54.

PARR, C. (1963). Māori Literacy 1843–1867. *Journal of the Polynesian Society*, 72(3), pp. 211–234.

PARSONAGE, W. (1952). Maori language teaching in New Zealand Schools. In M. Black (Ed.), *Report of the seventh science congress, Christchurch, May 15–21, 1951* (pp. 191–197). Royal Society of New Zealand.

PATERSON, L. (2006). *Colonial discourses: Niupepa Māori, 1855–1863*. University of Otago Press.

PATERSON, L. (2013). Te Hōkioi and the legitimization of the Māori nation. In B. Hokowhitu and V. Devadas (Eds.), *The fourth eye: Māori media in Aotearoa New Zealand* (pp. 124–142). University of Minnesota Press.

PIHAMA, L., & MIKA, C. (2013). The Treaty of Waitangi and policy in Māori broadcasting. In V. Tawhai & K. Gray-Sharp (Eds.), *Always speaking: The Treaty of Waitangi and public policy* (pp. 175–189). Huia.

POOL, I. (2015). *Colonization and Development in New Zealand Between 1769 and 1900: The Seeds of Rangiatea*. Springer.

REWETI, D. (2006). Māori and broadcasting. In M. Mulholland (Ed.), *State of the Māori nation: Twenty-first century issues in Aotearoa* (pp. 179–186). Reed.

REWI, P. (2010). *Whaikōrero: The world of Māori oratory*. Auckland University Press.

REWI, T., & REWI, P. (2015). The ZePA model of Māori language revitalization: Key considerations for empowering indigenous language educators, students, and communities. In J. Reyhner, L. Martin, L. Lockard, & W. Gilbert (Eds.), *Honoring our elders* (pp. 136–153). Northern Arizona University.

SCANLAN, C. (2000). *Reporting and writing: Basics for the 21st century*. Oxford University Press.

SCHUDSON, M. (2011). *The sociology of news* (2nd ed.). WW Norton & Co.

SCHWIMMER, E. (2004). The local and the universal: Reflections on contemporary Maori literature in response to 'Blood Narrative' by Chadwick Allen. *Journal of the Polynesian Society*, 113(1), pp. 7–36.

SCOTT, J. (2014). Radio journalism. In G. Hannis (Ed.), *Intro: A beginner's guide to journalism in 21st-century Aotearoa/New Zealand* (1st ed, pp. 253–267). New Zealand Journalists Training Organisation.

SHIRRES, M. P. (1997). *Te tangata: The human person*. Accent Publications.

SMITH, C. (2000). Straying beyond the boundaries of belief: Māori epistemologies inside the curriculum. *Educational Philosophy & Theory*, 32(1), pp. 43–51.

SMITH, J., & RUCKSTUHL, K. (2011). The case of *Te Karaka*: Ngāi Tahu print media before and after settlement. *AlterNative*, 6(1), pp. 25–37.

SMITH, L., & PIRIPI, H. (2012). *Ngā whetū kapokapo Māori language evaluation framework*. Te Māngai Pāho.

STEPHENS, T. (2004). Māori television. In R. Horrocks & N. Perry (Eds.), *Television in New Zealand: Programming the nation* (pp. 107–115). Oxford University Press.

STEPHENS, T. (2014). He kura takitahi he kura takimano. In R. Higgins, P. Rewi, & V. Olsen-Reeder (Eds.), *The value of the Māori language Te hua o te reo Māori* (pp. 369–383). Huia.

STUART, I. (2002). Māori and mainstream: Towards bicultural reporting. *Pacific Journalism Review*, 11(1), pp. 42–58.

STURM, J. (1993, April). Three men and their mags. *Landfall*, 185, pp. 6–7.

SULLIVAN, J. (1987). *A history of broadcasting news 1921–1962*. Radio New Zealand Sound Archives.

TAUROA, H., & TAUROA, P. (2009). *Te marae: A guide to customs & protocol*. Raupo.

TE UA, H. (2005). *Hēnare te Ua: In the air*. Reed.

WALKER, R. (1978). The relevance of Māori myth and tradition. In *Tihe mauri ora: Aspects of Māoritanga* (pp. 19–32). Methuen.

WALKER, R. (2004). *Ka whawhai tonu mātou: Struggle without end*. Penguin.

WHAANGA, P. (1990). Radio: Capable of carrying a bicultural message? In P. Spoonley & W. Hirsh (Eds.), *Between the lines: Racism and the New Zealand media*. Heinemann Reed.

WHAANGA, P. (1994). Ngā piki me ngā heke The ups and downs of Maori radio. In P. Ballard (Ed.), *Power and responsibility: Broadcasters striking a balance* (pp. 137–145). Broadcasting Standards Authority. bsa.govt.nz

WILLIAMS, H. W. (1971). *A dictionary of the Māori language* (7th ed.). Legislation Direct.

WILSON, H. (Ed.). (1994). Whakarongo mai e ngā iwi. In *The radio book 1994* (pp. 99–114). New Zealand Broadcasting School.

WINITANA, C. (2011). *My language, my inspiration*. Huia Publishers and Te Taura Whiri i te Reo Māori.

YOUNG, M. (2018). Tā moko and the cultural politics of appropriation. *Sites: A Journal of Social Anthropology and Cultural Studies*, 15(2), pp. 1–15.

## UNPUBLISHED THESES

AUGUST, W. T. (2004). 'The Māori female: Her body, spirituality, sacredness and mana. A space within spaces'. Unpublished MA thesis, Waikato University.

DURIE, M. K. (2011). 'He kawa oranga: Māori achievement in the 21st century'. Unpublished PhD thesis, Massey University.

KELLY, J. (2015). 'Ngā tikanga o te uhunga i Te Nehenehenui'. Unpublished MA thesis, Auckland University of Technology.

LASCELLES, P. (2014). 'Remembering Seafarers: The (missing) history of New Zealanders employed in the mercantile marine during World War I'. Unpublished MA thesis, Massey University.

LEMKE, C. (1995) 'Maori involvement in sound recording and broadcasting 1919 to 1958'. Unpublished MA thesis, University of Auckland.

MACDONALD, J. S. (2008). 'Who talks, what they talk about, and how much they say: A study of bulletin structure and source use in New Zealand free-to-air television news programmes'. Unpublished MA thesis, Massey University.

MAHUTA, R. T. (1974). 'Whaikoorero: A study of formal Māori speech'. Unpublished MA thesis, University of Auckland.

MATAMUA, R. (2006). 'Te reo pāho: Māori radio and language revitalisation'. Unpublished PhD thesis, Massey University.

MIDDLETON, A. (2020). 'Kia hiwa rā! The influence of tikanga and the language revitalisation agenda on the practices and perspectives of Māori journalists working in reo-Māori news'. Unpublished PhD thesis, Auckland University of Technology.

PETERS, R. J. (2000). 'Tika, pono and aroha in three novels by Patricia Grace'. Unpublished MA thesis, Massey University.

REWI, P. (2005). 'Te ao o te whaikorero'. Unpublished PhD thesis, University of Otago.

SULLIVAN, C. L. T. (2012). 'Te okiokinga mutunga kore – The eternal rest: Investigating Māori attitudes towards death.' Unpublished MA thesis, University of Otago.

TATE, H. (2010). 'Towards some foundations of a systematic Māori theology'. Unpublished PhD thesis, Melbourne College of Divinity.

TE HUIA, A. (2013). 'Whāia te iti kahurangi, ki te tuohu koe me he maunga teitei: Establishing psychological foundations for higher levels of Māori language proficiency'. Unpublished PhD thesis, Victoria University of Wellington.

THOMAS, R. (2008). 'The making of a journalist: The New Zealand way'. Unpublished PhD thesis, Auckland University of Technology.

WHELAN, B. (2021). 'He whakangungu kairīpoata nō Aotearoa: Journalism education of this place'. Unpublished PhD thesis, Auckland University of Technology.

WIRI, R. (2001). 'The prophecies of the great canyon of Toi: A history of Te Whāiti-nui-a-Toi in the western Urewera mountains of New Zealand'. Unpublished PhD thesis, University of Auckland.

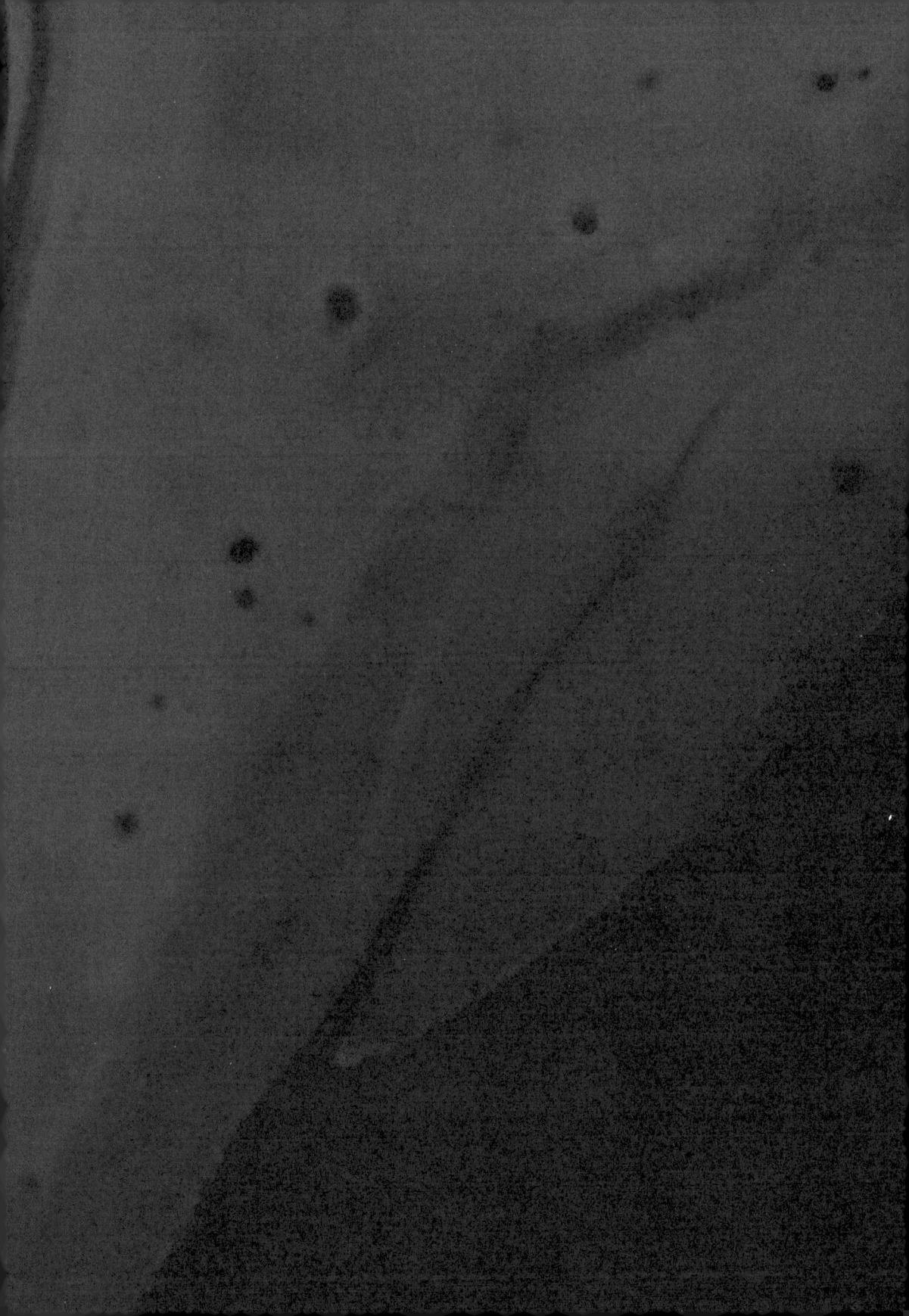

# INDEX

INDEX

Entries in *italics* refer to illustrations. Māori *te*, like its English equivalent "the", is ignored in alphabetisation.

*1 News* 13, 143, 152

**A**
āhuatanga tapu 266
Ake, Jason 59, 79, 274
Ake Ngāti Whātua 281n145
Amoroa, Lynette 111
Anderson, Kura 73
Anglo-American journalistic tradition 139, 141
*Te Ao Hou* 28, *44*, 45–6, 201
te ao Māori: in journalism training 104, 118; public interest in 13, 65; respect for elders in 232; tika, pono and aroha in 216; whanaungatanga in 226
*Te Ao Māori News* 96
Te Ao Mārama 20–1
*Te Ao Mārama* (news bulletins) 9, *10*
*Te Ao Tapatahi* 96
*Te Ao with Moana* 96
*Aotearoa* (newspaper) 42, *43*
Aotearoa Television Network 89
Te Arawa 216
Archie, Carol 55, 79
Ardern, Jacinda 95
aroha 215–23, 231
Te Atairangikaahu, tangihanga of 255, 256
Ātea 10–11, *14*, 60–1
ATI *see* Auckland University of Technology (AUT)
atua 20, 189, 196, 207, 209
*Auckland Star* 101, 109
Auckland University of Technology (AUT) 18, 103, 105–8, 110–11
audio-visuals, as news value 142, 151, 161
Aukaha – Te Tai Puukoorero 16
Te Aute College 129
Awa FM 16, 109

**B**
Babington, Kirsty 111, *113*
bad news, as news value 141, 151
Barclay, Barry 83
Bateson, Sonya 121
Beazley, Manuel 220–1
Bennett, Frederick 64, 69
Bensemann, Paul 55
biculturalism: and journalism training 104; in print media 45, 51; on radio 65; and television 91
Biddle, Purewa 85, 105
Bidois, Eliza 108
Bidois-Stephens, Vanessa 52
birds: in Māori worldview 19–20; and reo Māori newspapers 28–9, 32–7
Black, Taroi 170
Black Lives Matter 11
Black Power 51, 111
Blank, Arapera 46
booster courses 110, 115
Boucher, Sinead 11
Boynton, John 98
brevity: as news value 143; in oratory 212
Broadcasting Assets Case 76–7
Broadcasting Standards Authority (BSA) 14; and Te Kōhanga Reo National Trust 235–8
Broadhead, Bruce 110
Brown, Harata 124, *181*, 182
Brown, Heeni 121, 124
Buller, Walter 27
BusinessDesk 136

**C**
Carlyon, Ric 110
carvings 23, 84, 247
celebrity, as news value 142

305

Christianity 25, 32, 139, 205
church newspapers 26–7, 40
citizen journalism 30
clarity: as news value 143, 160; in oratory 212
cognitive dissonance 241–2
commercial radio 65; Māori-owned 77
conflict, as news value 141
Cook Islands 156–7
Cooper, Whina 55
corpses, and tapu 258–60; *see also* tapu, of death
cosmology, Māori 205
COVID-19 14, 96, 136, 274
creation stories 20–2, 154
Crosbie, Sharon 79
cultural appropriation 262
cultural knowledge 22, 92, 140, 185
culture, in Māori worldview 140

## D

Dalton, Tania 263
Daniels, Ngarimu 78, 131
Dansey, Harry 101
Davis, Charles 27
Department of Māori Affairs: and Māori journalism 45–6, 49; and television 91; *see also* Te Puni Kōkiri
Dick, Maurice 110
Diploma in Bicultural Journalism 118
Diploma in Radio Broadcasting 135
Dittmer, George 47
diversity, in Māori worldview 140
*Dominion Post* 12
drama, as news value 142, 151
drop intro 203–4
Durie, Meihana 23, 207, 209

## E

editorial independence 231
Edwards: Brian 110; Hone 105, *107*, 164, 167, 255–6, 264–5
elders, in Māori worldview 139
emotions, as news value 142
English language 9–10; Māori print media in 44–60; Māori radio news in 80; in te reo news 167–8; translating Māori concepts into 187–8; *see also* New Zealand English

English-language journalism: Māori trained in 105; te reo Māori in 161
English-language newspapers 40, 277n20; style of writing 37–8; translations into te reo Māori 29
entertainment, as news value 142
Epiha, Mana 78
Eriksen, Alanah 121
*E-Tangata* 10
ethics of journalism 238
Evans, Ripeka 238
exclusivity, as news value 141

## F

Facebook 174, 258
*Feathering the Nest* 235
Festinger, Leon 241–2
Fishman, Joshua 176
Flavell, Te Ururoa 155–7
follow-up, as news value 142, 160
Forbes, Michael 110
Forbes, Mihingarangi *15*, 97, *98*, 132–3, 230, *233*; and hard questions 234–6
Fowler, Leo 68–70
Fox, Derek *56*, *88*; and journalism training 105, 107, 113; and *Koha* 84; and *Mana* magazine 54–7; and radio news 77, 79; and TV news 85–7
Fuatai, Teuila 11
Fuimaono, Mahia 75

## G

Galtung, Johan 141
gestures, symbolic 265–7
Gilbert, Te Rangihau 125
God (Christian) 192, 206
good news, as news value 142, 160
Goodman, Hinerangi 105, *108*, 122, 169, 252, 254, 259
Gorst, John 29
government newspapers 26
Grace, Patricia 46
Grant, Mere 75
greetings and sign-offs 13–14
Grennell, Airini 65
Grey, George 29

## H

Haami, Bradford 108
Haddon, Ōriwa Tahupōtiki 65
Haggie, Sonya 110
haka *147*, 152
Hall, Sarah 98
Hao'uli, Sefita 110
Harawira, Tumamao 155, 173, *200*; on aroha 221; karakia of 210–11; on manaakitanga 222–3; and mihi mate 197, 199–200; on tapu 208; whakaaraara by 187; and whakataukī 203
Harawira, Wena 55, 87–9, *88*, 94, 95, 105, 118
Harcup, Tony 141
Hastings, David 38
Haunui-Thompson, Shannon *102*, 103, 160–1; on aroha 221; on cognitive dissonance 243; on interviewing kaumātua 240; on tapu 248; on tikanga 216
Hawaiki 38, 195, 206, 210–11
*Hawera Star* 101
*Hawke's Bay Today* 59–60
*He Kupu Whakamarama* 27
*He Rourou* 173
Heat 99.1FM 281n145
Hemmingsen, Erana 75
Henare, Erima 256
Henare, Hēmi 92
Henry, Ella 273
Herewini, Bill 47
Hetaraka, Henare 75
*Te Hēteri* 94
Higgins, Rawinia 165
Hineahuone 21
Hine-nui-te-pō 21, 146, 154, 196, 211
Hīroa, Te Rangi 45
Hoani Waititi Marae 126, 252
Hodges, Kevin 75
Hoey, Nicole 274
hōhā, being the 232
*Te Hokioi o Niu Tireni e Rere atu na* 28–9, 59
Holland, Semiramis 111, 254, 259–60
Holmes, Huata 260
hongi 169–70, 207, 245, 249
Hongi, Hāre 64
hononga 227

*Te Hookioi* 59
Horomia, Parekura, tangihanga of 256
*The Hui* 10, 78, 97, 98; and sector review 273–4
*Huia Tangata Kotahi* 29
Te Huki, Tama 73
Human Rights Commission 14
Huria, Gabrielle 58
Huta-Martin, Wiremu 124

## I

Ihaka, James 121
Ihaka, Jodi 111
Īhaka, Kīngi 260
Ihimaera, Witi 46
Ikin, Keith 120, 236–7
Indigenous journalism 238
intellectual property 261–2
internet, Māori use of 52–3
internet publications 60–1
interviews: with kaumātua 240; preserving mana in 223; in te reo Māori 168–9, 181–3; tika, pono and aroha in 217–19
inverted pyramid style 38, 152, 160
Iosefa, Renee Kahukura 250
iwi 9
iwi newspapers 57–60
*Te Iwi o Aotearoa* 51, 111
iwi radio 16; commercial 281n145; and COVID-19 136; genesis of 73–6; and journalism training 121, 124, 135; news on 77–8, 124, 273

## J

Jackson, Hikurangi Kimiora 96
Jackson, Simon 78
Jackson, Willie 273–4
Johnston, Sarah 67
Jones, Michael Rotohiko 68
Jones, Peter-Lucas 273
Jones, Shane 202
journalism: investigative 235–8; monocultural 140–1; *see also* Māori journalism
journalism training 18, 77, 101; Māori participation in 104–9; new pathways into 135–7; personal stories of 102–3, 107, 113–17, 122, 125–34;

journalism training (*Continued ...*)
    polytechnic-based 284n232; and te reo
    Māori education 121–4, 135; taster courses
    in 49, 109–10; at Waiariki 111, 118–21
journalists: celebrification of 142; *see also* Māori
    journalists
Journalists Training Board 49
*The Jubilee Te Tiupiri* 30

## K

Kaa, Hone 90, 91–2, 95, 259–60
Kaa, Jasmine 58
*Te Kaea* (magazine) 46, 47
*Te Kāea* (TV programme) 93–4, 96, 109, 166;
    conclusions on 205–6; karakia on 192;
    mihi on 193–4, 196, 198; whakaaraara on
    187; and Whetū Tirikātene-Sullivan 225
Kāhu 11–13
*Kahungunu* 58
Kaipara, Oriini 78, *130*, 131, 227; on attitudes to
    journalists 228–9; on cognitive dissonance
    241–3; pulling people out of ceremonial
    occasions 253; on use of te reo 167–8,
    172, 176; on whanaungatanga 226, 228
Te Kanawa, Ata 52, 53
Te Kanawa, Wepiha 169, 223, 248
kapa haka 124
*Te Karaka* 58–9
karakia 20, 215, 288n348; and cognitive
    dissonance 242; leading 121; personal
    248, 250–1, 254, 266; in te reo Māori
    news 189–92, 207–12; in te reo Māori
    newspapers 32
karanga 207, 227, 249
*Te Karere* (*Māori*) *News* (newspaper) 52
*Te Karere* (TV programme) 9, 85–90, *88*,
    *89*, 94; conclusions on 206–7; filming
    tangihanga 255; funding of 163; and
    journalism training 105, 107, 109, 117,
    133; mihi on 193–4, 196–8; new words
    used on 180–1; news values on 143–55;
    screenshots of *144–51*; scripts for 152–5;
    and sector review 273–4; stories on tikanga
    261–2; use of te reo on 164, 167–8, 176–9;
    whakaaraara on 187, 189
*Te Karere o Poneke* 27

Kāretu, Tīmoti 57, 177, 239
kaumātua 50; interviewing 219, 240; and Māori
    broadcasting 69–70; and te reo 90; and
    *Waka Huia* 92
kawa 207, 209
*Kawe Kōrero – Reporters* 95–6, 167, 262–7, 263
Kawea Te Rongo 118–19
Kawiti, N. P. 40
Kearney, Stephen 225–6
Kennedy, Marcus 121
Kia Ora FM 16
*Kia Ora News* 58
King, Donald 75
King, Michael 83, 110, 277n20
King Movement *see* Kīngitanga
Kingi, Henare 75, 200–1
Kīngitanga 26, 28–9, 59, 161, 192
kinship structure 140
kirimate 256–7
Knight, Richard 134
*Ko Aotearoa or the Maori Recorder* 27
*Ko te Karere o Nui Tireni* 26
Koea, George 101
*Koha* (TV programme) 84–5
*Te Kohanga o te Tui* 111
kōhanga reo 121
Te Kōhanga Reo National Trust 234–9
Kōkako dashboard 77, 179, *180*
Kōmiromiro 137
*Te Kopara* 27
kōrero take 201
*Te Korimako* 27, 32–9, *33*, 35, 36
Korimako 35
Te Korimako o Taranaki 16
Kōwhai Media 57
*Te Kupenga* 91
Kupu Taea 141
kupu whakarite 46, 193, 196
kura kaupapa 121
Te Kura Kaupapa Māori o Hoani Waititi Marae 126
Te Kura Pāpāho o te Motu 135
kurahautū Māori 80

## L

Labour Party 64, 176, 273
Lacey, Megan 121

language anxiety 223
language plans 77, 164
language revitalisation 163–4, 171, 176, 185, 238, 274
LDR (Local Democracy Reporting) 16
lecturettes 63–4
Lee-Mather, Annabelle 78, 98, 131, *171*, 233; and Anthony Ratahi 259; on hard questions 232, 239; and journalism training 127, 137; and manaakitanga 223–4; and te reo 170–1, 176; and sector review 274; and *The Hui* 97
Lee-Morgan, Eruera 111, 125, 189, *190*; farewells by 205; on figures of speech 202; on karakia 211; mihi by 193, 195–6; and whakataukī 204
legacy media 101, 136
Leilua, Iulia 108, 111, *114*, 115
Leonard, Ernie 92–3, 108
Locke, Helen 78
Lyndon, Pierre 105

# M

MACCESS (Māori Access) 111
McGregor, Judy 110, 141
MacKenzie, Raewyn 110
Mackey, Bailey 274
McLean, Mere 78, 251, 253, 257, 259
McRae, Jane 26, 32
magnitude, as news value 142, 160
Mahuta, Nanaia 204, 273
Mai FM 77
Maihi, Rehutai 42, 43
mainstream media 11–14; cooperation with Māori producers 15; coverage of Māori issues 93, 104; government funding for 16–17; interview style of 223; portrayal of Māori in 48, 50, 52, 55, 140, 231; racism in 141
Maitai, Caleb 55, 79
Maitai, Pere 87, *88*, 108, 124
Mākiha, Rereata 55, 105
mana 28, 31; and journalism 217, 222–4, 234, 260; and karakia 207, 209; of mountains 194; and pōwhiri 249; of te reo learners 165, 170, 173, 175–6, 223

*Mana* magazine 54, 55–7
Mana Māori Media 54, 77, 79
mana matua 180
*Mana News* 79
*Mana Tangata* 58
manaakitanga 175–6, 215; and aroha 221; and journalism 222–4, 232–4, 243
*Manako* 9, 155, 157; conclusions on 205; karakia on 189, 210–11; mihi on 193, 195–7; use of te reo on 164, 166, 173, 178–9; whakaaraara on 187
Manawaiti, Okeroa 133
Manawaiti, Petiwaea 133
Manawaiti, Ringiringi 133
Maniapoto FM 16
Maniapoto-Jackson, Moana 73, 96, *97*
Manu Kōrero competition 124
Manukau Technical Institute 111
*Te Māori* (exhibition) 92
Māori Battalion 47, 68, 70, 92, 101
Māori establishment 94, 236
Māori journalism: funding of 274; languages of 9–13; as less adversarial 230; and news values 141; skills shortage in 137; *see also* journalism training; te reo Māori journalism
Māori journalists 14–17; and cognitive dissonance 240–3; community feedback for 228–32; greetings by 169; and hard questions 232–40; as language coaches 176; leading journalism training 119; in mainstream media 48; and manaakitanga 222–6; Piripi Whaanga and 48–9; in post-war years 101; and tika, pono and aroha 216–22; and tikanga 215–16, 267–70; using new words 180; and whaikōrero 22; and whanaungatanga 226–8; *see also* Kawea Te Rongo
Māori Land Court 109, 125
Māori language *see* te reo Māori
Māori Language Act 1987 73
Māori Language Act 2016 281n137
Māori Language Commission *see* Te Taura Whiri i te Reo Māori
Māori Language Week 13
Māori media 9, 11, 78; regional news in 16;

309

Māori media (*Continued ...*)
    review of 136, 273–4; *see also* newspapers; radio; television
*Māori News* 52
*Te Maori News* 52
Māori organisations 51, 161; and investigative journalism 235, 238; tapu and noa at 246
*The Māori Programme* 71–2
Māori reporters *see* Māori journalists
Māori Television *see* Whakaata Māori
Māori women 31, 43, 52, 143
Māori Women's Welfare League 45, 48, 92
Māori worldview 18–19, 21–2, 84, 237, 259; indicators to understanding 139–40; and unmarked signification 34, 36; *see also* te ao Māori
Māori–Pākehā relations 94
*Marae* (magazine) 68
*Marae* (TV programme) 10, 92–3, 175, 273–4
marae: following tikanga on 215–16, 242, 249; tapu areas of 246
Marsden, Māori 245
Martin, D'Angelo 98
Mata'aho, Halaevalu 263
Mataira, Katerina Te Heikōkō 46, 133
Matamua, Rangi 65, 177
mātauranga Māori 18, 22–3, 208–9, 260
Mather, Jim 235–6
*Te Maunga Kōrero* 58
Maxwell, Paora 236–7
Mead, Aroha 124
Mead, Hirini Moko 23, 57, 208, 219
Meads, Colin 196–201
Melbourne, Hirini 75
Melbourne, Peata 10, *181*, 263; dealing with death 263, 265; interviewing kaumātua 240; and news values 143–4, 151–3; and stories on tikanga 261–2; and tapu 252–3
metaphors 22; in early newspapers 26, 32, 34, 37, 41; in mihi mate 198–9; in te reo Māori news 185, 193; translation of 154; *see also* kupu whakarite
Metge, Joan 202
middle class, Māori 55
Middleton, Atakohu 17, *18*
mihi 32; on radio 64; in te reo Māori news 192–200; on television 85, 95

mihi mate and mihi ora 194–200, 264–5
Mihinui, Mata 110
Milroy, Te Wharehuia 177, 239
Misa, Tapu *60*, 110
mita 153, 178
Te Moana, Lucy 75
Moana Radio 16, 134
mokomokai 261
Molyneux, Tini 105, *108*, 117, 122, *222*; on aroha 221; on use of te reo 170, 175
Montague, J. F. 64
Morgan, Eruera *see* Lee-Morgan, Eruera
Morgan, Reikura 126
Morrison, Howard 46, *47*, 83
Morrison, Scotty 89, 125, 143, *210*; karakia of 209; on language and tikanga 198, 207; and sector review 274; and stories on tikanga 261–2; use of te reo 172, 181
Morrison, Temuera 108
Mounter, Julian 91
MTS (Māori Television Service) *see* Whakaata Māori
Murchie, Fiona 108
Murchie, Malcolm 111, *120*
Murray, Justine 111, 134, 222, *251*; and tapu 246, 249–50
Muru, Selwyn 46, *71*, 72, 85
musicians, Māori 208

# N

Nathan, Te Anga 93, 111
Nathan, Dean 125, 167, *174*, 175
National Diploma in Journalism 111, 118
*Native Affairs* 94, 96; and Anthony Ratahi 259; and Te Kōhanga Reo National Trust 234–40
native schools 40
Nēpia, Ted 70, *71*
New Zealand Company 277n20
New Zealand English, Māori words in 161, 189
*New Zealand Gazette* 277n20
*New Zealand Herald* 11–13, 110, 121, 134
New Zealand Journalists Training Board 109
New Zealand Journalists Training Organisation 118
*New Zealand Listener* 66, 91
New Zealand Māori Council 48, 76

New Zealand Media Council 14, 238
New Zealand Qualifications Authority 135
New Zealand Radio Training School 135
New Zealand Wars 29
*News in Māori* 68–70
news organisations, agenda of 142
News Publishers' Association 16
news values 119, 140–2; and manaakitanga 224–6; on radio news 155–7; on television news 143–55; on websites 157–61
Newshub 17, 78, 97, 137, 227
newspapers: church-published 26–7; government-published 26, 44–50; Māori-owned 28–30, 50–60; Pākehā-owned 27; *see also* te reo Māori newspapers
Newsroom 136
Ngā Iwi FM 16
Ngā Kaiwhakapūmau i te Reo 73, 76
*Nga Kohinga o Ngati Porou* 58
*Ngā Take Māori* 90–1
Ngāi Tahu: magazine of 58–9; radio station of 16
Ngata, Whai 68, 71–2, 85–7, 86, 88, 101, 105
Ngāti Kahungunu, iwi radio station 75
Ngāti Porou 66, 129, 278n39
Ngāti Whakatōhea (radio station) 281n145
Ngāti Whātua, radio stations of 77
Niniwa-i-te-rangi 29, 31
noa *see* tapu and noa
nonelite sources 94
Nuri, Roihana 131
*NZ Wars: Stories of Tainui* 15
NZBC (New Zealand Broadcasting Corporation) 71, 83–4
nzherald.co.nz 11
NZME (New Zealand Media and Entertainment) 11; and journalism training 17, 137
NZOA (New Zealand On Air) 11, 77; and PIJF 137; projects funded by 15–17, 274

## O

O'Donnell, Bernie 173, 226
Olsen, Olly 110
O'Neill, Deirdre 141
oratory *see* whaikōrero
Orbell, Margaret 34

O'Regan: Hana 172; Tipene 59
Te Owai, Henare 288n352

## P

Pacific Islanders, and journalism training 110
Pacific Media Network 17, 137
*Pacific Viewpoint* 84
*Paepae* 95
Pākehā, use of term 14
Pākehā journalists 45, 83, 140, 231
Paki, Raiha 215, 247, 254
Te Panekiretanga o te Reo Māori 177–8, 239
Pango Productions 93
pan-tribal newspapers 50–7
pan-tribal radio 78, 163
*Panui* 92
Paora, Uramo 65
Papatūānuku 20–1, 192, 211
Parahi, Carmen 11, 228–30, 229
Paraone, Te Hemara Te Rerehau 28
Parker, Wiremu 66, 67, 68–71
Paterson, Lachy 30
Paul, Maanu 111, *120*
pepeha 46, 121
Perera, Ruwani 98
perspective 139
Pewhairangi, Irene 133
Pihama, Amomai 126
*Te Pihoihoi Mokemoke i Runga i te Tuanui* 29
PIJF (Public Interest Journalism Fund) 17, 137
Pikia, Anzac 121
*Pikiao Pānui* 58
*Te Pīpīwharauroa* 27, 30, *31*
Pītama, Te Aritaua 65
Te Pō 20
pono 216–22, 231, 243, 253
poroporoaki 46, 48, 85, 201, 225
Pōtatau Te Wherowhero 28
Pou Tiaki 11
Poutu, Hinurewa 261
power elite, as news value 142, 157, 160
pōwhiri 161; asking people to leave 252–5; journalists at 242, 249–50; skipping 250–2; at tangihanga 253; tapu and noa in 245
print journalism, decline of 119
printing presses 28, 132

311

Te Puke ki Hikurangi 29
Te Puna Wai Korero 72
Te Puni Kōkiri 48; and Māori media review 274
pūrākau 20–2, 185
Pūriri, Paraone Kawiti 46

## Q

qualification creep 104
A Question of Trust 235

## R

racism 11, 60, 141
radio: early Māori voices on 63–5; *see also* commercial radio; iwi radio; pan-tribal radio; RNZ; state radio
Radio Aotearoa 72–3
radio news, in te reo Māori *see* te reo Māori news, on radio
Radio Ngāti Porou 75
*The Radio Record* 64
Radio Waatea 9–10; funding of 163; news values on 155–7; PIJFO funding for 17; and RNZ 80; and sector review 273
rāhui 245, 267–9
Raihania, Murray 75
Rakuraku, Martin 109, 122
rangatahi 50, 97, 109
rangatira, images of 261
Te Rangi Hīroa 45, 186
Rangihau, Boy 133
Rangihau, Tāwini 105, 238
Ranginui 20, 192, 211
Rasch, Raewyn 17, *136*, 137
Ratahi, Anthony 259
Rātana faith 64
Raukawa FM *16*
*Re:* 97
reciprocity 140
Reedy, Amster 209
Reedy, Erana 108
regional news 16
relevance, as news value 142, 151, 157, 160
Reo FM 281n145
te reo irirangi, use of term 65
Te Reo Irirangi o Te Arawa 16
Te Reo Irirangi o Te Hiu 76

Te Reo Irirangi o Te Upoko o Te Ika 73–4, 75
Te Reo Irirangi o Waatea 78, 274
reo journey 165–6, 172
te reo Māori: continuum of use 164, 274; ethics of journalists helping with 175–7; everyday and formal registers of 185; health of 10; on independent radio 73–4; and journalism training 129; macrons in 31–2, 161; in mainstream media 13; mana of 209; and Māori worldview 21–2, 139; negotiating use of 169–70; new words in 88–9, 177, 180–1; number of speakers 25, 40, 164–5; and PIJF funding 17; quality and quantity in broadcasting 165–9, 177–80; on state-owned radio 64–73, 78–80; supporting learners 170–5; on television 85, 89–90, 94–6; use in interviews 181–3
Reo Māori Claim 9, 73
te reo Māori education 10, 170; and journalism 121–4, 135; *see also* kōhanga reo; kura kaupapa
te reo Māori journalism 9–10, 17–19, 141, 163, 181–3
te reo Māori news: bidding farewell on 204–7; and cultural appropriation 262; karakia in 189–92; and Māori worldview 21–2; mihi in 192–200; on radio 65–72, 77–80, 155–7; scripts for 152, 173; on television 9, 85–9, 93–4, 105, 143–54, 177–80; whakaaraara on 185–9; whakataukī and whakatauāki in 201–4, 206
te reo Māori newspapers 25–30; decline of 38–43; journalists for 30–2; oral arts in 32–7; writing style 37–8
Te Reo o Aotearoa (radio station) 72
Te Reo o Raukawa 75
Te Reo o Te Māori (programme) 70–1
Te Reo o Te Uru 16
te reo ōkawa 185, 189
te reo ōpaki 185
reporting, good 179
Repudiation movement 29
*Rereātea – Midday News Bytes* 95–6
Reweti, Debra 84
Rewi, Poia 22, 165, 187, 245

Rewi Maniapoto 29
Rickard, Eva 46
Rikihana, Damiane 111, *120*
Ringatū faith 259
ritenga pai 27
*Te Rito* (insert) 57
Te Rito (journalism training) 17, 137
RNZ (Radio New Zealand): Hēnare te Ua Māori Journalism Internship 136; and LDR 16; Māori news in English on 80; and Te Reo o Aotearoa 72; use of te reo on 13, 79–80; website of *158–9*, 160
Robb, Andrew 55
Roderick, Maramena 111, 119, *220*; on aroha 221; on negative community feedback 229, 231, 238, 240; on tika 219–20; on tikanga guidance 257
Roes, Kawe 263, *264*, 265–7
Rolleston, Lance Kahu 78
Rongo 20
Royal, Te Ahukaramū Charles 207–8
Rūaumoko 20
Ruge, Mari Holmboe 141
Ruia Mai Te Ratonga Irirangi o te Motu 77–8, 124–7, 131

## S

sacred speech 192, 207
Saffery, Philip 75
Savage, Michael Joseph 64
Scadden, David 119–21
Scanlan, Christopher 37
Schuler, Annabel 118–19, 121
Schwimmer, Erik 45
self-determination 45, 119, 140
Serious Fraud Office 235
sexism 236
shareability, as news value 142, 161
Shaw, Barry 110
Shearer, Ian 86
Shelley, James 70
Sherman, Maiki 121, 256
Shortland, Waihoroi 55, 95, 105, 118, 120
signification, unmarked 34
Smith, Cherryl Waerea-i-te-rangi 19
Smith, Irena *117*, 121, 163, 169, 172, 198, *199*, 223, 246
Snow, W. P. 27, 32, 36, 37
social media: new Māori words on 181; news on 87, 95, 97; news stories about 263; shareability on 142
soundbites 94, 157, 182–3
South Seas Film and Television School 124, 131
Southern Institute of Technology 118, 284n232
*The Spinoff* 11, 60–1
spiritual health 263
spirituality, in Māori worldview 139, 185, 205
Stafford, Moari 105
state radio 64, 72, 77–8; *see also* RNZ
Stephens, Tainui 22, 83–4, 87, 90
Stirling, George 108
Stuart, Ian 50
studio panels, live 176
*Stuff* (stuff.co.nz) 11; apology of *12*; Māori journalists at 137; PIJF funding for 17; te reo on 14
Sturm, J. C. 45
subject experts 163, 165, 168, 173
subtitles 13, 144–51, 156, 174; translation of 152, 154, 187–8
Summerville, Larry 135
Sun FM 281n145
*Sunday News* 110
Sunshine FM 281n145
surprise, as news value 141, 151
Szászy, Mira 92

## T

taha wairua 247, 257, 259
Tāhiwi, Kīngi 65
Tahu FM 16, 76
Tahuparae, John 105
Tai FM 281n145
Tainui Live 16
Tait, Wena 55, 79, 109
*Talks in Māori* 70
Tāne (atua) 20–2; in karakia 190–1, 211–12; in mihi 196, 198; in whakaaraara 187
Tangaroa 20, 22, 208, 258
*Tangata Whenua* (TV series) 83
Tangatarua (marae) 118, 120
tangihanga 46, 267; journalists at 220, 242,

253–6; lack of 224–5; and tapu 245
Tanirau, Katrina 121
Tapiata, Ana 173, 215–16; on pono 220; and tapu 248; and whanaungatanga 227–8
tapu 19; of death 253–7, 259–60, 262–7; karakia invoking 189, 207; places as 242; and pōwhiri 249; and time 250–2; and whakaaraara 187
tapu and noa 19, 208–9, 245–6; in creation story 21; in the newsroom and in the field 246–9; in pōwhiri 249–50
*Taranaki Herald* 101, 118
*Tatau te Iwi* 51, 111
Tate, Pā Henare 216, 219
taumaha 266
Taumata, Arana 109, 153, *166*; on metaphor 194; on pono 220; and tangihanga 254; and tapu 248; on tika 219; on tikanga 215; on translations into English 187–8; on use of te reo 167–8; on whakawhanaungatanga 227
Taumaunu, Gloria 126, *263*; on community attitudes to journalism 231; dealing with death 263, 266; and hard questions 233–4; on manaakitanga 224; pulling people out of ceremonial occasions 253; on tikanga 215
tauparapara 189–92
Te Taura Whiri i te Reo Māori 73; coining words 177, 180; licensing interpreters 178; on macrons 32, 161
Taurima, Shane 78, 96, 131, 260
Taurua, Kingi 124
Tautoko Radio 75
Tawhai, Rapaera *197*
Tāwhirimātea 20–2
Taylor, Piripi 78, *188*, 192, 194
telegraphy 37–8
television 18–19, 71, 83; Māori programming on 84–5, 90–3; Māori-run 76; *see also* Three; TVNZ; Whakaata Māori
television news 83–5, 95–7; in te reo Māori *see* te reo Māori news, on television
Temara, Pou 177
*Te Tēpu* 95
tertiary education, Māori participation in 104
Thiel, Peter 155–6

Three (television network) 10, 17, 97, 137
*Tīhei Kahungunu* 59
tika 23, 216–22, 231, 235, 243, 253
tikanga Māori 18–19, 23; and colonisation 40; education grounded in 121; iwi radio and 75; journalists on 215–16; of mihi mate and mihi ora 195, 197–8; modern reworking of 207–12; and news work 234, 236–7, 239–41, 251–2; in newspapers 45–6, 261; on radio 65, 72; seeking guidance on 257–61; as the story 261–2; studying 118; tapu and noa in 245, 247, 250; on television 83, 85, 189; transmission of 40; and whakaaraara 187
Timu, Johnny 55
Tirikātene: Eruera 64; Kukupa 225
Tirikātene-Sullivan, Whetū 224–5
Te Tiriti o Waitangi 9, 84, 104, 118, 140, 160; *see also* Waitangi Tribunal
TMP (Te Māngai Pāho) 9, 77; funding policy 163–5, 167–8, 274; language assessment framework 178–9; and Māori language news 79; and regional news 16
*Te Toa Takitini* 27, 75
tohunga 40, 207, 248
Tostee, Gable 143–4, 149–51, 154
tōtara 22, 196, 198–9
TPO (Te Pātaka Ōhanga) 234–5
Tremewan, Philip 140
tribal identity 139–40
*Tu Mai* 52–3
*Tu Tangata* 48–50, 88; and journalism training 110–11
Te Tuhi, Wiremu Pātara 28
Tūhoe 105, 153, 251–3, 259
Tully, Jim 94
Tumahai, Anaru 51–2
Tūmatauenga 20–1, 245
Tumohe, Wiremu Toetoe 28
Tūpaea, Hori 69
Tūranga FM 16
Turei, Lois 13
Turei, Metiria 238, 260
Tūwharetoa FM *16*
TVNZ (Television New Zealand) 9; and journalism training 103, 105–8; Māori

journalists at 137; Māori programming on 84–93; newsroom 152; online news 97; PIJF funding for 17; te reo on 13–14 (*see also Te Karere*)

TVNZ Māori Programmes Department 91, 108–9, 135

## U

te Ua, Hēnare 63–5, 69, 72
Uetahi 34, 278n39

## V

value judgments 20, 179
voice-overs 166–8
von Hochstetter, F. R. 28

## W

*Waatea News* 9; and *Manako* 155; mihi on 192, 196, 198–9; use of te reo on 164, 166, 178–9; whakataukī on 203–4
Wade, Ngahuia 131
waewae tapu 242, 249–52
te wāhi ngaro 205–6, 266
wāhi tapu, reporting in 267–70
Waiariki Community College, journalism training at 108, 110–21, 124, 134–5
waiata 32, 185, 215, 249
waiata tautoko 204
*Waikato Times* 110
Waikato-Tainui: magazine of 59; pakeke and Whakaata Māori 261; use of macrons 32, 161
Waikerepuru, Huirangi 73, 74, 75, 259–60
*Wairere* 40, *41*
Waitangi Tribunal 40, 52, 57–8, 286n261; claim WAI11 *see* Reo Māori Claim
*Waka Huia* 92–3, 125
*Te Waka Maori o Ahuriri* 26, 288n352
*Te Waka Maori o Niu Tireni* 26
*Te Waka o te Iwi* 27
Walker, Piripi 73–4, 75
Walker, Ranginui 20, 141
*Te Wananga* 29
weaving 23, 195
Webby, Kim 119
*Weekly News Summary in Māori* 67

Western Institute of Technology 284n232
Whaanga, Iris Te Ari 75
Whaanga, John *102*
Whaanga, Piripi *49*, 75, 77; and iwi radio 75; and journalism training 110–11, 113, 118; and *Mana* magazine 54; and *Tu Tangata* 48–50
whaikōrero 22; conclusion of 204; for the dead and the living 195–6; and te reo Māori broadcasting 187; and te reo Māori newspapers 31–2, 46, 48; and te reo ōkawa 185; rituals in marae setting 192, 207; structure of *186*; tapu of 189
whakaaraara 185–8; in te reo Māori news 185–9
Whakaata Māori 10; dealing with death 263; funding of 163; and investigative journalism 230, 235–7; and journalism training 17, 137; Kaunihera Kaumātua at 259–61; manaakitanga and news values 224–5; news and current affairs on 93–6; reo Māori news on 9, 164, 167, 178–9; and sector review 273; tapu and noa at 246; value statement of 217; whakaaraara on 188–9; and whakataukī 202–3
whakanoa 192, 266
whakapapa 19–20; discussing 241; and news values 152; primacy of 209; recitation of 248
Te Whakaruruhau o Ngā Reo Irirangi Māori 76, 135
whakatau hā 196, 210–12
whakatauākī 201
whakataukī 37, 185, 215; in te reo Māori news 201–4, 206
whakawhanaungatanga 226–7, 253
whanaungatanga 221, 226–8, 231
whare nui 84, 192, 205, 252
Te Whare Wānanga o Awanuiārangi 135
Wharerau, Laurence 111, *120*
Wharewaka, Abraham 51, 111
Whelan, Bernie 104
*Te Whetu o te Tau* 27
Whitireia Institute of Technology 135
Wickliffe, Tina 78, 94, 131
Wikaira, Chris 79, 115, 118
Wikaira, Pete 115
Wilcox, Julian *128*, 129, 172, *218*; and Anthony

Ratahi 259; on cognitive dissonance 241; on journalism in te ao Māori 230–1; on mana 223; on manaakitanga 224–6; on tika, pono and aroha 217–18; on whakawhanaungatanga 226
Williams, H. W. 177
Williams, Haare 71
Wills, Mike 75
Wilson, Gary 54, 57, *60*, 77, 79, 109–11, 113, *120*
Winitana, Chris 95, 110, 118
Winitana, Tūpoutahi 95
Wiremu, Graham 46
Wiri, Robert 22
women: in reo Māori newspapers 31; and tapu and noa 247; *see also* Māori women
Wong, Ruth 60
Wood, John 110
World War I 41–2

World War II 43–4, 66, 101
Wright, Kereama *122*, 124, *172*; on community responsibility of journalists 229; and hard questions 232–3; on pōwhiri 250; on te reo 168, 171; seeking guidance 257–9; and tangihanga 256; on tika, pono and aroha 217; on whakawhanaungatanga 227
Wright, Manawa 124
Wright, Rawiri 118, 124, 257–9
Wright, Warriena 143–5, 150–2

# Y

Young, David 110

# Z

ZePA model *164*, 165
Zukina, Igor 78